THE
80/20
PRINCIPLE

THE
80/20
PRINCIPLE

THE SECRET OF

ACHIEVING MORE

WITH LESS

RICHARD KOCH

CURRENCY

DOUBLEDAY
NEW YORK LONDON TORONTO SYDNEY AUCKLAND

A CURRENCY BOOK
PUBLISHED BY DOUBLEDAY
a division of Bantam Doubleday Dell Publishing Group, Inc.
1540 Broadway, New York, New York 10036

CURRENCY and DOUBLEDAY are trademarks of Doubleday,
a division of Bantam Doubleday Dell Publishing Group, Inc.

First published in the U.K. by Nicholas Brealey Publishing.

Although the author expresses a view on the likely future performance of certain investment instruments, this should not be taken as an incitement to deal in any of them, nor is it to be regarded as investment advice. Each individual should consider their investment position in relation to their own circumstances with the benefit of professional advice. No responsibility can be assumed by either the author or the publisher for investment or any other decisions taken on the basis of views expressed in this book.

Library of Congress Cataloging-in-Publication Data
Koch, Richard, 1950–
The 80/20 principle: the secret of achieving more with less / by
Richard Koch. — 1st Currency ed.
p.   cm.
Includes bibliographical references and index.
1. Time management.   2. Labor productivity—Psychological aspects.
3. Industrial efficiency—Psychological aspects.   4. Conduct of
life.   I. Title.
HD69.T54K63   1998
650.1—dc21   97-37959
                                                                    CIP

ISBN 0-385-49170-0
Printed in the United States of America
First Currency edition: March 1998
5 7 9 10 8 6

To Lee

CONTENTS

ACKNOWLEDGMENTS

This has been the most painful and well-researched book I have ever written. There is a certain irony here, since the 80/20 Principle tells us that I could have obtained a book 80 percent as good in 20 percent of the time. This would certainly have been my inclination, and only the reader can tell whether the extra effort has been worthwhile. I think it has, but I have lost all objectivity.

The effort involved has been much more collective than for any of my previous books. Don't believe the false modesty of those who write generously that their books have been "team efforts." In the end only an author (or authors) can write a book. But I want to thank some individuals without whom this book would either not have existed or would have been vastly inferior.

First is Mark Allin, then at Pitman Publishing and now my partner in Capstone Publishing, who first had the idea of the book.

Second is Nicholas Brealey, who has put so much intelligent effort into this book that I sincerely hope it pays off for him! According to the Von Manstein principle (see Chapter 13), people like Nicholas who are smart and industrious will not be as successful as those who are smart and lazy. To become a real star, Nicholas must work a great deal less. I have a theory that if he published half the number of books, and put all his effort into these, he'd make even more money. I hope my next book will not be one to get the axe! I am very grateful for his persistence on this book.

Sally Lansdell Yeung has been the "third person" collaborating to get the structure and text right. She is clearly a gifted publisher in her own right.

Next, my researcher on the book, Nick Oosterlinck, did a terrific job of reconstructing the history of the 80/20 Principle from 1897 to 1997. He has now disappeared from my radar screen, but if he would like to get in touch I would be delighted to dispense some champagne his way.

I should also thank not only Mr. Pareto for originating the 80/20 Principle, but also Mr. Juran, Mr. Zipf, Mr. Krugman, and the unsung heroes at IBM in the 1960s for elaborating it. And also the hundreds of people from all walks of life and disciplines who have written magazine articles about the 80/20 Principle, many of whom I have quoted extensively as evidence of the way in which the principle can be used. I have made every effort to acknowledge these people in the references, but if there are any omissions please accept my apologies and let me know so that correction can by made in any future editions. I am particularly grateful to David Parker, lecturer in managerial economics and business strategy at the University of Birmingham Business School, whose work on the application of chaos theory to business strategy is full of brilliant insights, many of which I have appropriated.

Finally, every true believer needs his trusted skeptics. Patrick Weaver and Lee Dempsey have fulfilled this role admirably, and it is much appreciated.

PART
ONE

OVERTURE

1

WELCOME TO THE
80/20 PRINCIPLE

For a very long time, the Pareto law [the 80/20 Principle] has lumbered the economic scene like an erratic block on the landscape; an empirical law which nobody can explain.

JOSEF STEINDL[1]

The 80/20 Principle can and should be used by every intelligent person in their daily life, by every organization, and by every social grouping and form of society. It can help individuals and groups achieve much more, with much less effort. The 80/20 Principle can raise personal effectiveness and happiness. It can multiply the profitability of corporations and the effectiveness of any organization. It even holds the key to raising the quality and quantity of public services while cutting their cost. This book, the first ever on the 80/20 Principle,[2] is written from a burning conviction, validated in personal and business experience, that this principle is one of the best ways of dealing with and transcending the pressures of modern life.

WHAT IS THE 80/20 PRINCIPLE?

The 80/20 Principle asserts that a minority of causes, inputs, or effort usually lead to a majority of the results, outputs, or rewards. Taken literally, this means that, for example, 80 percent of what you achieve in your job comes from 20 percent of the time spent. Thus for all practical purposes, four-fifths of the effort—a dominant part of it—is largely irrelevant. This is contrary to what people normally expect.

So the 80/20 Principle states that there is an inbuilt imbalance between causes and results, inputs and outputs, and effort and reward. A good benchmark for this imbalance is provided by the 80/20 relationship: a typical pattern will show that 80 percent of outputs result from 20 percent of inputs; that 80 percent of consequences flow from 20 percent of causes; or that 80 percent of results come from 20 percent of effort. Figure 1 shows these typical patterns.

In business, many examples of the 80/20 Principle have been validated. Twenty percent of products usually account for about 80 percent of dollar sales value; so do 20 percent of customers. Twenty percent of products or customers usually also account for about 80 percent of an organization's profits.

In society, 20 percent of criminals account for 80 percent of the value of all crime. Twenty percent of motorists cause 80 percent of accidents. Twenty percent of those who marry comprise 80 percent of the divorce statistics (those who consistently remarry and redivorce distort the statistics and give a lopsidedly pessimistic impression of the extent of marital fidelity). Twenty percent of children attain 80 percent of educational qualifications available.

In the home, 20 percent of your carpets are likely to get 80 percent of the wear. Twenty percent of your clothes will be worn 80 percent of the time. And if you have an intruder alarm, 80 percent of the false alarms will be set off by 20 percent of the possible causes.

The internal combustion engine is a great tribute to the 80/20 Principle. Eighty percent of the energy is wasted in combustion and only 20 percent gets to the wheels; this 20 percent of the input generates 100 percent of the output![3]

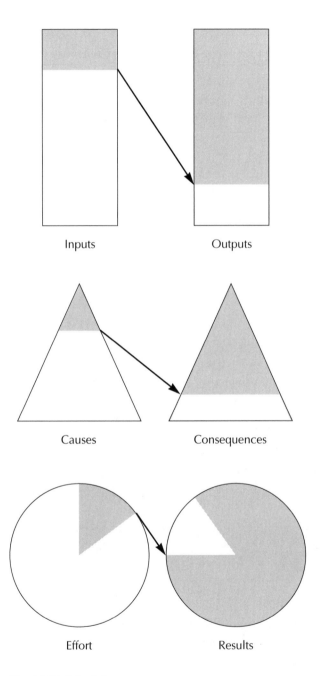

Inputs

Outputs

Causes

Consequences

Effort

Results

Figure 1   The 80/20 Principle

Pareto's discovery: systematic and predictable lack of balance

The pattern underlying the 80/20 Principle was discovered in 1897, about 100 years ago, by Italian economist Vilfredo Pareto (1848–1923). His discovery has since been called many names, including the Pareto Principle, the Pareto Law, the 80/20 Rule, the Principle of Least Effort, and the Principle of Imbalance; throughout this book we will call it the 80/20 Principle. By a subterranean process of influence on many important achievers, especially business people, computer enthusiasts and quality engineers, the 80/20 Principle has helped to shape the modern world. Yet it has remained one of the great secrets of our time—and even the select band of cognoscenti who know and use the 80/20 Principle only exploit a tiny proportion of its power.

So what did Vilfredo Pareto discover? He happened to be looking at patterns of wealth and income in nineteenth-century England. He found that most income and wealth went to a minority of the people in his samples. Perhaps there was nothing very surprising in this. But he also discovered two other facts that he thought highly significant. One was that there was a consistent mathematical relationship between the proportion of people (as a percentage of the total relevant population) and the amount of income or wealth that this group enjoyed.[4] To simplify, if 20 percent of the population enjoyed 80 percent of the wealth,[5] then you could reliably predict that 10 percent would have, say, 65 percent of the wealth, and 5 percent would have 50 percent. The key point is not the percentages, but the fact that the distribution of wealth across the population was *predictably unbalanced*.

Pareto's other finding, one that really excited him, was that this pattern of imbalance was repeated consistently whenever he looked at data referring to different time periods or different countries. Whether he looked at England in earlier times, or whatever data were available from other countries in his own time or earlier, he found the same pattern repeating itself, over and over again, with mathematical precision.

Was this a freak coincidence, or something that had great importance for economics and society? Would it work if applied to sets of data relating to things other than wealth or income? Pareto was a terrific innovator, because before him no one had looked at two related sets of data—in this case, the distribution of incomes or wealth, compared to the number of income earners or property owners—and compared percentages between the two sets of data. (Nowadays this method is commonplace and has led to major breakthroughs in business and economics.)

Sadly, although Pareto realized the importance and wide range of his discovery, he was very bad at explaining it. He moved on to a series of fascinating but rambling sociological theories, centering on the role of élites, which were hijacked at the end of his life by Mussolini's fascists. The significance of the 80/20 Principle lay dormant for a generation. While a few economists, especially in the US,[6] realized its importance, it was not until after the Second World War that two parallel yet completely different pioneers began to make waves with the 80/20 Principle.

1949: Zipf's Principle of Least Effort

One of these pioneers was the Harvard professor of philology, George K Zipf. In 1949 Zipf discovered the "Principle of Least Effort," which was actually a rediscovery and elaboration of Pareto's principle. Zipf's principle said that resources (people, goods, time, skills, or anything else that is productive) tended to arrange themselves so as to minimize work, so that approximately 20–30 per cent of any resource accounted for 70–80 per cent of the activity related to that resource.[7]

Professor Zipf used population statistics, books, philology, and industrial behavior to show the consistent recurrence of this unbalanced pattern. For example, he analyzed all the Philadelphia marriage licenses granted in 1931 in a 20-block area, demonstrating that 70 percent of the marriages occurred between people who lived within 30 percent of the distance.

Incidentally, Zipf also provided a scientific justification for the messy desk by justifying clutter with another law: frequency of use draws near to us things that are frequently used. Intelligent secretaries have long known that files in frequent use should not be filed!

1951: Juran's Rule of the Vital Few and the rise of Japan

The other pioneer of the 80/20 Principle was the great quality guru, Romanian-born U.S. engineer Joseph Moses Juran (born 1904), the man behind the Quality Revolution of 1950–90. He made what he alternately called the "Pareto Principle" and the "Rule of the Vital Few" virtually synonymous with the search for high product quality.

In 1924, Juran joined Western Electric, the manufacturing division of Bell Telephone System, starting as a corporate industrial engineer and later setting up as one of the world's first quality consultants.

His great idea was to use the 80/20 Principle, together with other statistical methods, to root out quality faults and improve the reliability and value of industrial and consumer goods. Juran's path-breaking *Quality Control Handbook* was first published in 1951 and extolled the 80/20 Principle in very broad terms:

> The economist Pareto found that wealth was nonuniformly distributed in the same way [as Juran's observations about quality losses]. Many other instances can be found—the distribution of crime amongst criminals, the distribution of accidents among hazardous processes, etc. Pareto's principle of unequal distribution applied to distribution of wealth and to distribution of quality losses.[8]

No major U.S. industrialist was interested in Juran's theories. In 1953 he was invited to Japan to lecture, and met a receptive audience. He stayed on to work with several Japanese corporations, transforming the value and quality of their consumer goods. It was only once the Japanese threat to U.S. industry had become apparent, after 1970, that Juran was taken seriously in the West. He moved back to do for U.S. industry what he had done for the Japanese. The 80/20 Principle was at the heart of this global quality revolution.

From the 1960s to the 1990s: progress from using the 80/20 Principle

IBM was one of the earliest and most successful corporations to spot and use the 80/20 Principle, which helps to explain why most computer systems specialists trained in the 1960s and 1970s are familiar with the idea.

In 1963, IBM discovered that about 80 percent of a computer's time is spent executing about 20 percent of the operating code. The company immediately rewrote its operating software to make the most-used 20 percent very accessible and user friendly, thus making IBM computers more efficient and faster than competitors' machines for the majority of applications.

Those who developed the personal computer and its software in the next generation, such as Apple, Lotus, and Microsoft, applied the 80/20 Principle with even more gusto to make their machines cheaper and easier to use for a new generation of customers, including the now celebrated "dummies" who would previously have given computers a very wide berth.

Winner take all

A century after Pareto, the implications of the 80/20 Principle have surfaced in a recent controversy over the astronomic and ever-rising incomes going to superstars and those very few people at the top of a growing number of professions. Film director Steven Spielberg earned $165 million in 1994. Joseph Jamial, the most highly paid trial lawyer, was paid $90 million. Merely competent film directors or lawyers, of course, earn a tiny fraction of these sums.

The twentieth century has seen massive efforts to level incomes, but inequality, removed in one sphere, keeps popping up in another. In the United States from 1973 to 1995, average real incomes rose by 36 percent, yet the comparable figure for nonsupervisory workers fell by 14 percent. During the 1980s, all of the gains went to the top 20 percent of earners, and a mind-boggling 64 percent of the total increase went to the top 1 percent! The ownership of shares in the United States is also heavily concentrated within a small minority of households: 5 percent of U.S. households own about 75 percent of the household sector's equity. A similar effect may be seen in the role of the dollar: almost 50 percent of world trade is invoiced in dollars, far above America's 13 percent share of world exports. And, while the dollar's share of foreign exchange reserves is 64 percent, the ratio of American GDP to global output is just over 20 percent. The 80/20

Principle will always reassert itself, unless conscious, consistent, and massive efforts are made and sustained to overcome it.

WHY THE 80/20 PRINCIPLE IS SO IMPORTANT

The reason that the 80/20 Principle is so valuable is that it is counter-intuitive. We tend to expect that all causes will have roughly the same significance. That all customers are equally valuable. That every bit of business, every product, and every dollar of sales revenue is as good as any other. That all employees in a particular category have roughly equivalent value. That each day or week or year we spend has the same significance. That all our friends have roughly equal value to us. That all inquiries or phone calls should be treated in the same way. That one university is as good as another. That all problems have a large number of causes, so that it is not worth isolating a few key causes. That all opportunities are of roughly equal value, so that we treat them all equally.

We tend to assume that 50 percent of causes or inputs will account for 50 percent of results or outputs. There seems to be a natural, almost democratic, expectation that causes and results are generally equally balanced. And, of course, sometimes they are. But this "50/50 fallacy" is one of the most inaccurate and harmful, as well as the most deeply rooted, of our mental maps. The 80/20 Principle asserts that when two sets of data, relating to causes and results, can be examined and analyzed, the most likely result is that there will be a pattern of imbalance. The imbalance may be 65/35, 70/30, 75/25, 80/20, 95/5, or 99.9/0.1, or any set of numbers in between. However, the two numbers in the comparison don't have to add up to 100 (see page 24).

The 80/20 Principle also asserts that when we know the true relationship, we are likely to be surprised at how unbalanced it is. Whatever the actual level of imbalance, it is likely to exceed our prior estimate. Executives may suspect that some customers and some products are more profitable than others, but when the extent of the difference is proved, they are likely to be surprised and sometimes dumbfounded. Teachers may know that the majority of their disciplinary troubles or most truancy arises from a minority of pupils, but if records are analyzed the extent of the imbalance will probably be larger than expected. We may feel that some of our time is more valuable than the rest, but if we measure inputs and outputs the disparity can still stun us.

Why should you care about the 80/20 Principle? Whether you realize it or not, the principle applies to your life, to your social world, and to the place where you work. Understanding the 80/20 Principle gives you great insight into what is really happening in the world around you.

The overriding message of this book is that our daily lives can be greatly improved by using the 80/20 Principle. Each individual can be more effective and happier. Each profit-seeking corporation can become very much more profitable. Each nonprofit organization can also deliver much more useful outputs. Every government can ensure that its citizens benefit much more from its existence. For everyone and every institution, it is possible to obtain much more that is of value and avoid what has negative value, with much less input of effort, expense, or investment.

At the heart of this progress is a process of substitution. Resources that have weak effects in any particular use are not used, or are used sparingly. Resources that have powerful effects are used as much as possible. Every resource is ideally used where it has the greatest value. Wherever possible, weak resources are developed so that they can mimic the behavior of the stronger resources.

Business and markets have used this process, to great effect, for hundreds of years. The French economist J-B Say coined the word "entrepreneur" around 1800, saying that "the entrepreneur shifts economic resources out of an area of lower productivity into an area of higher productivity and yield." But one fascinating implication of the 80/20 Principle is how far businesses and markets still are from producing optimal solutions. For example, the 80/20 Principle asserts that 20 percent of products, or customers or employees, are really responsible for about 80 percent of profits. If this is true—and detailed investigations usually confirm that some such very unbalanced pattern exists—the state of affairs implied is very far from being efficient or optimal. The implication is that 80 percent of products, or customers or employees, are only contributing 20 percent of profits; that there is great waste; that the most powerful resources of the company are being held back by a majority of much less effective resources; that profits could be multiplied if more of the best sort of products could be sold, employees hired, or customers attracted (or convinced to buy more from the firm).

In this kind of situation one might well ask: why continue to make the 80 percent of products that only generate 20 percent of profits? Companies rarely ask these questions, perhaps because to answer them would mean very radical action: to stop doing four-fifths of what you are doing is not a trivial change.

What J-B Say called the work of entrepreneurs, modern financiers call arbitrage. International financial markets are very quick to correct anomalies in valuation, for example between exchange rates. But business organizations and individuals are generally very poor at this sort of entrepreneurship or arbitrage, at shifting resources from where they have weak results to where they have powerful results, or at cutting off low-value resources and buying more high-value resources. Most of the time, we do not realize the extent to which some resources, but only a small minority, are superproductive—what Joseph Juran called the "vital few"—while the majority—the "trivial many"—exhibit little productivity or else actually have negative value. If we did realize the difference between the vital few and the trivial many in all aspects of our lives and if we did something about it, we could multiply anything that we valued.

THE 80/20 PRINCIPLE AND CHAOS THEORY

Probability theory tells us that it is virtually impossible for all the applications of the 80/20 Principle to occur randomly, as a freak of chance. We can only explain the principle by positing some deeper meaning or cause that lurks behind it.

Pareto himself grappled with this issue, trying to apply a consistent methodology to the study of society. He searched for "theories that picture facts of experience and observation," for regular patterns, social laws, or "uniformities" that explain the behavior of individuals and society.

Pareto's sociology failed to find a persuasive key. He died long before the emergence of chaos theory, which has great parallels with the 80/20 Principle and helps to explain it.

The last third of the twentieth century has seen a revolution in the way that scientists think about the universe, overturning the prevailing wisdom of the past 350 years. That prevailing wisdom was a machine-based and rational view, which itself was a great advance on the mystical and random view of the world held in the Middle Ages. The machine-based view converted God from being an irrational and unpredictable force into a more user-friendly clockmaker-engineer.

The view of the world held from the seventeenth century and still prevalent today, except in advanced scientific circles, was immensely comforting and useful. All phenomena were reduced to regular, predictable, *linear* relationships. For example, *a* causes *b*, *b* causes *c*, and *a* + *c* cause *d*. This worldview enabled any individual part of the universe—the operation of the human heart, for example, or of any individual market—to be analyzed separately, because the whole was the sum of the parts and vice versa.

But in the second half of the twentieth century it seems much more accurate to view the world as an evolving organism where the whole system is more than the sum of its parts, and where relationships between the parts are nonlinear. Causes are difficult to pin down, there are complex interdependencies between causes, and causes and effects are blurred. The snag with linear thinking is that it doesn't always work, it is an oversimplification of reality. Equilibrium is illusory or fleeting. The universe is wonky.

Yet chaos theory, despite its name, does not say that everything is a hopeless and incomprehensible mess. Rather, there is a self-organizing logic lurking behind the disorder, a *predictable nonlinearity*— something which economist Paul Krugman has called "spooky," "eerie," and "terrifyingly exact."[9] The logic is more difficult to describe than to detect and is not totally dissimilar to the recurrence of a theme in a piece of music. Certain characteristic patterns recur, but with infinite and unpredictable variety.

Chaos theory and the 80/20 Principle illuminate each other

What have chaos theory and related scientific concepts got to do with the 80/20 Principle? Although no one else appears to have made the link, I think the answer is: a great deal.

The principle of imbalance

The common thread between chaos theory and the 80/20 Principle is the issue of *balance*—or, more precisely, *imbalance*. Both chaos theory and the 80/20 Principle assert (with a great deal of empirical backing) that the universe is unbalanced. They both say that the world is not linear; cause and effect are rarely linked in an equal way. Both also place great store by self-organization: some forces are always more forceful than others and will try to grab more than their fair share of resources. Chaos theory helps to explain why and how this imbalance happens by tracing a number of developments over time.

The universe is not a straight line

The 80/20 Principle, like chaos theory, is based around the idea of nonlinearity. A great deal of what happens is unimportant and can be disregarded. Yet there are always a few forces that have an influence way beyond their numbers. These are the forces that must be identified and watched. If they are forces for good, we should multiply them. If they are forces we don't like, we need to think very carefully about how to neutralize them. The 80/20 Principle supplies a very powerful empirical test of nonlinearity in any system: we can ask, do 20 percent of causes lead to 80 percent of results? Is 80 percent of any phenomenon associated with only 20 percent of a related phenomenon? This is a useful method to flush out nonlinearity, but it is even more useful because it directs us to identifying the unusually powerful forces at work.

Feedback loops distort and disturb balance

The 80/20 Principle is also consistent with, and can be explained by, reference to the feedback loops identified by chaos theory, whereby small initial influences can become greatly multiplied and produce highly unexpected results, which nevertheless can be explained in retrospect. In the absence of feedback loops, the natural distribution of phenomena would be 50/50—inputs of a given frequency would lead to commensurate results. It is only because of positive and negative feedback loops that causes do not have equal results. Yet it also seems to be true that powerful positive feedback loops only affect a small minority of the inputs. This helps to explain why those small minority of inputs can exert so much influence.

We can see positive feedback loops operating in many areas, explaining how it is that we typically end up with 80/20 rather than 50/50 relationships between populations. For example, the rich get richer, not just (or mainly) because of superior abilities, but because riches beget riches. A similar phenomenon exists with goldfish in a pond. Even if you start with goldfish almost exactly the same size, those that are slightly bigger become very much bigger, because, even with only slight initial advantages in stronger propulsion and larger mouths, they are able to capture and gobble up disproportionate amounts of food.

The tipping point

Related to the idea of feedback loops is the concept of the tipping point. Up to a certain point, a new force—whether it is a new product, a disease, a new rock group, or a new social habit such as jogging or roller blading—finds it difficult to make headway. A great deal of effort generates little by way of results. At this point many pioneers give up. But if the new force persists and can cross a certain invisible line, a small amount of additional effort can reap huge returns. This invisible line is the tipping point.

The concept comes from the principles of epidemic theory. The tipping point is "the point at which an ordinary and stable phenomenon—a low-level flu outbreak—can turn into a public-health crisis,"[10] because of the number of people who are infected and can therefore infect others. And since the behavior of epidemics is non-linear and they don't behave in the way we expect, "small changes—like bringing new infections down to thirty thousand from forty thousand—can have huge effects . . . It all depends when and how the changes are made."[11]

First come, best served

Chaos theory advocates "sensitive dependence on initial conditions"[12]—what happens first, even something ostensibly trivial, can have a disproportionate effect. This resonates with, and helps to explain, the 80/20 Principle. The latter states that a minority of causes exert a majority of effects. One limitation of the 80/20 Principle, taken in isolation, is that it always represents a snapshot of what is true now (or, more precisely, in the very recent past when the snapshot was taken). This is where chaos theory's doctrine of sensitive dependence on initial conditions is helpful. A small lead early on can turn into a larger lead or a dominant position later on, until equilibrium is disturbed and another small force then exerts a disproportionate influence.

A firm that, in the early stages of a market, provides a product that is 10 percent better than its rivals may end up with a 100 or 200 percent greater market share, even if the rivals later provide a better product. In the early days of motoring, if 51 percent of drivers or countries decide to drive on the right rather than the left side of the road, this will tend to become the norm for nearly 100 percent of road users. In the early days of using a circular clock, if 51 percent of clocks go what we now call "clockwise" rather than "counterclockwise," this convention will become dominant, although clocks could just as logically have moved to the left. In fact, the clock over Florence cathedral moves counterclockwise and shows 24 hours.[13] Soon after 1442 when the cathedral was built, the authorities and clockmakers standardized on a 12-hour, "clockwise" clock, because the majority of clocks had those features. Yet if 51 percent of clocks had ever been like the clock over Florence cathedral, we would now be reading a 24-hour clock backwards.

These observations regarding sensitive dependence on initial conditions do not exactly illustrate the 80/20 Principle. The examples given involve *change over time*, whereas the 80/20 Principle involves a *static* breakdown of causes *at any one time*. Yet there is an important link between the two. Both phenomena help to show how the universe abhors balance. In the former case, we see a natural flight away from a 50/50 split of competing phenomena. A 51/49 split is inherently unstable and tends to gravitate towards a 95/5, 99/1, or even 100/0 split. Equality ends in dominance: that is one of the messages of chaos theory. The 80/20 Principle's message is different yet complementary. It tells us that, at any one point, a majority of any phenomenon will be explained or caused by a minority of the actors participating in the phenomenon. Eighty percent of the results come from 20 percent of the causes. A few things are important; most are not.

The 80/20 Principle sorts good movies from bad

One of the most dramatic examples of the 80/20 Principle at work is with movies. Two economists have just made a study of the revenues and lifespans of 300 movies released over an 18-month period.[14] They found that four movies—just 1.3 percent of the total—earned 80 percent of box office revenues; the other 296 movies or 98.7 percent earned only 20 percent of the gross. So movies, which are a good example of unrestricted markets at work, produce virtually an 80/1 rule, a very clear demonstration of the principle of imbalance.

Even more intriguing is why. It transpires that movie goers behave just like gas particles in random motion. As identified by chaos theory, gas particles, Ping-Pong balls, or movie goers all behave at random but produce a predictably unbalanced result. Word of mouth, from reviews and the first audiences, determines whether the second set of audiences will be large or small, which determines the next set and so on. Movies like *Independence Day* or *Mission Impossible* continue to play to packed houses, while other star-studded and expensive movies, like *Waterworld* or *Daylight*, very quickly play to smaller and smaller houses, and then none at all. This is the 80/20 Principle working with a vengeance.

A GUIDE TO THIS GUIDEBOOK

Chapter 2 explains how you can put the 80/20 Principle into practice and explores the distinction between 80/20 Analysis and 80/20 Thinking, both of which are useful methods derived from the 80/20 Principle. 80/20 Analysis is a systematic, quantitative method of comparing causes and effects. 80/20 Thinking is a broader, less precise, and more intuitive procedure, comprising the mental models and habits that enable us to hypothesize what are the important causes of anything important in our lives, to identify these causes, and to make sharp improvements in our position by redeploying our resources accordingly.

Part Two: Corporate Success Needn't be a Mystery summarizes the most powerful business uses of the 80/20 Principle. These uses have been tried and tested and found to be of immense value yet remain curiously unexploited by most of the business community. There is little in my summary that is original, but anyone seeking major profit improvement, whether for a small or large business, should find this a very useful primer and the first ever to appear in a book.

Part Three: Work Less, Earn and Enjoy More shows how the 80/20 Principle can be used to raise the level at which you are operating in both your work and personal life. This is a pioneering attempt to apply the 80/20 Principle on a novel canvas; and the attempt, although I am sure it is imperfect and incomplete in many ways, does lead to some surprising insights. For example, 80 percent of the typical person's happiness or achievement in life occurs in a small proportion of that life. The peaks of great personal value can usually be greatly expanded. The common view is that we are short of time. My application of the 80/20 Principle suggests the reverse: that we are actually awash with time and profligate in its abuse.

Part Four: Crescendo—Progress Regained draws the themes together and positions the 80/20 Principle as the greatest secret engine of progress available to us all. It hints at the uses that could be made of the 80/20 Principle for the public good as well as for corporate wealth creation and personal advancement.

WHY THE 80/20 PRINCIPLE BRINGS GOOD NEWS

I want to end this introduction on a personal rather than a procedural note. I believe that the 80/20 Principle is enormously hopeful. Certainly, the principle brings home what may be evident anyway: that there is a tragic amount of waste everywhere, in the way that nature operates, in business, in society, and in our own lives. If the typical pattern is for 80 percent of results to come from 20 percent of inputs, it is necessarily typical too that 80 percent, the great majority, of inputs are having only a marginal—20 percent—impact.

The paradox is that such waste can be wonderful news, if we can use the 80/20 Principle creatively, not just to identify and castigate low productivity but to do something positive about it. There is enormous scope for improvement, by rearranging and redirecting both nature and our own lives. Improving on nature, refusing to accept the status quo, is the route of all progress: evolutionary, scientific, social, and personal. George Bernard Shaw put it well: "The reasonable man adapts himself to the world. The unreasonable one persists in trying to adapt the world to himself. Therefore all progress depends on the unreasonable man."[15]

The implication of the 80/20 Principle is that output can be not just increased but multiplied, if we can make the low-productivity inputs nearly as productive as the high-productivity inputs. Successful experiments with the 80/20 Principle in the business arena suggest that, with creativity and determination, this leap in value can usually be made.

There are two routes to achieving this. One is to reallocate the resources from unproductive to productive uses, the secret of all entrepreneurs down the ages. Find a round hole for a round peg, a square hole for a square peg, and a perfect fit for any shape in between. Experience suggests that every resource has its ideal arena, where the resource can be tens or hundreds of times more effective than in most other arenas.

The other route to progress—the method of scientists, doctors, preachers, computer systems designers, educationalists, and trainers—is to find ways to make the unproductive resources more effective, even in their existing applications; to make the weak resources behave as though they were their more productive cousins; to mimic, if necessary by intricate rote-learning procedures, the highly productive resources.

The few things that work fantastically well should be identified, cultivated, nurtured, and multiplied. At the same time, the waste—the majority of things that will always prove to be of low value to man and beast—should be abandoned or severely cut back.

As I have been writing this book and observed thousands of examples of the 80/20 Principle, I have had my faith reinforced: faith in progress, in great leaps forward, and in mankind's ability, individually and collectively, to improve the hand that nature has dealt. Joseph Ford comments: "God plays dice with the universe. But they're loaded dice. And the main objective is to find out by what rules they were loaded and how we can use them for our own ends."[16]

The 80/20 Principle can help us achieve precisely that.

2

HOW TO THINK 80/20

Chapter 1 explained the concept behind the 80/20 Principle; this chapter will discuss how the 80/20 Principle works in practice and what it can do for you. Two applications of the principle, 80/20 Analysis and 80/20 Thinking, provide a practical philosophy which will help you understand and improve your life.

DEFINITION OF THE 80/20 PRINCIPLE

The 80/20 Principle states that there is an inbuilt imbalance between causes and results, inputs and outputs, and effort and reward. Typically, causes, inputs, or effort divide into two categories:

- the majority, that have little impact
- a small minority, that have a major, dominant impact.

Typically also, results, outputs, or rewards are derived from a small proportion of the causes, inputs, or effort aimed at producing the results, outputs, or rewards.

The relationship between causes, inputs, or efforts on the one hand, and results, outputs, or rewards on the other, is therefore typically unbalanced.

When this imbalance can be measured arithmetically, a good benchmark for the imbalance is the 80/20 relationship—80 percent of results, outputs, or rewards are derived from only 20 percent of the causes, inputs, or effort. About 80 percent of the world's energy is consumed by 15 percent of the world's population, for example.[1] Eighty percent of the world's wealth is possessed by 25 percent of the world's people.[2] In health care, "20 percent of your population base and/or 20 percent of its disease elements will consume 80 percent of your resources."[3]

Figures 2 and 3 show this 80/20 pattern. Let us imagine that a company has 100 products and has found out that the most profitable 20 products account for 80 percent of all profits. In Figure 2, the bar on the left comprises the 100 products, each occupying an equal hundredth of the space.

In the bar on the right are the total profits of the company from the 100 products. Imagine that the profits from the one most profitable product are filled in from the top of the right-hand bar downwards. Let us say that the most profitable product makes 20 percent of total profits. Figure 2 therefore shows that one product, or 1

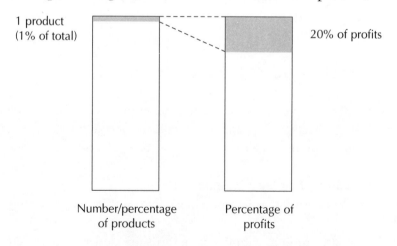

1 product
(1% of total)   20% of profits

Number/percentage   Percentage of
    of products   profits

1 product—1% of the total—makes 20% of total profits
Figure 2   Shows a 20/1 pattern

percent of the products, occupying one hundredth of the space on the left, makes 20 percent of the profits. The shaded areas represent this relationship.

If we continue counting the next most profitable product and so on down the bar, until we have the profits from the top 20 products, we can then shade in the right-hand bar according to how much of the total profit these top 20 products make. We show this in Figure 3, where we see (in our fictitious example) that these 20 products, 20 percent of the number of products, comprise 80 percent of the total profits (in the shaded area). Conversely, in the white area, we can see the flip side of this relationship: 80 percent of the products only make, in total, 20 percent of the profits.

The 80/20 numbers are only a benchmark, and the real relationship may be more or less unbalanced than 80/20. The 80/20 Principle asserts, however, that in most cases the relationship is much more likely to be closer to 80/20 than to 50/50. If all of the products in our example made the same profit, then the relationship would be as shown in Figure 4.

The curious but crucial point is that, when such investigations are conducted, Figure 3 turns out to be a much more typical pattern than Figure 4. Nearly always, a small proportion of total products produces a large proportion of profits.

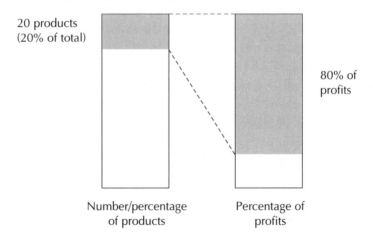

20 products—20% of total—make 80% of the profits
Figure 3   A typical 80/20 pattern

Figure 4   An unusual 50/50 pattern

Of course, the exact relationship may not be 80/20. 80/20 is both a convenient metaphor and a useful hypothesis, but it is not the only pattern. Sometimes, 80 percent of the profits come from 30 percent of the products; sometimes 80 percent of the profits come from 15 percent or even 10 percent of the products. The numbers compared do not have to add up to 100, but the picture usually looks unbalanced, much more like Figure 3 than Figure 4.

It is perhaps unfortunate that the numbers 80 and 20 add up to 100. This makes the result look elegant (as, indeed, would a result of 50/50, 70/30, 99/1, or many other combinations) and it is certainly memorable, but it makes many people think that we are dealing with just one set of data, one 100 percent. This is not so. If 80 percent of people are right-handed and 20 percent are left-handed, this is not an 80/20 observation. To apply the 80/20 Principle you have to have two sets of data, both adding up to 100 per cent, and one measuring a variable quantity owned, exhibited, or caused by the people or things making up the other 100 percent.

WHAT THE 80/20 PRINCIPLE CAN DO FOR YOU

Every person I have known who has taken the 80/20 Principle seriously has emerged with useful, and in some cases life-changing, insights. You have to work out your own uses for the principle: they will be there if you look creatively. Part Three (Chapters 9 to 15) will guide you on your odyssey, but I can illustrate with some examples from my own life.

How the 80/20 Principle has helped me

When I was a raw student at Oxford, my tutor told me never to go to lectures. "Books can be read far faster," he explained. "But never read a book from cover to cover, except for pleasure. When you are working, find out what the book is saying much faster than you would by reading it through. Read the conclusion, then the introduction, then the conclusion again, then dip lightly into any interesting bits." What he was really saying was that 80 percent of the value of a book can be found in 20 percent or fewer of its pages and absorbed in 20 percent of the time most people would take to read it through.

I took to this study method and extended it. At Oxford there is no system of continuous assessment, and the class of degree earned depends entirely on finals, the examinations taken at the end of the course. I discovered from the "form book," that is by analyzing past examination papers, that at least 80 percent (sometimes 100 percent) of an examination could be well answered with knowledge from 20 percent or fewer of the subjects that the exam was meant to cover. The examiners could therefore be much better impressed by a student who knew an awful lot about relatively little, rather than a fair amount about a great deal. This insight enabled me to study very efficiently. Somehow, without working very hard, I ended up with a congratulatory First Class degree. I used to think this proved that Oxford dons were gullible. I now prefer to think, perhaps improbably, that they were teaching us how the world worked.

I went to work for Shell, serving my time at a dreadful oil refinery. This may have been good for my soul, but I rapidly realized that the best-paying jobs for young and inexperienced people such as I lay in management consultancy. So I went to Philadelphia and picked up an effortless MBA from Wharton (scorning the boot-camp style so-called learning experience from Harvard). I joined a leading U.S. consultancy that on day one paid me four times what Shell had paid me when I left. No doubt 80 percent of the money to be had by people of my tender age was concentrated in 20 percent of the jobs.

Since there were too many colleagues in the consultancy who were smarter than me, I moved to another U.S. strategy "boutique." I identified it because it was growing faster than the firm I had joined, yet had a much smaller proportion of really smart people.

Who you work for is more important than what you do

Here I stumbled across many paradoxes of the 80/20 Principle. Eighty percent of the growth in the strategy consultancy industry— then, as now, growing like gangbusters—was being appropriated by firms that then had, in total, fewer than 20 percent of the industry's professional staff. Eighty percent of rapid promotions were also available in just a handful of firms. Believe me, talent had very little to do with it. When I left the first strategy firm and joined the second, I raised the average level of intelligence in both.

Yet the puzzling thing was that my new colleagues were more effective than my old ones. Why? They didn't work any harder. But they followed the 80/20 Principle in two key ways. First, they realized that for most firms, 80 percent of profits come from 20 percent of clients. In the consulting industry that means two things: large clients and long-term clients. Large clients give large assignments, which means you can use a higher proportion of lower-cost, younger consultants. Long-term client relationships create trust and raise the cost to the client of switching to another consulting firm. Long-term clients tend not to be price sensitive.

In most consulting firms, the real excitement comes from winning new clients. In my new firm, the real heroes were those who worked on the largest existing clients for the longest possible time. They did this by cultivating the top bosses of those client corporations.

The second key insight the consulting firm had was that in any client, 80 percent of the results available would flow from concentrating on the 20 percent of most important issues. These were not necessarily the most interesting ones from a curious consultant's viewpoint. But, whereas our competitors would look superficially at a whole range of issues and then leave them for the client to act (or not) on the recommendations, we kept plugging away at the most important issues until we had bludgeoned the client into successful action. The clients' profits often soared as a result, as did our consulting budgets.

Are you working to make others rich or is it the reverse?

I soon became convinced that, for both consultants and their clients, effort and reward were at best only loosely linked. It was better to be in the right place than to be smart and work hard. It was best to be cunning and focus on results rather than inputs. Acting on a few key insights produced the goods. Being intelligent and hard working did not. Sadly, for many years, guilt and conformity to peer-group pressure kept me from fully acting on this lesson; I worked far too hard.

By this time, the consulting firm had several hundred professional staff and about 30 people, including myself, who were called partners. But 80 percent of the profits went to one man, the founder, even though numerically he constituted less than 4 percent of the partnership and a fraction of 1 percent of the consulting force.

Instead of continuing to enrich the founder, two other junior partners and I spun off to set up our own firm doing exactly the same thing. We in turn grew to have hundreds of consultants. Before long, although the three of us, on any measure, did less than 20 percent of the firm's valuable work, we enjoyed over 80 percent of the profits. This, too, caused me guilt. After six years I quit, selling my shares to the other partners. At this time, we had doubled our revenues and profits every year, and I was able to secure a good price for my shares. Shortly after, the recession of 1990 hit the consulting industry. Although I will counsel you later to give up guilt, I was lucky with my guilt. Even those who follow the 80/20 Principle need a bit of luck, and I have always enjoyed far more than my share.

Wealth from investment can dwarf wealth from working

With 20 percent of the money received, I made a large investment in the shares of one corporation, Filofax. Investment advisers were horrified. At the time I owned about 20 shares in quoted public companies, but this one stock, 5 percent of the number of shares I owned, accounted for about 80 percent of my portfolio. Fortunately, the proportion proceeded to grow still further, as over the next three years Filofax shares multiplied several times in value. When I sold some shares, in 1995, it was at nearly 18 times the price I had paid for my first stake.

I made two other large investments, one in a start-up restaurant called Belgo and the other in MSI, a hotel company that at the time owned no hotels. Together, these three investments at cost comprised about 20 percent of my net worth. But they have accounted for more than 80 percent of my subsequent investment gains and now comprise over 80 percent of a much larger net worth.

As Chapter 14 will show, 80 percent of the increase in wealth from most long-term portfolios comes from fewer than 20 percent of the investments. It is crucial to pick this 20 percent well and then concentrate as much investment as possible into it. Conventional wisdom is not to put all your eggs in one basket. 80/20 wisdom is to choose a basket carefully, load all your eggs into it, and then watch it like a hawk.

HOW TO USE THE 80/20 PRINCIPLE

There are two ways to use the 80/20 Principle, as shown in Figure 5.

Traditionally, the 80/20 Principle has required 80/20 Analysis, a quantitative method to establish the precise relationship between causes/input/effort and results/outputs/rewards. This method uses the possible existence of the 80/20 relationship as a hypothesis and then gathers the facts so that the true relationship is revealed. This is an empirical procedure which may lead to any result ranging from 50/50 to 99.9/0.1. If the result does demonstrate a marked imbalance between inputs and outputs (say a 65/35 relationship or an even more unbalanced one), then normally action is taken as a result (see below).

A new and complementary way to use the 80/20 Principle is what I call 80/20 Thinking. This requires deep thought about any issue that is important to you and asks you to make a judgment on whether the 80/20 Principle is working in that area. You can then act on the insight. 80/20 Thinking does not require you to collect data or actually test the hypothesis. Consequently, 80/20 Thinking may on occa-

Figure 5   Two ways to use the 80/20 Principle

sion mislead you—it is dangerous to assume, for example, that you already know what the 20 percent is if you identify a relationship—but I will argue that 80/20 Thinking is much less likely to mislead you than is conventional thinking. 80/20 Thinking is much more accessible and faster than 80/20 Analysis, although the latter may be preferred when the issue is extremely important and you find it difficult to be confident about an estimate.

We look first at 80/20 Analysis and then at 80/20 Thinking.

80/20 ANALYSIS

80/20 Analysis examines the relationship between two sets of comparable data. One set of data is always a universe of people or objects, usually a large number of 100 or more, that can be turned into a percentage. The other set of data relates to some interesting characteristic of the people or objects that can be measured and also turned into a percentage.

For example, we might decide to look at a group of 100 friends, all of whom are at least occasional beer drinkers, and compare how much beer they drank last week.

So far, this method of analysis is common to many statistical techniques. What makes 80/20 Analysis unique is that the measurement ranks the second set of data in descending order of importance and makes comparisons between percentages in the two sets of data.

In our example, then, we will ask all our 100 friends how many glasses of beer they drank last week and array the answers in a table in descending order. Figure 6 shows the top 20 and bottom 20 from the table.

80/20 Analysis can compare percentages from the two sets of data (the friends and the amount of beer drunk). In this case, we can say that 70 percent of the beer was drunk by just 20 percent of the friends. This would therefore give us a 70/20 relationship. Figure 7 introduces an 80/20 frequency distribution chart (or 80/20 chart for short) to summarize the data visually.

Why is this called 80/20 Analysis?

When comparing these relationships, the most frequent observation, made long ago (probably in the 1950s), was that 80 percent of the quantity being measured came from 20 percent of the people or objects. 80/20 has become shorthand for this type of unbalanced relationship, whether or not the precise result is 80/20 (statistically, an exact 80/20 relationship is unlikely). It is the convention of 80/20 that it is the *top* 20 percent of causes that is cited, not the bottom. 80/20 Analysis is my name for the way that the 80/20 Principle has generally been used to date, that is, in a quantitative and empirical way, to measure possible relationships between inputs and outputs.

We could equally well observe from the data on our beer-drinking friends that the bottom 20 percent of people only consumed 30 glasses, or 3 percent of the total. It would also be perfectly legitimate to call this a 3/20 relationship, although this is rarely done. The emphasis is nearly always on the heavy users or causes. If a brewery was conducting a promotion or wanted to find out what beer drinkers

Rank	Name	Glasses drunk	Cumulative
		Our top 20 beer drinkers	
1	Charles H	45	45
2	Richard J	43	88
3=	George K	42	130
3=	Fred F	42	172
5	Arthur M	41	213
6	Steve B	40	253
7	Peter T	39	292
8	Reg C	37	329
9=	George B	36	365
9=	Bomber J	36	401
9=	Fatty M	36	437
12	Marian C	33	470
13	Stewart M	32	502
14	Cheryl W	31	533
15=	Kevin C	30	563
15=	Nick B	30	593
15=	Ricky M	30	623
15=	Nigel H	30	653
19	Greg H	26	679
20	Carol K	21	700
		Our bottom 20 beer drinkers	
81=	Rupert E	3	973
81=	Patrick W	3	976
81=	Anne B	3	979
81=	Jamie R	3	982
85=	Stephanie F	2	984
85=	Carli S	2	986
87=	Roberta F	1	987
87=	Pat B	1	988
87=	James P	1	989
87=	Charles W	1	990
87=	Jon T	1	991
87=	Edward W	1	992
87=	Margo L	1	993
87=	Rosabeth M	1	994
87=	Shirley W	1	995
87=	Greg P	1	996
87=	Gilly C	1	997
87=	Francis H	1	998
87=	David C	1	999
87=	Darleen B	1	1000

Figure 6   The 80/20 Principle applied to beer drinkers

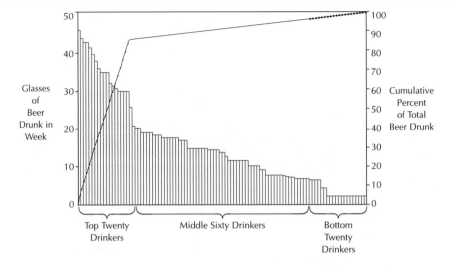

Figure 7   80/20 frequency distribution chart of beer drinkers

thought about their range of beers, it would be most useful to go to the top 20.

We might also want to know what percentage of our friends combined to account for 80 percent of total beer consumption. In this case, inspection of the part of the table not displayed (the middle part) would show that Mike G, the 28th biggest drinker with 10 glasses, took the cumulative total to 800 glasses. We could express this relationship, therefore, as 80/28: 80 percent of total beer was drunk by just 28 percent of our friends.

It should be clear from this example that 80/20 Analysis may result in any set of findings. Clearly, individual findings are more interesting and potentially more useful where there is an imbalance. If, for example, we had found that all of our friends had drunk exactly eight glasses each, the brewery would not have been very interested in using our group for a promotion or research. In this case, we would have had a 20/20 relationship (20 percent of beer was drunk by the "top" 20 percent of friends) or an 80/80 relationship (80 percent of beer was drunk by 80 percent of friends).

Bar charts show 80/20 relationships best

An 80/20 Analysis is best displayed pictorially, by looking at two bars—as is particularly appropriate for our example! (Figures 2–4 above were bar charts.) The first bar in Figure 8 contains our 100 beer-drinking friends, each filling 1 percent of the space, starting with the biggest beer drinker at the top and ending with the smallest beer drinkers at the bottom. The second bar contains the total amount of beer drunk by each (and all) of our friends. At any point, we can see for a given percentage of our friends how much beer they accounted for.

Figure 8 shows what we discovered from the table (and could also see from Figure 7): the top 20 percent of beer drinkers accounted for 70 percent of the beer drunk. The simple bars in Figure 8 take the data from Figure 7 and display them from top to bottom instead of from left to right. It doesn't matter which display you prefer.

If we wanted to illustrate what percentage of our friends drank 80 percent of the beer, we would draw the bar charts slightly differently, as in Figure 9, to show the 80/28 relationship: 28 percent of our friends drank 80 percent of the beer.

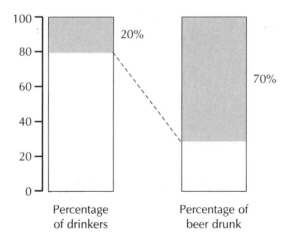

Figure 8   Beer / beer drinking ratios

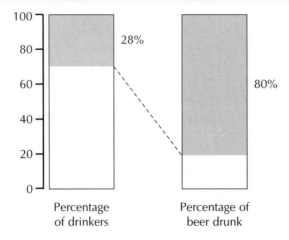

Shows an 80/28 rule
Figure 9   Beer / beer drinking ratios

What is 80/20 Analysis used for?

Generally, to change the relationship it describes, or to make better use of it!

One use is to concentrate on the key causes of the relationship, the 20 percent of inputs that lead to 80 percent (or whatever the precise number is) of the outputs. If the top 20 percent of beer drinkers account for 70 percent of beer consumed, this is the group that a brewery should concentrate on reaching, in order to attract as high a share as possible of the business from the 20 percent, and possibly also to increase their beer consumption still further. For all practical purposes, the brewery may decide to ignore the 80 percent of beer drinkers who only consume 30 percent of the beer; this simplifies the task immensely.

Similarly, a firm that finds that 80 percent of its profits come from 20 percent of its customers should use this information to concentrate on keeping that 20 percent happy and increasing the business carried out with them. This is much easier, as well as more rewarding, than paying equal attention to the whole customer group. Or, if the firm finds that 80 percent of its profits come from 20 percent of its products, it should put most of its efforts behind selling more of those products.

The same idea applies to nonbusiness applications of 80/20 Analysis. If you analyzed the enjoyment you derived from all your leisure activities and found that 80 percent of the enjoyment derived from 20 percent of the activities, which currently took only 20 percent of your leisure time, it would make sense to increase the time allocation from 20 to at least 80 percent.

Take transport as another example. 80 percent of traffic jams occur on 20 percent of roads. If you drive on the same route to work each day, you will know that roughly 80 percent of delays usually occur at 20 percent of the intersections. A sensible reaction would be for traffic authorities to pay particular attention to traffic phasing on those 20 percent of jam-creating intersections. While the expense of such phasing might be too much for 100 percent of junctions 100 percent of the time, it would be money well spent in the key 20 percent of locations for 20 percent of the day.

The second main use of 80/20 Analysis is to do something about the "underperforming" 80 percent of inputs that contribute only 20 percent of the output. Perhaps the occasional beer drinkers can be persuaded to drink more, for example by providing a blander product. Perhaps you could work out ways to get greater enjoyment out of the "underperforming" leisure activities. In education, interactive teaching systems now replicate the technique used by college professors where questions are addressed randomly to any student, in order to combat the 80/20 rule, where 80 percent of classroom participation comes from 20 percent of the trainees. In U.S. shopping malls it has been found that women (some 50 percent of the population) account for 70 percent of the dollar value of all purchases.[4] One way to increase the 30 percent of sales to men might be to build stores specifically designed for them. Although this second application of 80/20 Analysis is sometimes very useful and has been put to great effect in industry in improving the productivity of underperforming factories, it is generally harder work and less rewarding than the first use.

Don't apply 80/20 Analysis in a linear way

In discussing the uses of 80/20 Analysis, we must also briefly address its potential abuses. Like any simple and effective tool, 80/20 Analysis can also be misunderstood, misapplied, and, instead of being the means to an unusual insight, serve as the justification for conventional thuggery. 80/20 Analysis, applied inappropriately and in a linear way, can also lead the innocent astray—you need constantly to be vigilant against false logic.

Let me illustrate this with an example from my own new profession, the book trade. It is easy to demonstrate that, in most times and places, about 20 percent of book titles comprise about 80 percent of books sold. For those who are steeped in the 80/20 Principle, this is not surprising. It might seem a short hop to the conclusion that bookshops should cut the range of books they stock or, indeed, that they should concentrate largely or exclusively on "bestsellers." Yet what is interesting is that in most cases, instead of sending profits up, restricting range has sent profits down.

This does not invalidate the 80/20 Principle, for two reasons. The key consideration is not the distribution of books sold, but what customers want. If customers go to the trouble of visiting a bookstore, they want to find a reasonable range of books (as opposed to a kiosk or supermarket, where they don't expect range). Bookstores should concentrate on the 20 percent of customers who account for 80 percent of their profits and find out what those 20 percent of customers want.

The other reason is that what matters even when considering books (as opposed to customers) is not the distribution of sales—the 20 percent of books that represent 80 percent of sales—but the distribution of profits—the 20 percent of titles that generate 80 percent of profits. Very often, these are not the so-called bestsellers, books written by well-known authors. In fact, a study in the United States revealed that "best sellers represent about 5% of total sales."[5] The true bestsellers are often those books that never make it into the charts but sell a reliable quantity year in and year out, often at high margins. As the same U.S. research comments, "Core inventory represents those books that sell season-in and season-out. They are the

'80' in the 80/20 rule, often accounting for the lion's share of sales in a particular subject."

This illustration is salutary. It does not invalidate 80/20 Analysis at all, since the key questions should always be which customers and products generate 80 percent of profits. But it does show the danger of not thinking clearly enough about how the analysis is applied. When using the 80/20 Principle, be selective and be contrarian. Don't be seduced into thinking that the variable that everyone else is looking at—in this case, the books on the latest bestseller list—is what really matters. This is linear thinking. The most valuable insight from 80/20 Analysis will always come from examining nonlinear relationships that others are neglecting. In addition, because 80/20 Analysis is based on a freezeframe of the situation at a particular point rather than incorporating changes over time, you must be aware that if you inadvertently freeze the wrong or an incomplete picture, you will get an inaccurate view.

80/20 THINKING AND WHY IT IS NECESSARY

80/20 Analysis is extremely useful. But most people are not natural analysts, and even analysts cannot stop to investigate the data every time they have to make a decision—it would bring life to a shuddering halt. Most important decisions have never been made by analysis and never will be, however clever our computers become. Therefore, if we want the 80/20 Principle to be a guide in our daily lives, we need something less analytical and more instantly available than 80/20 Analysis. We need *80/20 Thinking*.

80/20 Thinking is my phrase for the application of the 80/20 Principle to daily life, for nonquantitative applications of the principle. As with 80/20 Analysis, we start with a hypothesis about a possible imbalance between inputs and outputs, but, instead of collecting data and analyzing them, we estimate them. 80/20 Thinking requires, and with practice enables, us to spot the few really important things that are happening and ignore the mass of unimportant things. It teaches us to see the wood for the trees.

80/20 Thinking is too valuable to be confined to causes where data and analysis are perfect. For every ounce of insight generated quantitatively, there must be many pounds of insight arrived at intuitively and impressionistically. This is why 80/20 Thinking, although helped by data, must not be constrained by it.

To engage in 80/20 Thinking, we must constantly ask ourselves: what is the 20 percent that is leading to 80 percent? We must never assume that we automatically know what the answer is but take some time to think creatively about it. What are the vital few inputs or causes, as opposed to the trivial many? Where is the haunting melody being drowned out by the background noise?

80/20 Thinking is then used in the same way as the results from 80/20 Analysis: to change behavior and, normally, to concentrate on the most important 20 percent. You know that 80/20 Thinking is working when it multiplies effectiveness. Action resulting from 80/20 Thinking should lead us to get much more from much less.

When we are using the 80/20 Principle we do not *assume* that its results are good or bad or that the powerful forces we observe are necessarily good. We *decide* whether they are good (from our own perspective) and either determine to give the minority of powerful forces a further shove in the right direction or work out how to frustrate their operation.

THE 80/20 PRINCIPLE TURNS CONVENTIONAL WISDOM UPSIDE DOWN

Application of the 80/20 Principle implies that we should do the following:

- celebrate exceptional productivity, rather than raise average efforts
- look for the short cut, rather than run the full course
- exercise control over our lives with the least possible effort
- be selective, not exhaustive
- strive for excellence in few things, rather than good performance in many
- delegate or outsource as much as possible in our daily lives and be encouraged rather than penalized by tax systems to do this (use

gardeners, car mechanics, decorators, and other specialists to the maximum, instead of doing the work ourselves)
- choose our careers and employers with extraordinary care, and if possible employ others rather than being employed ourselves
- *only* do the thing we are best at doing and enjoy most
- look beneath the normal texture of life to uncover ironies and oddities
- in every important sphere, work out where 20 percent of effort can lead to 80 percent of returns
- calm down, work less and target a limited number of very valuable goals where the 80/20 Principle will work for us, rather than pursuing every available opportunity
- make the most of those few "lucky streaks" in our life where we are at our creative peak and the stars line up to guarantee success.

There are no boundaries to the 80/20 Principle

No sphere of activity is immune from the influence of the 80/20 Principle. Like the six wise, blind Indian men who tried to discern the shape of an elephant, most users of the 80/20 Principle only know a fraction of its scope and power. Becoming an 80/20 thinker requires active participation and creativity on your part. If you want to benefit from 80/20 Thinking, *you* have to do it!

Now is a good time to start. If you want to begin with applications for your organization, go straight on to Part Two, which documents most of the important business applications of the 80/20 Principle. If you are more immediately interested in using the principle to make major improvements in your life, skip to Part Three, a novel attempt to relate the 80/20 Principle to the fabric of our daily lives.

PART TWO

CORPORATE SUCCESS NEEDN'T BE A MYSTERY

3

THE UNDERGROUND CULT

Now we see in a mirror dimly, but then we shall see face to face. Now I know in part; then I shall understand fully.

1 CORINTHIANS 13:12

It is difficult to gauge the extent to which the 80/20 Principle is already known in business. This is almost certainly the first book on the subject, yet in my research I was easily able to find several hundred articles referring to the use of 80/20 in all kinds of businesses, all over the world. Many successful firms and individuals swear by the use of the 80/20 Principle, and most holders of MBAs have heard of it.

Yet considering that the 80/20 Principle has affected the lives of hundreds of millions of people even though they may be unaware of it, it remains strangely uncelebrated. It is time to put this right.

THE FIRST 80/20 WAVE:
THE QUALITY REVOLUTION

The quality revolution which took place between 1950 and 1990 transformed the quality and value of branded consumer goods and other manufactures. The quality movement has been a crusade to obtain consistently higher quality at lower cost, by the application of statistical and behavioral techniques. The objective, now almost reached with many products, is to obtain a zero rate of product defects. It is possible to argue that the quality movement has been the most significant driver of higher living standards throughout the world since 1950.

The movement has an intriguing history. Its two great messiahs, Joseph Juran (born 1904) and W. Edwards Deming (born 1900), were both Americans (although Juran was born in Romania). Respectively an electrical engineer and a statistician, they developed their ideas in parallel after the Second World War but found it impossible to interest any major U.S. corporation in the quest for extraordinary quality. Juran published the first edition of his *Quality Control Handbook,* the bible of the quality movement, in 1951, but it received a very flat reception. The only serious interest came from Japan and both Juran and Deming moved there in the early 1950s. Their pioneering work took an economy known at the time for shoddy imitations and transformed it into a powerhouse of high quality and productivity.

It was only when Japanese goods, such as motorcycles and photocopiers, began to invade the U.S. market that most American (and other Western) corporations began to take the quality movement seriously. From 1970, and especially after 1980, Juran, Deming, and their disciples undertook an equally successful transformation of Western quality standards, leading to huge improvements in the level and consistency of quality, dramatic reductions in fault rates, and large falls in manufacturing costs.

The 80/20 Principle was one of the key building blocks of the quality movement. Joseph Juran was the most enthusiastic messiah of the principle, although he called it "the Pareto Principle" or "the

Rule of the Vital Few." In the first edition of the *Quality Control Handbook,* Juran commented that "losses" (that is, manufactured goods that have to be rejected because of poor quality) do not arise from a large number of causes:

> Rather, the losses are always maldistributed in such a way that a small percentage of the quality characteristics always contributes a high percentage of the quality loss.

The footnote to the text commented that

> the economist Pareto found that wealth was non-uniformly distributed in the same way. Many other instances can be found—the distribution of crime amongst criminals, the distribution of accidents among hazardous processes, etc. Pareto's principle of unequal distribution applied to distribution of wealth and to distribution of quality losses.[1]

Juran applied the 80/20 Principle to statistical quality control. The approach is to identify the problems causing lack of quality and to rank them from the most important—the 20 percent of defects causing 80 percent of quality problems—to the least important. Both Juran and Deming came to use the phrase 80/20 increasingly, encouraging diagnosis of the few defects causing most of the problems.

Once the "vital few" sources of off-quality product have been identified, effort is focused on dealing with these issues, rather than trying to tackle all the problems at once.

As the quality movement has progressed from an emphasis on quality "control" through to the view that quality must be built into products in the first place, by all operators, and to total quality management and increasingly sophisticated use of software, the emphasis on 80/20 techniques has grown, so that today almost all quality practitioners are familiar with 80/20. Some recent references illustrate the ways in which the 80/20 Principle is now being used.

In a recent article in the *National Productivity Review,* Ronald J. Recardo asks:

> Which gaps adversely affect your most strategic consumers? As with many other quality problems, Pareto's Law prevails here too: if you

remedy the most critical 20 percent of your quality gaps, you will realize 80 percent of the benefits. This first 80 percent typically includes your breakthrough improvements.[2]

Another writer, focusing on corporate turnarounds, comments:

> For every step in your business process, ask yourself if it adds value or provides essential support. If it does neither, it's waste. Cut it. [This is] the 80/20 rule, revisited: You can eliminate 80 percent of the waste by spending only 20 percent of what it would cost you to get rid of 100 percent of the waste. Go for the quick gain now.[3]

The 80/20 Principle was also used by Ford Electronics Manufacturing Corporation in a quality program that won the Shingo prize:

> Just-in-time programs have been applied using the 80/20 rule (80 percent of the value is spread over 20 percent of the volume) and top-dollar usages are analyzed constantly. Labor and overhead performance were replaced by Manufacturing Cycle Time analysis by product line, reducing product cycle time by 95 percent.[4]

New software incorporating the 80/20 Principle is being used to raise quality:

> [With the ABC DataAnalyzer] the data is entered or imported into the spreadsheet area, where you highlight it and click on your choice of six graph types: histograms, control charts, run charts, scatter diagrams, pie charts and Pareto charts.
>
> The Pareto chart incorporates the 80 to 20 rule, which might show, for instance, that out of 1,000 customer complaints roughly 800 can be eliminated by correcting only 20 per cent of the causes.[5]

The 80/20 Principle is also being increasingly applied to product design and development. For example, a review of the use that the Pentagon has made of total quality management explains that

> decisions made early in the development process fix the majority of life-cycle costs. The 80/20 rule describes this outcome, since 80 per-

cent of the life-cycle costs are usually locked in after only 20 percent of the development time.[6]

The impact of the quality revolution on customer satisfaction and value, and on the competitive positions of individual firms and indeed of whole nations, has been little noted but is truly massive. The 80/20 Principle was clearly one of the "vital few" inputs to the quality revolution. But the underground influence of the 80/20 Principle does not stop there. It also played a key role in a second revolution that combined with the first to create today's global consumer society.

THE SECOND 80/20 WAVE: THE INFORMATION REVOLUTION

The information revolution that began in the 1960s has already transformed work habits and the efficiency of large tracts of business. It is just beginning to do more than this: to help change the nature of the organizations that are today's dominant force in society. The 80/20 Principle was, is, and will be a key accessory of the information revolution, helping to direct its force intelligently.

Perhaps because they were close to the quality movement, the computing and software professionals behind the information revolution were generally familiar with the 80/20 Principle and used it extensively. To judge by the number of computing and software articles that refer to the 80/20 Principle, most hardware and software developers understand and use it in their daily work.

The information revolution has been most effective when using the 80/20 Principle's concepts of selectivity and simplicity. As two separate project directors testify:

Think small. Don't plan to the nth degree on the first day. The return on investment usually follows the 80/20 rule: 80 percent of the benefits will be found in the simplest 20 percent of the system, and the final 20 percent of the benefits will come from the most complex 80 percent of the system.[7]

Apple used the 80/20 Principle in developing the Apple Newton Message Pad, an electronic personal organizer:

> The Newton engineers took advantage of a slightly modified version [of 80/20]. They found that .01 percent of a person's vocabulary was sufficient to do 50 percent of the things you want to do with a small handheld computer.[8]

Increasingly, software is substituting for hardware, using the 80/20 Principle. An example is the RISC software invented in 1994:

> RISC is based on a variation of the 80/20 rule. This rule assumes that most software spends 80 percent of its time executing only 20 percent of the available instructions. RISC processors . . . optimize the performance of that 20 percent, and keep chip size and cost down by eliminating the other 80 percent. RISC does in software what CISC [the previously dominant system] does in silicon.[9]

Those who apply software know that, even though it is incredibly efficient, usage follows 80/20 patterns. As one developer states:

> The business world has long abided by the 80/20 rule. It's especially true for software, where 80 percent of a product's uses take advantage of only 20 percent of its capabilities. That means that most of us pay for what we don't want or need. Software developers finally seem to understand this, and many are betting that modular applications will solve the problem.[10]

Design of software is crucial, so that the most used functions are the easiest to use. The same approach is being used for new database services:

> How do WordPerfect and other software developers [do] it? First, they identify what customers want most of the time and how they want to do it—the old 80/20 rule (people use 20 percent of a program's functions 80 percent of the time). Good software developers make high-use functions as simple and automatic and inevitable as possible.
> Translating such an approach to today's database services would

mean looking at key customer use all the time . . . How many times do customers call search service support desks to ask which file to pick or where a file can be found? Good design could eliminate such calls.[11]

Wherever one turns, effective innovations in information—in data storage, retrieval, and processing—focus heavily on the 20 percent or fewer of key needs.

THE INFORMATION REVOLUTION HAS A LONG WAY TO RUN

The information revolution is the most subversive force business has ever known. Already the phenomenon of "information power to the people" has given knowledge and authority to front-line workers and technicians, destroying the power and often the jobs of middle management who were previously protected by proprietary knowledge. The information revolution has also decentralized corporations physically: the phone, the fax, the PC, the modem, and the increasing miniaturization and mobility of these technologies have already begun to destroy the power of corporate palaces and those who sit, or increasingly sat, in them. Ultimately, the information revolution will help to destroy the profession of management itself, thus enabling much greater direct value creation by "doers" in corporations for their key customers.[12] The value of automated information is increasing exponentially, much faster than we can use it. The key to using this power effectively, now and in the future, lies in selectivity: in applying the 80/20 Principle.

Peter Drucker points the way:

A database, no matter how copious, is not information. It is information's ore . . . The information a business most depends on is available, if at all, only in a primitive and disorganized form. For what a business needs the most for its decisions—especially its strategic ones—are data about what goes on outside of it. It is only outside the business where there are results, opportunities, and threats.[13]

Drucker argues that we need new ways of measuring wealth creation. Ian Godden and I call these new tools "automated performance measures";[14] they are just beginning to be created by some corporations. But well over 80 percent (probably around 99 percent) of the information revolution's resources are still being applied to counting better what we used to count ("paving over the cowpats") rather than creating and simplifying measures of genuine corporate wealth creation. The tiny proportion of effort that uses the information revolution to create a different sort of corporation will have an explosive impact.

THE 80/20 PRINCIPLE IS STILL
THE BEST-KEPT BUSINESS SECRET

Considering the importance of the 80/20 Principle and the extent to which it is known by managers, it remains extremely discreet. Even the 80/20 term itself caught on very slowly and without any visible landmarks. Given the piecemeal use and gradual spread of the 80/20 Principle, it remains underexploited, even by those who recognize the idea. It is extremely versatile. It can be profitably applied to any industry and any organization, any function within an organization and any individual job. The 80/20 Principle can help the chief executive, line managers, functional specialists, and any knowledge worker, down to the lowest level or the newest trainee. And although its uses are manifold, there is an underlying, unifying logic that explains why the 80/20 Principle works and is so valuable.

WHY THE 80/20 PRINCIPLE WORKS IN BUSINESS

The 80/20 Principle applied to business has one key theme—to generate the most money with the least expenditure of assets and effort.

The classical economists of the nineteenth and early twentieth centuries developed a theory of economic equilibrium and of the firm that has dominated thinking ever since. The theory states that under perfect competition firms do not make excess returns, and profitability is either zero or the "normal" cost of capital, the latter usually being defined by a modest interest charge. The theory is internally consistent and has the sole flaw that it cannot be applied to real economic activity of any kind, and especially not to the operations of any individual firm.

The 80/20 theory of the firm

In contrast to the theory of perfect competition, the 80/20 theory of the firm is both verifiable (and has, in fact, been verified many times) and helpful as a guide to action. The 80/20 theory of the firm goes like this:

- In any market, some suppliers will be much better than others at satisfying customer needs. These suppliers will obtain the highest price realizations and also the highest market shares.
- In any market, some suppliers will be much better than others at minimizing expenditure relative to revenues. In other words, these suppliers will cost less than other suppliers for equivalent output and revenue or, alternatively, be able to generate equivalent output with lower expenditure.
- Some suppliers will generate much higher surpluses than others. (I use the phrase "surpluses" rather than "profits," because the latter normally implies the profit available for shareholders. The concept of surplus implies the level of funds available for profits or reinvestment, over and above what is needed normally to keep the wheels turning.) Higher surpluses will result in one or more of the following: (1) greater reinvestment in product and service, to produce greater superiority and appeal to customers; (2) investment in gaining market share through greater sales and marketing effort, and/or takeovers of other firms; (3) higher returns to employees, which will tend to have the effect of retaining and attracting the best people in the market; and/or (4) higher returns to shareholders, which will tend to raise share prices and lower the cost of capital, facilitating investment and/or takeovers.
- Over time, 80 percent of the market will tend to be supplied by 20 percent or fewer of the suppliers, who will normally also be more profitable.

  At this point it is possible that the market structure may reach an equilibrium, although it will be a very different kind of equilibrium from that beloved of the economists' perfect competition model. In the 80/20 equilibrium, a few suppliers, the largest, will offer customers better value for money and have higher profits than smaller rivals. This is frequently observed in real life, despite being impossible according to the theory of perfect competition. We may term our more realistic theory the 80/20 law of competition.

But the real world does not generally rest long in a tranquil equilibrium. Sooner or later (usually sooner), there are always changes to market structure caused by competitors' innovations. Both existing suppliers and new suppliers will seek to innovate and obtain a high share of a small but defensible part of each market (a "market segment"). Segmentation of this kind is possible by providing a more specialized product or service ideally suited to particular types of customer. Over time, markets will tend to comprise more market segments.

Within each of these segments, the 80/20 law of competition will operate. The leaders in each specialist segment may either be firms operating largely or exclusively in that segment or industry generalists, but their success will be dependent, in each segment, on obtaining the greatest revenue with the lowest expenditure of effort. In each segment, some firms will be much better than others at doing this and will tend to accumulate segment market share as a result.

Any large firm will operate in a large number of segments, that is, in a large number of customer/product combinations where a different formula is required to maximize revenue relative to effort and/or where different competitors are met. In some of these segments, the individual large firm will generate large surpluses and in other segments much lower surpluses (or even deficits). It will tend to be true, therefore, that 80 percent of surpluses or profits are generated by 20 percent of segments and by 20 percent of customers and by 20 percent of products. The most profitable segments will tend to (but will not always) be where the firm enjoys the highest market shares and where the firm has the most loyal customers (loyalty being defined by being longstanding and least likely to defect to competitors).

- Within any firm, as with all entities dependent on nature and human endeavour, there is likely to be an inequality between inputs and outputs, an imbalance between effort and reward. Externally, this is reflected in the fact that some markets, products, and customers are much more profitable than others. Internally, the same principle is reflected by the fact that some resources, be they people, factories, machines, or permutations of these will produce very much more value relative to their cost than will other resources. If we were able to measure it (as we can with some jobs, such as those of salespeople), we would find that some people generate a very large surplus (their attributable share of revenue is very much greater than their full cost), whereas many people generate a small surplus or a deficit. Firms that generate the largest surpluses also tend to have the highest average surplus per employee, but in all firms the true surplus generated by each employee tends to be very unequal: 80 percent of the surplus is usually generated by 20 percent of employees.
- At the lowest level of aggregation of resources within the firm, for example an individual employee, 80 percent of the value created is likely to be generated in a small part, approximately 20 percent, of the time when, through a combination of circumstances including personal characteristics and the exact nature of the task, the employee is operating at several times his or her normal level of effectiveness.
- The principles of unequal effort and return therefore operate at all levels of business: markets, market segments, products, customers, departments, and employees. It is this lack of balance, rather than a notional equilibrium, that characterizes all economic activity. Apparently small differences create large consequences. A product has to be only 10 percent better value than that of a competing product to generate a sales difference of 50 percent and a profit difference of 100 percent.

Three action implications

One implication of the 80/20 theory of firms is that successful firms operate in markets where it is possible for that firm to generate the highest revenues with the least effort. This will be true both absolutely, that is, relative to monetary profits, and relatively, that is, in relation to competition. A firm cannot be judged successful unless it has a high absolute surplus (in traditional terms, a high return on investment) and also a higher surplus than its competitors (higher margins).

A second practical implication for all firms is that it is always possible to raise the economic surplus, usually by a large degree, by focusing only on those market and customer segments where the largest surpluses are currently being generated. This will always imply redeployment of resources into the most surplus-generating segments and will normally also imply a reduction in the total level of resource and expenditure (in plain words, fewer employees and other costs).

Firms rarely reach the highest level of surplus that they could attain, or anywhere near it, both because managers are often not aware of the potential for surplus and because they often prefer to run large firms rather than exceptionally profitable ones.

A third corollary is that it is possible for every corporation to raise the level of surplus by reducing the inequality of output and reward within the firm. This can be done by identifying the parts of the firm (people, factories, sales offices, overhead units, countries) that generate the highest surpluses and reinforcing these, giving them more power and resources; and, conversely, identifying the resources generating low or negative surpluses, facilitating dramatic improvements and, if these are not forthcoming, stopping the expenditure on these resources.

These principles constitute a useful 80/20 theory of the firm, but they must not be interpreted too rigidly or deterministically. The principles work because they are a reflection of relationships in nature, which are an intricate mixture of order and disorder, of regularity and irregularity.

LOOK FOR "IRREGULAR" INSIGHTS FROM THE 80/20 PRINCIPLE

It is important to try to grasp the fluidity and force driving 80/20 relationships. Unless you appreciate this, you will interpret the 80/20 Principle too rigidly and fail to exploit its full potential.

The world is full of small causes that, when combined, can have momentous consequences. Think of a saucepan of milk that when heated above a certain temperature suddenly changes form, swelling up and bubbling over. One moment you have a nice, orderly pan of hot milk; the next moment you can either have a wonderful cappucino or, if you are a second too late, a mess on top of your stove. Things take a little more time in business, but one year you can have an excellent and very profitable IBM dominating the computer industry and, before long, a combination of small causes results in a blinded monolith staggering to avoid destruction.

Creative systems operate away from equilibrium. Cause and effect, input and output, operate in a nonlinear way. You do not usually get back what you put in; you may sometimes get very much less and sometimes get very much more. Major alterations in a business system can flow from apparently insignificant causes. At any one time, people of equal intelligence, skill, and dedication can produce quite unequal results, as a result of small structural differences. Events cannot be predicted, although predictable patterns tend to recur.

Identify lucky streaks

Control is therefore impossible. But it is possible to influence events, and, perhaps even more important, it is possible to detect irregularities and benefit from them. The art of using the 80/20 Principle is to identify which way the grain of reality is currently running and to exploit that as much as possible.

Imagine you are in a crazy casino, full of unbalanced roulette wheels. All numbers pay odds of 35 to 1, but individual numbers come up more or less frequently at different tables. At one, number five comes up one time in twenty, at another table it only comes up one time in fifty. If you back the right number at the right table, you can make a fortune. If you stubbornly keep backing number five at a table where it comes up one time in fifty, your money will all disappear, regardless of how high your starting bank.

If you can identify where your firm is getting back more than it is putting in, you can up the stakes and make a killing. Similarly, if you can work out where your firm is getting back much less than it is investing, you can cut your losses.

In this context, the "where" can be anything. It can be a product, a market, a customer or type of customer, a technology, a channel of distribution, a department or division, a country, a type of transaction or an employee, type of employee or team. The game is to spot the few places where you are making great surpluses and to maximize them and to identify the places where you are losing and get out.

We have been trained to think in terms of cause and effect, of regular relationships, of average levels of return, of perfect competition, and of predictable outcomes. This is not the real world. The real world comprises a mass of influences, where cause and effect are blurred, and where complex feedback loops distort inputs; where equilibrium is fleeting and often illusory; where there are patterns of repeated but irregular performance; where firms never compete head to head and prosper by differentiation; and where a few favored souls are able to corner the market for high returns.

Viewed in this light, large firms are incredibly complex and constantly changing coalitions of forces, some of which are going with the grain of nature and making a fortune, while others are going against the grain and stacking up huge losses. All this is obscured by our inability to disentangle reality and by the calming, averaging (and highly distorting) effects of accounting systems. The 80/20 Principle is rampant but largely unobserved. What we are generally allowed to see in business is the net effect of what happens, which is by no means the whole picture. Beneath the surface there are warring positive and negative inputs that combine to produce the effect we can observe above the surface. The 80/20 Principle is most useful when we can identify all the forces beneath the surface so that we can stop the negative influences and give maximum power to the most productive forces.

HOW COMPANIES CAN USE THE 80/20 PRINCIPLE TO RAISE PROFITS

Enough of history, philosophy, and theory! We now switch gears to the intensely practical. Any individual business can gain immensely through practical application of the 80/20 Principle. It is time to show you how.

Chapters 4 to 7 cover the most important ways to raise profits via the 80/20 Principle. Chapter 8 closes Part Two with hints on how to embed 80/20 Thinking into your business life so that you can gain an unfair advantage over colleagues and competitors alike.

We start in the next chapter with the most important use of the 80/20 Principle in any firm: to isolate where you are really making the profits and, just as important, where you are really losing money. Every business person thinks they know this already, and nearly all are wrong. If they had the right picture, their whole business would be transformed.

4

WHY YOUR
STRATEGY IS WRONG

Unless you have used the 80/20 Principle to redirect your strategy, you can be pretty sure that the strategy is badly flawed. Almost certainly, you don't have an accurate picture of where you make, and lose, the most money. It is almost inevitable that you are doing too many things for too many people.

Business strategy should not be a grand and sweeping overview. It should be more like an underview, a peek beneath the covers to look in great detail at what is going on. To arrive at a useful business strategy, you need to look carefully at the different chunks of your business, particularly at their profitability and cash generation.

Unless your firm is very small and simple, it is almost certainly true that *you make at least 80 percent of your profits and cash in 20 percent of your activity, and in 20 percent of your revenues.* The trick is to work out *which* 20 percent.

WHERE ARE YOU MAKING THE MOST MONEY?

Identify which parts of the business are making very high returns, which are just about washing their faces, and which are disasters. To do this we will conduct an 80/20 Analysis of profits by different categories of business:

· by product or product group/type
· by customer or customer group/type
· by any other split which appears to be relevant for your business for which you have data; for example, by geographical area or distribution channel
· by competitive segment.

Start with *products.* Your business will almost certainly have information by product or product group. For each, look at the sales over the last period, month, quarter, or year (decide which is most reliable) and work out the profitability after allocating all costs.

How easy or difficult this will be depends on the state of your management information. What you need may all be readily available, but if not you will have to build it up yourself. You are bound to have sales by product or product line and almost certainly the gross margin (sales less cost of sales). You will also know the total costs for the whole business (all the overhead costs). What you then have to do is to allocate all the overhead costs to each product group on some reasonable basis.

The crudest way is to allocate costs on a percentage of turnover. A moment's thought, however, should convince you that this will not be very accurate. Some products take a great deal of salespeople's time relative to their value, for example, and others take very little. Some are heavily advertised and others not at all. Some require a lot of fussing around in manufacturing whereas others are straightforward.

Take each category of overhead cost and allocate it to each product group. Do this for all the costs, then look at the results.

Typically some products, representing a minority of turnover, are very profitable; most products are modestly or marginally profitable; and some are really making large losses once you allocate all the costs.

Figure 10 shows the numbers for a recent study I conducted of an electronic instrumentation group. Figure 11 gives the same data visually; look at this if you prefer pictures to numbers.

Product	$000 Sales	Income	Return on sales (%)
Product group A	3,750	1,330	35.5
Product group B	17,000	5,110	30.1
Product group C	3,040	601	25.1
Product group D	12,070	1,880	15.6
Product group E	44,110	5,290	12.0
Product group F	30,370	2,990	9.8
Product group G	5,030	(820)	(15.5)
Product group H	4,000	(3,010)	(75.3)
Total	119,370	13,380	11.2

Figure 10   Electronic Instruments Inc. sales and profits table by product group

We can see from the two figures that Product group A accounts for only 3 percent of sales, but for 10 percent of profits. Product groups A, B, and C account for 20 percent of sales, but for 53 percent of profits. This becomes very clear if we compile an 80/20 Table or an 80/20 Chart, as in Figures 12 and 13 respectively.

We have not yet found the 20 percent of sales that account for 80 percent of profits, but we are on our way. If not 80/20, then 67/30: 30 percent of product sales account for almost 67 percent of profits. Already you may be thinking about what can be done to raise the sales of Product groups A, B, and C. For example, you might want to reallocate all sales effort from the other 80 percent of business, telling salespeople to concentrate on doubling the sales of Products A, B, and C and not to worry about the rest. If they succeeded in doing this, sales would only go up by 20 percent, but profits would rise more than 50 percent.

You might also already be thinking about cutting costs, or raising prices, in Product groups D, E, and F; or about radical retrenchment or total exit from Product groups G and H.

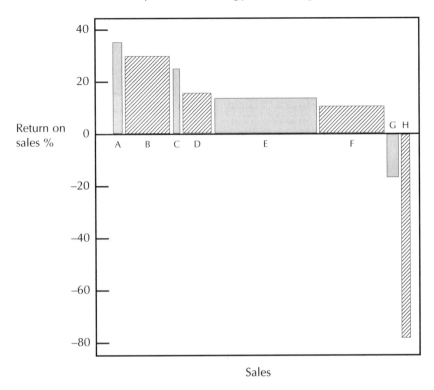

Figure 11   Electronic Instruments Inc. sales and profit chart by product group

Product	Percentage of sales		Percentage of profits	
	Group	Cumulative	Group	Cumulative
Product group A	3.1	3.1	9.9	9.9
Product group B	14.2	17.3	38.2	48.1
Product group C	2.6	19.9	4.6	52.7
Product group D	10.1	30.0	14.1	66.8
Product group E	37.0	67.0	39.5	106.3
Product group F	25.4	92.4	22.4	128.7
Product group G	4.2	96.6	(6.1)	122.6
Product group H	3.4	100.0	(22.6)	100.0

Figure 12   Electronic Instruments Inc. 80/20 Table

WHAT ABOUT CUSTOMER PROFITABILITY?

After products, go on to look at *customers*. Repeat the analysis, but look at total purchases by each customer or customer group. Some

Figure 13 Electronic Instruments Inc. 80/20 Chart

customers pay high prices but have a high cost to serve: these are often smaller customers. The very big customers may be easy to deal with and take large volumes of the same product, but screw you down on price. Sometimes these differences balance out, but often they do not. For the group we are calling Electronic Instruments Inc. the results are shown in Figures 14 and 15.

Customer	$000 Sales	Income	Return on sales (%)
Customer type A	18,350	7,865	42.9
Customer type B	11,450	3,916	34.2
Customer type C	43,100	3,969	9.2
Customer type D	46,470	(2,370)	(5.1)
Total	119,370	13,380	11.2

Figure 14 Electronic Instruments Inc. sales and profits table by customer group

A word of explanation about the customer groups. Type A customers are small, direct accounts paying very high prices and giving very fat gross margins. They are quite expensive to service but the margins more than compensate for this. Type B customers are distributors who tend to place large orders and have very low costs to serve, yet for one reason or another find it acceptable to pay fairly high prices, mainly because the electronic components bought are a tiny fraction of their total product costs. Type C customers are export accounts paying high prices. The snag with them, however, is that they are very expensive to service. Type D customers are large manufacturers who bargain very hard on price and also demand a great deal of technical support and many "specials."

Figures 16 and 17 show the 80/20 Table and 80/20 Chart respectively for the customer groups.

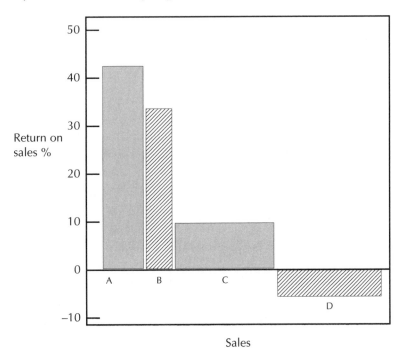

Figure 15   Electronic Instruments Inc. sales and profits chart by customer group

Customer	Percentage of sales		Percentage of profits	
	Type	Cumulative	Type	Cumulative
Customer type A	15.4	15.4	58.9	58.9
Customer type B	9.6	25.0	29.3	88.2
Customer type C	36.1	61.1	29.6	117.8
Customer type D	38.9	100.0	(17.8)	100.0

Figure 16   Electronic Instruments Inc. 80/20 Table by customer type

These figures reveal a 59/15 rule and an 88/25 rule: the most profitable customer category accounts for 15 percent of revenues but 59 percent of profits, and the most profitable 25 percent of customers yields 88 percent of profits. This is partly because the most profitable customers tend to take the most profitable products, but also because they pay more in relation to their cost to service.

The analysis led to a successful campaign to find more A and B customers: the small direct customers and the distributors. Even taking account of the cost of the campaign, the result was very profitable. Prices for C customers (the export accounts) were selectively raised and ways found to lower the cost of servicing some of them, particularly by greater use of telephone rather than face-to-face sell-

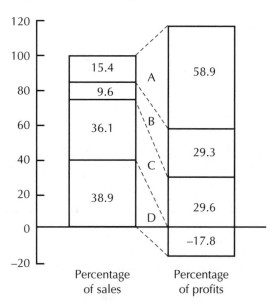

Figure 17   Electronic Instruments Inc. 80/20 Chart by customer type

ing. The D customers (large manufacturers) were dealt with individually: nine of these accounted for 97 percent of D sales. In some cases technical development services were charged for separately; in others prices were raised; and three accounts were tactically "lost" to the company's most hated competitor after a bidding war. The managers really wanted the competitor to enjoy these losses!

80/20 ANALYSIS APPLIED
TO A CONSULTANCY FIRM

After products and customers, take any other split of business that appears especially relevant to your business. There was no special analysis in the case of the instrumentation company, but to illustrate the point consider the simple split of sales and profits for a strategy consultancy shown in Figures 18 and 19.

Business split	$000 Sales	Profits	Return on sales (%)
Large projects	35,000	16,000	45.7
Small projects	135,000	12,825	9.5
Total	170,000	28,825	17.0

Figure 18 Strategy Consulting Inc. table of profitability of large versus small clients

These figures exhibit a 56/21 rule: large projects constitute only 21 percent of turnover but give 56 percent of profits.

Another analysis, shown in Figures 20 and 21, splits the business into "old" clients (more than three years old), "new" clients (less than six months old), and those in between.

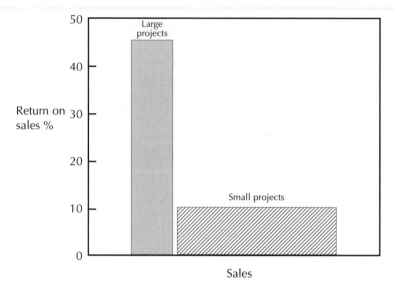

Figure 19   Strategy Consulting Inc. chart of profitability of large versus small clients

These figures tell us that 26 percent of the business (old clients) made up 84 percent of the profits: an 84/26 rule. The message here was to strive above all to keep and expand long-serving clients, who were the least price sensitive and who could be served most cheaply. New clients who do not turn into long-serving clients were recognized as being loss makers, leading to a much more selective approach to pitching for business: pitches were only made where it was believed the company concerned would turn into a long-term client.

| | $000 | | |
Business split	Sales	Profits	Return on sales (%)
Old clients	43,500	24,055	55.3
Intermediate clients	101,000	12,726	12.6
New clients	25,500	(7,956)	31.2
Total	170,000	28,825	17.0

Figure 20   Strategy Consulting Inc. table of profitability of old versus new clients

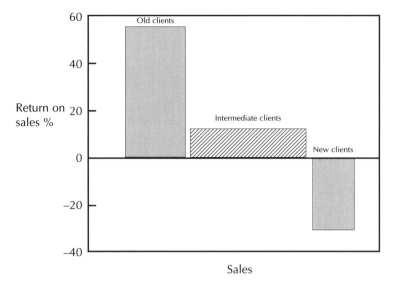

Figure 21   Strategy Consulting Inc. chart of profitability of old versus new clients

Figures 22 and 23 summarize a third analysis for the consultants, which divided projects into work on mergers and acquisitions (M&A), strategic analysis, and operational projects.

This split demonstrated an 87/22 rule: the M&A work was wildly profitable, giving 87 percent of profits for 22 percent of revenues. Efforts were redoubled to sell more M&A work!

Business split	$000 Sales	Profits	Return on sales (%)
M&A	37,600	25,190	67.0
Strategic analysis	75,800	11,600	15.3
Operational projects	56,600	7,965	14.1
Total	170,000	28,825	17.0

Figure 22   Strategy Consulting Inc. table of profitability by project type

Operational projects for old clients, when analyzed separately, turned out at about break-even, while large losses were made on operational projects for new clients. This led to a decision not to undertake the latter, while old clients were either charged much

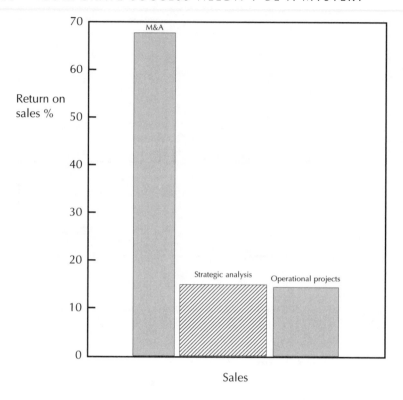

Figure 23   Strategy Consulting Inc. chart of possibility by project type

more for this kind of project or encouraged to farm them out to specialist operational consultancies.

SEGMENTATION IS THE KEY TO UNDERSTANDING AND DRIVING UP PROFITABILITY

The best way to examine the profitability of your business is to break it down into *competitive segments*. While analyses by product, customer, or any other relevant split are usually very valuable, the greatest insights come from a combination of customers and products into "dollops" of business defined with reference to your most important competitors. Although this is not as difficult as it may sound, very few organizations break up their business in this way, so a short exposition is necessary.

What is a competitive segment?

A competitive segment is a part of your business where you face a different competitor or different competitive dynamics.

Take any part of your business that comes to mind: a product, a customer, a product line sold to a customer type, or any other split that may be important to you (for example, consultants may think of M&A work). Now ask yourself two simple questions:

- *Do you face a different main competitor in this part of your business compared to the rest of it?* If the answer is yes, then that part of the business is a separate competitive segment (or simply segment for short).

    If you are up against a specialist competitor, your profitability will depend on the interaction of your product and service against theirs. Which do consumers prefer? And what is your total cost to deliver the product or service relative to your competitor's? Your profitability will be as much determined by your competitor as by anything else.

    It is therefore sensible to think of this area of your business separately, to determine a strategy for it that will beat (or collude with) your competitor. It is certainly sensible to look at its profitability separately too: you may have a surprise.

    But even if the part of your business you are looking at has the same competitor as another part of your business (for example, your main competitor in Product A is the same as in Product B), then you need to ask another question.

- *Do you and your competitor have the same ratio of sales or market share in the two areas, or are they relatively stronger in one area and you relatively stronger in another?*

    For example, if you have 20 percent market share in Product A and the largest competitor has 40 percent (they are twice as big as you), is it the same ratio in Product B: are they twice as big as you there? If you have 15 percent market share in Product B but your competitor only has 10 percent, then there is a different relative competitive position in the two products.

    There will be real reasons for this. Consumers may prefer your brand in Product B but your competitor's in Product A. Possibly the competitor doesn't care much about what happens in Product B. Perhaps you are efficient and price competitive in Product B, whereas the reverse is true in Product A. At this stage you don't need to know the reasons. All you need to do is observe that, although you face the same competitor, the balance of advantage is different in the two areas. They are therefore separate segments and will probably exhibit different profitability.

Thinking about competitors puts you straight on to the key business splits

Instead of starting with a conventional business definition, such as a product or the output from different parts of your organization, thinking about competitive segments lobs you straight at the most important way to split and think about your business.

At the instrumentation company referred to earlier, managers just could not agree among themselves how to analyze the business. Some thought that products were the key dimension. The view of others was that the most important split was whether the customers were in the pipeline business (broadly, oil companies) or in continuous process industries (such as food manufacturers). A third faction held that the U.S. business was very different from the export business. Since they started from different assumptions, all of which were to some degree valid, it was very difficult to make progress either in organizing the business or in communicating with each other.

Dividing the business into competitive segments demolished these arguments. The rule is simple: if you don't face different competitors, or different relative competitive positions, it's not a separate segment. We quickly arrived at a rather inelegant, but very clear, set of segments that everyone could understand.

For a start, it was clear that the competitors were very different in most, but not all, products. Where the competitors were the same, with similar relative competitive positions, we lumped the products together. In most other cases we kept the products apart.

Then we asked whether the competitive positions were different for pipeline customers as distinct from process customers. In all but one product, the answer was no. But in that one product, liquid density machines, the largest competitors were different. We therefore settled for two segments here: liquid density pipeline and liquid density process.

Finally, we asked whether the competitors or competitive positions were different in each segment in the United States and in international business. In most cases the answer was yes. If the international business was significant enough, we asked the same question for different countries: was it the same competitor in Great Britain as in France or Asia? Where the competitors were different, we subdivided the business into separate segments.

We ended up with a patchwork quilt of 15 large segments (very small ones we reaggregated to avoid unnecessary work), usually defined by product and geographic region, but in one case by product and customer type (this was liquid density, where the segments were liquid density pipeline worldwide and liquid density process worldwide). Each segment had a different competitor or different competitive positions. We then analyzed the split of sales and profits for each of the segments, and this is shown in Figures 24 and 25.

Segment	$000 Sales	Profits	Return on sales (%)
1	2,250	1,030	45.8
2	3,020	1,310	43.4
3	5,370	2,298	42.8
4	2,000	798	39.9
5	1,750	532	30.4
6	17,000	5,110	30.1
7	3,040	610	25.1
8	7,845	1,334	17.0
9	4,224	546	12.9
10	13,000	1,300	10.0
11	21,900	1,927	8.8
12	18,100	779	4.3
13	10,841	(364)	(3.4)
14	5,030	(820)	(15.5)
15	4,000	(3,010)	(75.3)
Total	119,370	13,380	11.2

Figure 24   Electronic Instruments Inc. table of profitability by segment

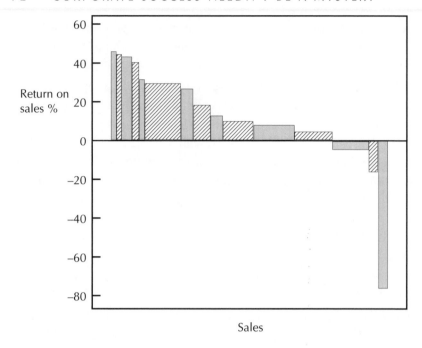

Figure 25   Electronic Instruments Inc. chart of possibility by segment

To highlight the imbalance between the split of revenues and profits, we can again construct either an 80/20 Table (Figure 26) or an 80/20 Chart (Figure 27).

We can see from these figures that the top six segments comprise only 26.3 percent of total sales, but 82.9 percent of profits: so here we have an 83/26 rule.

What did Electronic Instruments do to boost profits?

Figures 26 and 27 focused attention on three types of business.

The most profitable quarter of the business, segments 1–6, was classified initially as top priority A businesses, to be grown most aggressively. More than 80 percent of profits came from these segments, yet they were receiving only an average amount of management time in line with their turnover. A decision was made to raise the amount of time spent on these businesses to two-thirds of the total. The sales force focused on trying to sell more of these products, both to existing customers and to new ones. It was realized that the group could afford to offer extra services or to cut prices slightly and still enjoy very good returns.

Segment	Percentage of sales		Percentage of profits	
	Type	Cumulative	Type	Cumulative
1	1.9	1.9	7.7	7.7
2	2.5	4.4	9.8	17.5
3	4.5	8.9	17.2	34.7
4	1.7	10.6	6.0	40.7
5	1.5	12.1	4.0	44.7
6	14.2	26.3	38.2	82.9
7	2.5	28.8	4.6	87.5
8	6.6	35.4	10.0	97.5
9	3.5	38.9	4.1	101.6
10	10.9	49.8	9.7	111.3
11	18.3	68.1	14.4	125.7
12	15.2	83.3	5.8	131.5
13	9.1	92.4	−2.7	128.8
14	4.2	96.6	−6.0	122.6
15	3.4	100.0	−22.6	100.0

Figure 26   Electronic Instruments Inc. 80/20 Table of sales and profits by segment

The second set of businesses comprised segments 7–12. In total these made up 57 percent of total sales and 49 percent of total profits, in other words, on average, slightly below-average profitability. These segments were classified as B priority, although clearly some segments in this category (such as 7 and 8) were more interesting than others (such as 11 and 12). The priority to be accorded to these segments also depended on the answers to the two questions posed at the start of the chapter, that is, on whether each segment was a good market to be in and on how well the company was positioned in each segment. The answers to these questions are described in the final part of this chapter.

At this stage, a decision was made to cut the amount of management time spent on the B segments from around 60 percent to about half this level. Prices on some of the less profitable segments were also raised.

The third category, designated X priority, comprised the loss-making segments 13–15. A decision on what to do about these segments

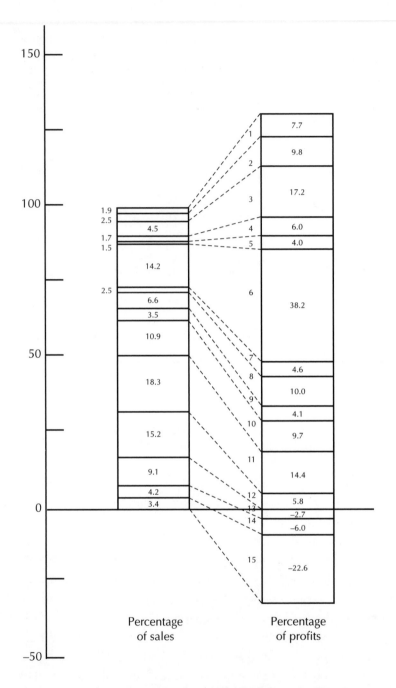

Figure 27 Electronic Instruments Inc. 80/20 Chart of profitability by segment

was deferred, as for the B category, until after analysis of market attractiveness and the strength of the company's position in each market.

Provisionally, however, it was possible to reset priorities as laid out in Figure 28.

Priority	Segments of sales	Percentage of profits	Percentage	Actions
A	1–6	26.3	82.9	Raise sales effort Raise management time Flexibility on price
B	7–12	57.0	48.5	Lower management time Lower sales effort Raise some prices
X	13–15	16.7	(31.4)	Review viability
Total		100.0	100.0	

Figure 28   Electronic Instruments Inc. result of 80/20 Analysis

Before reaching final decisions on any segment, however, the instrumentation group's top management examined the two other questions, besides profitability, that are key to strategy:

· Is the segment an attractive market to be in?
· How well is the firm positioned in each segment?

Figure 29 shows the final strategy conclusions for Electronic Instruments Inc.

Segment	Market attractive?	Firm well positioned?	Profitability
1	Yes	Yes	Very high
2	Yes	Yes	Very high
3	Yes	Yes	Very high
4	Yes	Yes	Very high
5	Yes	Yes	High
6	Yes	Yes	High
7	Yes	Moderately	High
8	Yes	Moderately	Fairly high
9	Yes	No	OK
10	Not very	Yes	OK

11	Not very	Yes	OK
12	No	Moderately	Poor
13	Yes	Improving	Loss making
14	No	Moderately	Loss making
15	No	No	Loss making

Figure 29   Electronic Instruments Inc. strategic diagnosis

What actions followed this diagnosis?

All of the A profit segments were also attractive markets—they were growing, had high barriers to entry for new competitors, had more demand than capacity, faced no threat from competing technologies, and had high bargaining power vis-à-vis both customers and component suppliers. As a result, nearly all the competitors in these markets made good money.

My client was also well positioned in each segment, meaning that it had a high market share and was one of the top three suppliers. Its technology was above average and its cost position better than average (that is, lower cost) compared to its competitors.

Since these were also the most profitable segments, the analysis confirmed the implications of the 80/20 profit comparison. Segments 1–6 therefore remained A segments and effort was concentrated on keeping all existing business and gaining market share in these segments by increasing sales to current customers and converting new ones.

The strategy could now be refined for some of the other segments in the B category. Segment 9 was interesting. Profitability was moderate, but this was not because the market was unattractive; on the contrary, it was highly attractive, with most of the other players making very good profits. But my client had a low market share and a high-cost position in this segment, largely because they were using old technology.

To update the technology would have taken a terrific effort and would have been very expensive. A decision was made, therefore, to "harvest" the segment, which meant cutting the effort going to protect the business and raising prices. This was expected to lead to a loss in sales but, for a time, to higher profits. In fact, cutting the effort and raising prices did raise margins, but led to very little loss of sales in the short term. It turned out that the customers were mainly locked in to the old technology themselves and had little choice of alternative suppliers until they switched over to the new technology. For my client profitability rose from 12.9 per cent to over 20 percent, although it was recognized that this might be a temporary development.

Segments 10 and 11 were ones where the instrumentation group had leading market shares, but they were structurally unattractive markets. Market size was declining; there was overcapacity, and the customers held all the cards and could negotiate very keen prices. Despite the fact that it was a market leader, my client decided to deemphasize these segments and all new investment was cancelled.

Although for different reasons, the same decision applied to segment 12. The market was even more unattractive and the firm had only a moderate market share. All new marketing programs, as well as investments, were sidelined.

What about the X category, the loss makers? Here it was found that two of the three segments, 14 and 15, were large but deeply unattractive markets in which the firm was in any case only a marginal player. A decision was made to leave both segments, in one case by selling part of a factory to a competitor. The price realized was very low, but at least there was some cash benefit and some jobs were preserved in addition to the losses being stopped. In the other case operations had to be closed altogether.

Segment 13, also in the X group, experienced a different fate. Although the group lost money in this business, it was a structurally attractive market: growing at 10 percent per annum and with most competitors making high returns. In fact, although the group was making a loss after allocating all costs, the gross margin in the segment was quite high. Its problem was that it had only entered the market the previous year and was having to make heavy investments in technology and sales effort. But it was gaining market share and, if it kept up its rate of progress, could hope to become one of the largest suppliers within three years. At that stage, with higher sales to spread the costs, it could expect to make high returns. It decided to put even more effort into segment 13 so that the group could become a "scale player" (that is, operate at the minimum size necessary to be profitable) as soon as possible.

DON'T TAKE 80/20 ANALYSIS
TO SIMPLISTIC CONCLUSIONS

Segment 13 in the above example helps to illustrate the point that
80/20 Analysis of profits does not give us all the right answers. The
analysis is bound to be a snapshot at a point in time and cannot (to
start with) provide a picture of the trend or of forces that could
change profitability. Profitability analysis of the 80/20 type is a necessary but not a sufficient condition of good strategy.

On the other hand, it is undoubtedly true that the best way to start
making money is to stop losing money. Note that, with the exception
of segment 13, the simple 80/20 profit analysis would have given
more or less the right result in 14 out of the 15 segments, comprising
over 90 percent of revenues. This does not mean that strategic analysis should stop with 80/20 Analysis, but that it should start with it.
For the full answer you must look at segment market attractiveness
and at how well the firm is positioned in each segment. The actions
taken by the instrumentation group are summarized in Figure 30.

Segments	Priority	Characteristics	Actions
1–6	A	Attractive markets Good market shares High profitability	Heavy management focus Sales effort raised Flexibility to gain sales
7–8	B	Attractive markets Moderate positions Good profitability	Hold position No special initiatives
9	C	Attractive market Poor technology and market share	Harvest (lower costs, raise prices)
10–11	C	Unattractive markets Good market shares Profitability OK	Less effort
12	C–	Unattractive market Moderate position Profitability poor	Much less effort

| 13 | A | Attractive market Subscale but improving position Loss making | Gain share quickly |
| 14–15 | Z | Unattractive markets Moderate/poor positions Loss making | Sell/close |

Figure 30   Electronic Instruments Inc. actions taken after all 80/20 Analyses

80/20 AS A GUIDE TO THE FUTURE—DEVELOPING YOUR FIRM INTO A DIFFERENT ANIMAL

This concludes our strategic review of existing business segments, where it is advisable to start with 80/20 profit analyses. As we have seen, these analyses are indispensable in arriving at segment strategy. But we have still not by any means exhausted the use of the 80/20 Principle in strategy. The principle is also of enormous value in identifying the next leaps forward for your business.

We tend to assume that our organizations, and our industries, are doing pretty much the best they can. We tend to think that our business world is highly competitive and has reached some sort of equilibrium or endgame. Nothing could be further from the truth!

It would be far better to start from the proposition that your industry is all screwed up and could be structured much more effectively to provide what customers want. And as far as your organization is concerned, your ambition could be to transform it within the next decade, so that in 10 years' time your people will look back, shake their heads ruefully, and say to each other: "I can't believe we used to do things that way. We must have been crazy!"

Innovation is the name of the game; it is absolutely crucial to future competitive advantage. We tend to think that innovation is difficult, but with creative use of the 80/20 Principle innovation can be both easy and fun! Consider, for example, the following ideas:

· 80 percent of the profits made by all industries are made by 20 percent of industries. Make a list of the most profitable industries

that you are aware of—such as pharmaceuticals or consulting—
and ask why your industry can't be more like these.

· 80 percent of the profits made in any industry are made by 20
percent of firms. If you aren't one of these, what are they doing
right that you're not?

· 80 percent of value perceived by customers relates to 20 percent
of what an organization does. What is that 20 percent in your case?
What is stopping you doing more of it? What is preventing you
from "making" an even more extreme version of that 20 percent?

· 80 percent of what an industry does yields no more than 20 percent of the benefit to its customers. What is that 80 percent? Why
not abolish it? For instance, if you are a banker, why do you have
branches? If you provide services, why not organize their provision
via the telephone and the personal computer? Where might less
be better, as with self-service? Could the customer be engaged in
providing some of the services?

· 80 percent of the benefit from any product or service can be
provided at 20 percent of the cost. Many consumers would buy a
stripped-down, very cheap product. Is anyone providing it in your
industry?

· 80 percent of any industry's profits come from 20 percent of its
customers. Do you have a disproportionate share of these? If not,
what would you need to do to get it?

Why do you need people?

Some examples of industry transformations may help. My grandmother used to run a corner grocery store. She received orders,
would pick them out, and then I (or some more reliable boy) would
deliver them on a bike. Then a supermarket opened in the town. It
engaged its customers in picking their own groceries and carting
them back home. In return the supermarket offered a wider range,
lower prices, and a car park. Soon my grandmother's customers were
flocking to the supermarket.

Some industries, such as petrol retailing, cottoned on to self-service quickly. Others, such as furniture retailing and banking, thought
it was not for them. Every few years a new competitor, such as Ikea

in furniture, proves that there is new life in the very old idea of self-service.

Discounting is also a perennial transformation strategy. Offer less choice, fewer frills, less service, and much cheaper prices. Eighty percent of sales are concentrated in 20 percent of products—just stock these. Another place I used to work, a wine merchant, stocked 30 different types of claret. Who needed that amount of choice? The firm was taken over by a discount chain and now a wine warehouse has opened up down the road.

Who would have thought 50 years ago that people would have wanted fast-food outlets? And today, who realizes that accessible mega-restaurants, the sort that offer a limited and predictable menu in glitzy surroundings at reasonable prices but insist that you give back the table after 90 minutes, constitute a death warrant for traditional owner-run restaurants?

Why do we insist on using people to do things that machines can do much more cheaply? When will airlines start to use robots to serve you? Most people prefer humans, but machines are more reliable and much cheaper. Machines may give 80 percent of the benefit at 20 percent of the cost. In some cases, as with cash machines (automatic teller machines, also known as holes in the wall), they provide a much better service, much faster, and at a fraction of the cost. In the next century only old fogies like me will prefer to deal with humans and even I will have my doubts.

Are carpets obsolete?

I want to leave you to your own imagination. Just one final example, where use of the 80/20 Principle has transformed a company's fortunes and could conceivably change a whole industry.

Consider the Interface Corporation of Georgia, now an $800 million carpet supplier. It used to sell carpets; now it leases them, installing carpet tiles rather than whole carpets. Interface realized that 20 percent of any carpet receives 80 percent of the wear. Normally a carpet is replaced when most of it is still perfectly good. Under Interface's leasing scheme, carpets are regularly inspected and any worn or damaged carpet tile is replaced. This lowers costs for both Interface and the customer. A trivial 80/20 observation has transformed one company and could lead to widespread future changes in the industry.

CONCLUSION

The 80/20 Principle suggests that your strategy is wrong. If you make most of your money out of a small part of your activity, you should turn your company upside down and concentrate your efforts on multiplying this small part. Yet this is only part of the answer. Behind the need for focus lurks an even more powerful truth about business, and it is to this theme that we turn next.

5

SIMPLE IS BEAUTIFUL

My effort is in the direction of simplicity. People in general have so little and it costs so much to buy even the barest necessities (let alone the luxuries to which I think everyone is entitled) because nearly everything we make is much more complex than it needs to be. Our clothing, our food, our household furnishings—all could be much simpler than they now are and at the same time be better-looking.

HENRY FORD[1]

We saw in the previous chapter that nearly all businesses have within them chunks of business with widely varying profitability. The 80/20 Principle suggests something quite outrageous as a working hypothesis: that one-fifth of a typical company's revenues account for four-fifths of its profits and cash. Conversely, four-fifths of the average company's revenues account for only one-fifth of profits and cash. This is a bizarre hypothesis. If we assume that one such business has sales of $100 million and total profits of $5 million, for the 80/20 Principle to be correct $20 million of sales has to produce $4 million of profits—a return on sales of 20 percent; while $80 million of sales has to produce just $2 million of profits, a return on sales of just 1.25 percent. This means that the top fifth of business is *sixteen* times more profitable than the rest of the business.

What is extraordinary is that when it is tested, the hypothesis generally turns out to be correct, or not very far wide of the mark.

How can this be true? It is intuitively obvious that some business chunks may be considerably more profitable than others. But 16 times better? It almost beggars belief. And, routinely, executives who commission product-line profitability exercises often do refuse to believe the results when first presented with them. Even when they have checked the assumptions and verified them, they still end up baffled.

The next stage is often for managers to refuse to get rid of the 80 percent of business that is unprofitable, on the apparently reasonable grounds that the 80 percent makes a very large contribution to over-heads. Removing the 80 percent, they say, would clearly decrease profits, because you simply couldn't remove 80 percent of your over-head in any sensible time frame.

When faced with these objections, corporate analysts or consultants generally give way to the managers. Only the most horribly unprofitable business is removed. And only minor efforts are made to increase the extremely profitable business.

Yet all this is a dreadful compromise, based on a misunderstanding. Few people stop to ask *why* the unprofitable business is so bad. Even fewer stop to think whether you could in practice, as well as in theory, have a business solely composed of the most profitable chunks and get rid of 80 percent of the overhead.

The truth is that the unprofitable business is so unprofitable *because* it requires the overheads and because having so many different chunks of business makes the organization horrendously complicated. It is equally true that the very profitable business does not require the overheads, or only a very small portion of them. You *could* have a business solely composed of the profitable business and it *could* make the same absolute returns, provided that you organized things differently.

And why is this so? The reason is the same. It is that simple is beautiful. Business people seem to love complexity. No sooner is a simple business successful than its managers pour vast amounts of energy into making it very much more complicated. But business returns abhor complexity. As the business becomes more complex, its returns fall dramatically. This is not just because more marginal business is being taken. It is also because the act of making a business more complex depresses returns more effectively than any other means known to humanity.

It follows that the process can be reversed. A complex business can be made more simple and returns can soar. All it takes is an understanding of the costs of complexity (or the value of simplicity) and courage to remove at least four-fifths of lethal managerial overhead.

SIMPLE IS BEAUTIFUL—COMPLEX IS UGLY

Those of us who believe in the 80/20 Principle will never succeed in transforming industry until we can demonstrate that simple is beautiful and why. Unless people understand this, they will never be willing to give up 80 percent of their current business and overheads.

So we need to go back to basics and revise the common view of the roots of business success. To do so, we must get involved in a current controversy over whether size in business is a help or a hindrance. By resolving this dispute, we will also be able to show why simple is beautiful.

Something very interesting, and unprecedented, is happening to our industrial structure. Since the Industrial Revolution companies have become both bigger and more diversified. Until the end of the nineteenth century, nearly all companies were national or subnational, having the vast bulk of their revenues confined to their home country; and nearly all were in just one line of business. The twentieth century has seen a series of transformations, changing the nature both of business and of our daily lives. First, thanks largely to Henry Ford's sensationally successful quest to "democratize" the automobile, there was the burgeoning power of the assembly line, multiplying the revenues of the average firm, creating mass branded consumer goods for the first time in history, slashing the real cost of those goods, and giving more and more power to the largest enterprises. Then there was the emergence of so-called multinational enterprises, which initially took the Americas and Europe, and later the whole world, as their canvas. Next came the conglomerates, a new breed of corporation that refused to confine itself to one line of business and rapidly spread its tentacles across many industrial sectors and a myriad of products. Then the invention and refinement of the hostile takeover, fuelled equally by management ambition and the financial lubrication of leverage, gave further impetus to size. Finally, in the last 30 years of the century, the determination of industrial leaders, mainly from Japan, to seize global leadership in their priority markets and as much market share as feasible provided the final reinforcement to the cult of corporate size.

For various reasons, therefore, the first 75 years of the twentieth century witnessed a progressive and apparently unstoppable expansion in the size of industrial enterprise and, until recently, in the proportion of business activity taken by the largest firms. But in the past two decades, the latter trend has suddenly, and dramatically, gone into reverse. In 1979, the Fortune 500 largest U.S. firms accounted for nearly 60 percent of U.S. gross national product, but by the early 1990s this had slumped to just 40 percent.

Does this mean that small is beautiful?

No. This is definitely the wrong answer. There is absolutely nothing wrong with the belief long held by business leaders and strategists that scale and market share are valuable. Extra scale gives greater volume over which to spread fixed costs, especially the overhead costs that make up the lion's share of all costs (now that factories have been made so efficient). Market share, too, helps to raise prices. The most popular firm, that with the highest market share, the best reputation and brands, and the most loyal customers, should command a price premium over lower-share competitors.

Yet why is that larger firms are losing market share to smaller firms? And why does it happen that in practice, as opposed to theory, the advantages of scale and market share fail to translate into higher profitability? Why is it that firms often see their sales mushroom yet their returns on sales and capital actually fall, rather than rise as the theory would predict?

The cost of complexity

The most important answer is the *cost of complexity*. The problem is not extra scale, but extra complexity.

Additional scale, without additional complexity, will always give lower unit costs. To deliver to one customer more of one product or service, provided that it is exactly the same, will always raise returns.

Yet additional scale is rarely just more of the same. Even if the customer is the same, the extra volume usually comes from adapting an existing product, providing a new product, and/or adding more service. This requires expensive overhead costs that are usually hidden, but always real. And if new customers are involved it is far worse. There are high initial costs in recruiting customers and they generally have different needs to existing customers, causing even greater complexity and cost.

Internal complexity has huge hidden costs

When new business is different from existing business, even if it is only slightly different, costs tend to go up, not just pro rata with the volume increase but well ahead of it. This is because complexity slows down simple systems and requires the intervention of managers to deal with the new requirements. The cost of stopping and starting again, of communication (and miscommunication) between extra people and above all the cost of the "gaps" between people, when partially completed work is set down to await someone else's intervention and later picked up and passed on into another gap—all these costs are horrendous and all the more insidious because they are largely invisible. If the communication needs to straddle different divisions, buildings, and countries, the result is even worse.

How this works is shown in Figure 31. Competitor B is larger than competitor A, yet has higher costs. This is not because the scale curve—additional volume equals lower costs—doesn't work. Rather, it is because B's extra volume has been bought at the cost of higher complexity. The effect of this is massive and much greater than the additional cost that is visible relative to A. The scale curve operates, but its benefits are overturned by the extra complexity.

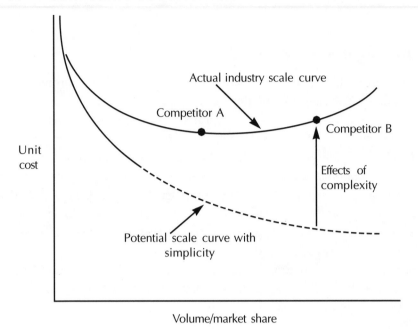

Figure 31   The cost of complexity

SIMPLE IS BEAUTIFUL EXPLAINS
THE 80/20 PRINCIPLE

Understanding the cost of complexity allows us to take a major leap forward in the debate about corporate size. It is not that small is beautiful. All other things being equal, big is beautiful. But all other things are not equal. Big is only ugly and expensive because it is complex. Big can be beautiful. But it is simple that is *always* beautiful.

Even management scientists are belatedly realizing the value of simplicity. A recent careful study of 39 middle-sized German companies, led by Gunter Rommel,[2] found that only one characteristic differentiated the winners from the less successful firms: simplicity. The winners sold a narrower range of products to fewer customers and also had fewer suppliers. The study concludes that a simple organization was best at selling complicated products.

This mental breakthrough helps to explain why and how the seemingly outrageous claims of the 80/20 Principle, applied to corporate profits, can actually be true. A fifth of revenues can produce four-fifths of profits. The top 20 percent of revenues can be 16 times more profitable than the bottom 20 percent (or, where the bottom 20 percent makes a loss, infinitely more profitable!). Simple is beautiful explains a large part of why the 80/20 Principle works:

- Simple and pure market share is much more valuable than has previously been recognized. The returns from pure scale have been obscured by the cost of complexity associated with impure scale. And different chunks of business have usually had different competitors and different relative strength vis-à-vis those competitors. Where a business is dominant in its narrowly defined niche, it is likely to make several times the returns earned in niches where one faces a dominant competitor (the mirror image).
- Parts of the business that are mature and simple can be amazingly profitable. Cutting the number of products, customers, and suppliers usually leads to higher profits, partly because you can have the luxury of just focusing on the most profitable activities and customers, but partly also because the costs of complexity—in the form of overheads and management—can be slashed.
- In different products, firms often have differences in the extent to which they buy in goods and services from the outside (in the jargon, outsourcing). Outsourcing is a terrific way to cut complexity and costs. The best approach is to decide which is the part of the value-adding chain (R&D/manufacturing/distribution/selling/marketing/servicing) where your company has the greatest comparative advantage—and then ruthlessly outsource everything else. This can take out most of the costs of complexity and enable dramatic reductions in head count, as well as speeding up the time it takes you to get a product to market. The result: much lower costs and often significantly higher prices too.
- It can enable you to do away with all central functions and costs. If you are just in one line of business, you don't need a head office, regional head offices, or functional offices. And the abolition of the head office can have an electric effect on profits. The key problem with head offices is not their cost; it is the way they take away real

responsibility and initiative from those who do the work and add the value to customers. For the first time, corporations can center themselves around customer needs rather than around the management hierarchy.

Before the head office is abolished, different chunks of business attract different degrees of head office cost and interference. The most profitable products and services are usually those that are left to get on with their own life without any "help" from the center. This is why, when 80/20 profitability exercises have been carried out, executives are often staggered to learn that the most neglected areas are the most profitable. It is no accident. (And one of the unfortunate byproducts of 80/20 Analysis is sometimes that the most profitable areas get a lot more attention from managers at the top. As a result, they can begin to drop down the profitability league table.)

· Finally, where a chunk of business is simple, the chances are that it is closer to the customer. There is less management to get in the way. Customers can be listened to and feel that they are important. People are willing to pay a lot more for this. For customers, the quest for self-importance is at least as important as the quest for value. Simplicity raises prices as well as lowering costs.

CONTRIBUTION TO OVERHEAD: ONE OF THE LAMEST EXCUSES FOR INACTION

Frequently, managers faced with the results of 80/20 Analysis protest that they cannot just focus on the most profitable segments. They point out that the less profitable segments, and even the loss-making segments, make a positive contribution to overheads. This is one of the lamest and most self-serving defence mechanisms ever contrived.

If you focus on the most profitable segments, you can grow them surprisingly fast—nearly always at 20 percent a year and sometimes even faster. Remember that the initial position and customer franchise are strong, so it's a lot easier than growing the business overall. The need for overhead coverage from unprofitable segments can disappear pretty quickly.

Yet the truth is that you don't need to wait. "If your eye offends you, pluck it out!" Just remove the offending overhead. If your will is strong, you can always do it. The less profitable segments can sometimes be sold, with or without their overheads, and always be closed. (Do not listen to accountants who bleat about "exit costs"; a lot of these are just numbers on a page with no cash cost. Even where there is a cash cost, there is normally a very quick payback, one that will be much quicker, because of the value of simplicity, than the bean counters will ever tell you.) A third option, often the most profitable, is to harvest these segments, deliberately losing market share. You let go of the less profitable customers and products, cut off most support and sales effort, raise prices, and allow sales to decline at 5–20 percent while you laugh all the way to the bank.

GO FOR THE MOST SIMPLE 20 PERCENT

What is most simple and standardized is hugely more productive and cost effective than what is complex. The simplest messages are the most appealing and universal: to colleagues, consumers, and suppliers. The simplest structures and process flows are at once the most attractive and the lowest cost. Letting the customer access your business system—as with all forms of self-service—creates choice, economy, speed, and spend.

Always try to identify the simplest 20 percent of any product range, process, marketing message, sales channel, product design, product manufacture, service delivery, or customer feedback mechanism. Cultivate the simplest 20 percent. Refine it until it is as simple as you can make it. Standardize delivery of a simple product or service on as universal and global a basis as possible. Pass up thrills, bells, and whistles. Make the simplest 20 percent as high quality and consistent as imaginable. Whenever something has become complex, simplify it; if you cannot, eliminate it.

REDUCING COMPLEXITY AT CORNING

How can a business in trouble use the 80/20 Principle to reduce complexity and raise profits? An excellent case study is provided by

Corning, which produces ceramic substrates for automobile exhaust systems in Greenville, Ohio, and Kaiserslautern, Germany.[3]

In 1992 the U.S. business was doing badly and the next year the German market fell sharply. Instead of panicking, the Corning executives took a long, hard look at the profitability of all their products.

As in almost every firm around the world, the Corning executives had used a standard cost approach to decide what to produce. But standard cost systems are one of the most important reasons the 80/20 Principle has so much to add: standard cost systems make it impossible to know true product profitability, largely because they do not differentiate between high- and low-volume products. When variable costs—such as overtime, training, equipment modifications, and downtime—were fully allocated at Corning, the results caused astonishment.

Take two products made at Kaiserslautern: a high-volume, simple, symmetrically shaped ceramic substrate, disguised here as the R10; and a much lower-volume product, the R5, an odd-shaped substrate. The standard cost of the R5 was 20 percent more than that of the R10. But when the extra engineering and shopfloor effort to produce the R5 were fully costed, it turned out to have an incredible cost, around 500,000 percent greater than the R10!

Yet, on reflection, the data could be believed. The R10 virtually made itself. The R5 required expensive engineers to hover over it, nudging it to keep within specification. Therefore, if only R10s were made, far fewer engineers would be needed. And that is what happened. By eliminating low-volume, unprofitable products, which contributed little to revenues and negative amounts of profit, engineering capacity was reduced by 25 percent.

The 50/5 Principle

The Corning analysis kept gravitating toward a very useful cousin of the 80/20 Principle—the 50/5 Principle.

The 50/5 Principle asserts that, typically, 50 percent of a company's customers, products, components, and suppliers will add less than 5 percent to revenues and profits. Getting rid of the low-volume (and negative value) 50 percent of items is the key to reducing complexity.

The 50/5 Principle worked at Corning. Out of 450 products produced at Greenville, half produced 96.3 percent of revenue; the other 50 percent yielded just 3.7 percent. Depending on the period analyzed, the German plant showed that the low-volume 50 percent of products produced only 2–5 per cent of sales. In both locations, the bottom 50 percent made losses.

More is worse

The road to hell is paved with the pursuit of volume. Volume leads to marginal products, marginal customers, and greatly increased managerial complexity. Since complexity is both interesting and rewarding to managers, it is often tolerated or encouraged until it can no longer be afforded. At Corning, they had filled up the plants with loss-making, complicating business. The solution was to cut the number of products by more than half. Instead of dealing with 1,000 suppliers, purchases were consolidated through the 200 suppliers who comprised 95 percent of total supplies (a 95/20 Principle). The organization was streamlined and flattened.

At the heart of the market meltdown, Corning turned away business. This might seem perverse, but it worked. A simpler, smaller operation rapidly restored profits. Less was more.

MANAGERS LOVE COMPLEXITY

At this point it is worth asking: why do supposedly profit-maximizing organizations become complex, when this plainly destroys value?

One important answer, alas, is that managers love complexity. Complexity is stimulating and intellectually challenging; it leavens boring routine; and it creates interesting jobs for managers. Some people believe that complexity obtrudes when no one is looking. No doubt—but complexity is also sponsored by managers, just as it sponsors them. Most organizations, even ostensibly commercial and capitalist ones, are conspiracies of management against the interests of customers, investors, and the outside world generally. Unless firms are facing an economic crisis, or have an unusual leader who favors investors and customers rather than his or her own managers, excess management activity is virtually guaranteed. It is in the interests of the managerial class in charge.[4]

COST REDUCTION THROUGH SIMPLICITY

There is thus a natural tendency for business, like life in general, to become overcomplex. All organizations, especially large and complex ones, are inherently inefficient and wasteful. They do not focus on what they should be doing. They should be adding value to their customers and potential customers. Any activity that does not fulfill this goal is unproductive. Yet most large organizations engage in prodigious amounts of expensive, unproductive activity.

Every person and every organization is the product of a coalition and the forces within the coalition are always at war. The war is between the trivial many and the vital few. The trivial many comprise the prevalent inertia and ineffectiveness. The vital few are the breakthrough streaks of effectiveness, brilliance, and good fit. Most activity results in little value and little change. A few powerful interventions have massive impact. The war is difficult to observe: it is the same person, the same unit, and the same organization that produces both a mass of weak (or negative) output and a smattering of highly valuable output. All we can discern is the overall result; we miss both the garbage and the gems.

It follows that any organization always has great potential for cost reduction and for delivering better value to customers: by simplifying what it does and by eliminating low- or negative-value activities.

Be mindful that:

· waste thrives on complexity; effectiveness requires simplicity
· the mass of activity will always be pointless, poorly conceived, badly directed, wastefully executed, and largely beside the point to customers
· a small portion of activity will always be terrifically effective and valued by customers; it is probably not what you think it is; it is opaque and buried within a basket of less effective activity
· all organizations are a mix of productive and unproductive forces: people, relationships, and assets

- poor performance is always endemic, hiding behind and succored by a smaller amount of excellent performance
- major improvements are always possible, by doing things differently and by doing less.

Always recall the 80/20 Principle: if you study the output your firm generates, the chances are that a quarter to a fifth of the activity accounts for three-quarters or four-fifths of profits. Multiply that quarter or fifth. Multiply the effectiveness of the rest, or cut it out.

REDUCING COSTS USING THE 80/20 PRINCIPLE

All effective techniques to reduce costs use three 80/20 insights: *simplification*, through elimination of unprofitable activity; *focus*, on a few key drivers of improvements; and *comparison of performance*. The last two deserve elaboration.

Be selective

Do not tackle everything with equal effort. Cost reduction is an expensive business!

Identify the areas (perhaps only 20 percent of the whole business) that have the greatest cost-reduction potential. Concentrate 80 percent of your efforts here.

> You don't want to get too bogged down in microanalysis. It can help to apply the 80/20 rule. Ask yourself what are the major time sinks that you can cut out, where are the 80 per cent of the time delays and costs in your current processes that you could target, and understand how you would attack those.[5]

> To be successful, one has to measure what really counts . . . most organizations fit Pareto's rule: 80 percent of what is important is supported by 20 percent of the costs . . . For example, a study in Pacific Bell's customer payment center found that 25 percent of the center's work was devoted to processing 0.1 percent of the payments. A third of the payments were processed twice, and occasionally several times.[6]

In reducing cost or raising product and service quality, remember above all that equal cost does not lead to equal customer satisfaction. A few parts of cost are tremendously productive; but most cost has little or no relationship to what customers value. Identify, treasure, and multiply the few productive costs, and get rid of the rest.

Using 80/20 Analysis to pinpoint improvement areas

80/20 Analysis can establish why particular problems arise and focus attention on the key areas for improvement. To take a simple example, let's imagine that you are running a book publishing firm and that your typesetting costs are 30 percent above budget. Your product manager tells you that there are 1,001 reasons for the overrun: sometimes the authors are late with the manuscript, sometimes the proofreaders or index compilers take longer than planned, in many cases the book is longer than planned, the charts and other figures often need correction, and there are many other special causes.

One thing you can do is to take a particular time period, say three months, and carefully monitor the causes of the all typesetting cost overruns. You should record the main reason for each overrun and also the financial cost penalty involved.

Figure 32 displays the causes in a table, ranking the most frequent cause at the top and so on.

Causes	Number	Percentage	Cumulative percentage
1 Authors late with corrections	45	30.0	30.0
2 Authors late with original manuscript	37	24.7	54.7
3 Authors make too many corrections	34	22.7	77.4
4 Figures need correction	13	8.6	86.0
5 Book longer than planned	6	4.0	90.0
6 Proofreader late	3	2.0	92.0
7 Index compiler late	3	2.0	94.0
8 Permissions received late	2	1.3	95.3
9 Typesetter's computer fault	1	0.67	96.0
10 Typesetter's correction errors	1	0.67	96.6
11 Schedule changed by editor	1	0.67	97.3
12 Schedule changed by marketing	1	0.67	98.0
13 Schedule changed by printer	1	0.67	98.7

14 Fire at typesetter's	1	0.67	99.3
15 Legal dispute with typesetter	1	0.67	100.0
Total	150	100	100

Figure 32   Causes of publisher's typesetting overruns

Figure 33 converts this information to an 80/20 Chart. To construct this, make the causes bars in descending order of importance, put the number of causes per bar on the left-hand vertical axis and put the cumulative percentage of causes on the right-hand vertical axis. This is easily done and the visual summary of the data is quite powerful.

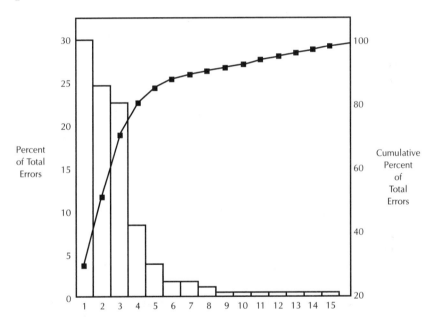

Figure 33   80/20 Chart of causes of publisher's typesetting overruns

We can see from Figure 33 that three of the fifteen problems (exactly 20 percent) cause nearly 80 percent of the overruns. The cumulative line flattens out quickly after the first five causes, telling you that you are reaching the "trivial many" causes.

The major three causes all relate to authors. The publishing house could solve this problem by writing into authors' contracts a clause making them liable for any extra typesetting costs caused by their being late or making too many corrections. A minor change like this would eliminate over 80 percent of the problem.

Sometimes it is more useful to draw an 80/20 Chart on the basis of the financial impact of the problem (or opportunity) rather than the number of causes. The method is exactly the same.

Compare performance

The 80/20 Principle states that there always are a few high-productivity areas and many low-productivity ones. All of the most effective cost-reduction techniques of the past 30 years have used this insight (often with conscious acknowledgment to the 80/20 Principle) to compare performance. The onus is placed on the majority of laggards to improve performance to the level of the best (sometimes taking the 90th percentile, sometimes the 75th, usually within this range) or else to retire gracefully from the field.

This is not the place to give chapter and verse on cost-reduction/ value-improvement techniques such as benchmarking, best demonstrated practice, or reengineering. All of these are systematic expansions of the 80/20 Principle, and all, if (a big if) pursued relentlessly, can raise value to customers by tremendous amounts. Too often, however, these techniques become the latest, evanescent management fad or self-contained programs. They stand a much greater chance of success if placed within the context of the very simple 80/20 Principle that should drive all radical action:

- a minority of business activity is useful
- value delivered to customers is rarely measured and always unequal
- great leaps forward require measurement and comparison of the value delivered to customers and what they will pay for it.

CONCLUSION: SIMPLICITY POWER

Because business is wasteful, and because complexity and waste feed on each other, a simple business will always be better than a complex business. Because scale is normally valuable, for any given level of complexity, it is better to have a larger business. The large and simple business is the best.

The way to create something great is to create something simple. Anyone who is serious about delivering better value to customers can easily do so, by reducing complexity. Any large business is stuffed full of passengers—unprofitable products, processes, suppliers, customers, and, heaviest of all, managers. The passengers obstruct the evolution of commerce. Progress requires simplicity, and simplicity requires ruthlessness. This helps to explain why simple is as rare as it is beautiful.

6

HOOKING THE
RIGHT CUSTOMERS

Those who analyze the reasons for their success know the 80/20 rule applies. Eighty percent of their growth, profitability and satisfaction comes from 20 percent of the clients. At a minimum, firms should identify the top 20 percent to get a clear picture of desirable prospects for future growth.

VIN MANAKTALA[1]

The 80/20 Principle is essential for doing the right kind of selling and marketing and for relating this to any organization's overall strategy, including the whole process of producing and delivering goods and services. We will show how to use the 80/20 Principle in this way. But first, we have an obligation to clear away a lot of pseudo-intellectual undergrowth about industrialization and marketing. For example, it is often said that we live in a postindustrial world, that firms should not be production led, that they should be marketing led and customer centered. These are, at best, half-truths. A short historical excursion is necessary to explain why.

In the beginning, most firms concentrated on their markets—their important customers—with little or no thought. Marketing as a separate function or activity was not necessary, yet the small business made sure that it looked after its customers.

Then came the Industrial Revolution, which created big business, specialization (Adam Smith's pin factory), and eventually the production line. The natural tendency of big business was to subordinate customer needs to the exigencies of low-cost mass production. Henry Ford famously said that customers could have his Model T in "any color as long as it's black." Until the late 1950s, big business everywhere was overwhelmingly production led.

It is easy for the sophisticated marketeer or businessperson today to sneer at the primitiveness of the production-led approach. In fact the Fordist approach was plainly the the right one for its time; the mission to simplify goods and lower their cost, while making them more attractive, is the foundation for today's wealthy consumer society. Products from the low-cost factory progressively made goods in higher and higher categories available (or, in the ghastly phrase, "affordable") to consumers previously excluded from the market. The creation of a mass market also created spending power that had not previously existed, leading to a virtuous circle of lower-cost production, higher consumption, greater employment, higher purchasing power, greater unit volumes, lower unit costs, higher consumption, . . . and so on in a progressive, if not unbroken, upward spiral.

Viewed in this light, Henry Ford was not a production-driven troglodyte: he was a creative genius who did signal service to ordinary citizens. In 1909, he said that his mission was to "democratize the automobile." At the time, the goal was laughable: only rich people had cars. But, of course, the mass-produced Model T, provided at a fraction of the cost of earlier cars, set the ball rolling. For good and ill, and on the whole much more good than ill, we enjoy the "horn of plenty"[2] provided by the Fordist world.

Mass industrialization and innovation did not stop with automobiles. Many products, from refrigerators to the Sony Walkman or the CD-Rom, could not have been commissioned as a result of market research. Nobody in the nineteenth century would have wanted frozen food, because there were no freezers to keep it in. All the great breakthroughs from the invention of fire and the wheel onward have been triumphs of production which then created their own markets.

And it is nonsense to say that we live in a postindustrial world. Services are now being industrialized in the same way that physical products were in the so-called industrial era. Retailing, agriculture, flower production, language, entertainment, teaching, cleaning, hotel provision, and even the art of restauranteering—all these used to be exclusively the province of individual service providers, nonindustrializable and nonexportable. Now all these areas are being rapidly industrialized and in some cases globalized.[3]

The 1960s rediscovered marketing and the 1990s rediscovered customers

The success of the production-driven approach, with the focus on making the product, expanding production, and driving down costs, eventually highlighted the approach's own deficiencies. In the early 1960s, business school professors like Theodore Levitt told managers to be marketing led. His legendary *Harvard Business Review* article in 1960 called "Marketing myopia" encouraged industry to be "customer satisfying" rather than "goods producing." The new gospel was electric. Business people fell over themselves to win the hearts and minds of customers; a relatively new branch of business studies, market research, was vastly expanded in order to discover which new products customers wanted. Marketing became the hot topic at business schools and marketing executives ousted those from production backgrounds as the new generation of CEOs. The mass market was dead; product and customer segmentation became the watchwords of the wise. More recently, in the 1980s and 1990s, customer satisfaction, customer centeredness, customer delight, and customer obsession have become the stated goals of most enlightened and successful corporations.

The customer-led approach is both right and dangerous

It is absolutely right to be marketing led and customer centered. But it can also have dangerous and potentially lethal side effects. If the product range is extended into too many new areas, or if the obsession with customers leads to recruiting more and more marginal consumers, unit costs will rise and returns fall. With additional product range, overhead costs rise sharply, as a result of the cost of complexity. Factory costs are now so low that they comprise only a small part of firms' value added—typically less than 10 percent of a product's selling price. The vast majority of firms' costs lie outside the factory. These costs can be penal if the product range is too large.

Similarly, chasing too many customers can escalate marketing and selling costs, lead to higher logistical costs, and very often, most dangerously of all, permanently lower prevailing selling prices, not just for the new customers, for the old ones too.

The 80/20 Principle is essential here. It can provide a synthesis of the production-led and marketing-led approaches, so that you concentrate only on profitable marketing and profitable customer centeredness (as opposed to the unprofitable customer centeredness very evident today).

THE 80/20 MARKETING GOSPEL

The markets and customers on which any firm should be centered must be the right ones, typically a small minority of those that the company currently owns. The conventional wisdom on being marketing led and customer centered is typically only 20 percent correct.

There are three golden rules:

· Marketing, and the whole firm, should focus on providing a stunning product and service in 20 percent of the existing product line—that small part generating 80 percent of fully costed profits.
· Marketing, and the whole firm, should devote extraordinary endeavor toward delighting, keeping forever, and expanding the sales to the 20 percent of customers who provide 80 percent of the firm's sales and/or profits.
· There is no real conflict between production and marketing. You will only be successful in marketing if what you are marketing is different and, for your target customers, either unobtainable elsewhere, or provided by you in a product/service/price package that is much better value than is obtainable elsewhere. These conditions are unlikely to apply in more than 20 percent of your current product line; and you are likely to obtain more than 80 percent of

your true profits from this 20 percent. And if these conditions apply in almost none of your product lines, your only hope is to innovate. At this stage, the creative marketeer must become product led. All innovation is necessarily product led. You cannot innovate without a new product or service.

Be marketing led in the few right product/market segments

Products accounting for 20 percent of your revenues are likely to comprise 80 percent of your profits, once you take into account all the costs, including overheads, associated with each product. It is even more likely that 20 percent of your products account for 80 percent of your profits. Bill Roatch, the cosmetics buyer for Raley's, a retailer in Sacramento, California, comments:

> Eighty percent of your profit comes from 20% of the products. The question [for a retailer] is, how much of the 80% can you afford to eliminate [without the risk of losing stature in cosmetics] . . . Ask the cosmetics franchisers and they say it'll hurt. Ask the retailers and they'll say you can cut some.[4]

The logical thing to do is to expand the area devoted to the 20 percent of most profitable and best-selling lipsticks and to delist some of the slowest-selling product. Major promotion can then be undertaken in-store on the most profitable 20 percent, in cooperation with the suppliers of these top products. Note that there are always apparently good reasons trotted out as to why you need the unprofitable 80 percent of products, in this case the fear of "losing stature" by having a smaller product line. Excuses like this rest on the strange view that shoppers like to see a lot of products they have no intention of buying, which distracts attention from the product they like to buy. Whenever this has been put to the test, the answer in 99 percent of cases is that delisting marginal products boosts profits while not harming customer perceptions one iota.

A company making automobile appearance products—waxes, polishes, and other car-cleaning accessories—marketed its products through car washes. In theory this was logical, since car-wash owners would make incremental profits through each sale of appearance products simply by putting them on display in space that would otherwise serve no useful function. The idea was that they would give the products premium floor space and make an effort to sell them.

But when the auto appearance product business was sold and new management conducted a comprehensive sales analysis, they found that "the classic 80/20 rule applied—meaning 80 percent of the company's revenues were generated at 20 percent of its retail sites."[5] When the new CEO turned up at 50 car washes generating minimal sales, he found his display hidden away in corners or other poor locations, allowing them to be mistreated and often badly understocked.

The CEO harangued the owners of the car washes not selling many of his products. He told them to pull their socks up and manage their point-of-sale displays properly. This didn't work. Instead, he should have concentrated on the best 20 percent of car washes. What were they doing right? Could they do more of it? What did they have in common? How could more such outlets be found? As the successful outlets were owned by large, professionally run chains, he should have cultivated these outlets rather than trying to improve the performance of the sole-proprietor sites.

Be customer centered for the few right customers

Important as focus on the few best products is, it is much less important than focusing on the few best customers. Many successful marketing professionals have learned this lesson. A few cases may be cited. In telecoms:

> Direct your attention where the real threat of competition exists. In most instances, the 80/20 rule still applies—80% of the revenue comes from 20% of the customers. Know who the top revenue-producing customers are and make sure you meet their needs.[6]

In contract management:

> Remember the old 80/20 rule. Keep in closest contact with the 20 percent of your clients who give you 80 percent of your business. Every Sunday evening, go through contract management files and jot a

note, send a card, or make a note to call anyone you haven't had contact with for too long.[7]

Since 1994 American Express has conducted many campaigns to strengthen its franchise with the merchants and their customers who generate the highest volume of Amex sales. Carlos Viera, director of sales for American Express in South Florida, explains:

> It's the old 80/20 rule: the bulk of your business comes from 20 percent of your market. This campaign is more of a PR campaign to get people to dine out more.[8]

Successful marketing is all about a focus on the relatively small number of customers who are the most active in consuming your product or service. A few customers buy a great deal while a great number buy very little. The latter can be ignored. It is the core customer group that matters: those that consume heavily and frequently. For example, Emmis Broadcasting, which owns WQHT and WRKS radio stations, has conducted successful marketing campaigns focused exclusively on its core audiences, to increase the time they spend listening:

> Instead of spending 12 hours a week with their favorite radio station, they are now spending 25 hours a week with it . . . we focus on the 80/20 rule of consumption with all of our stations . . . we get every single one of the listeners in our target audience and milk every single quarter-hour we can out of them.[9]

Focusing on 20 percent of your customers is a great deal easier than focusing on 100 percent of them. Being customer centered on all of your customers is pretty nigh impossible. But cherishing the core 20 percent is both feasible and highly rewarding.

Four steps to lock in your core customers

You cannot target the key 20 percent until you know who they are. Firms with a finite customer base can work this out individual customer by individual customer. Firms selling to tens of thousands or millions of consumers need to know who their key customers are (these might be channels of distribution) and also the profile of the heavy and frequent consumer.

Second, you need to provide quite exceptional or even "outrageous" service to them. To create a super insurance agency of the future, advises consultant Dan Sullivan, "you'd build 20 relationships and cover them like a run with service. Not regular service, not good service. Outrageous service. You'd anticipate their needs when you could and you'd rush like a SWAT team when they asked you for anything else."[10] The real key is to provide surprising service, above and beyond the call of duty and quite out of line with prevailing industry standards. This may have a short-term cost but it will have a long-term reward.

Third, target new products and services at the core 20 percent of customers, developing them solely for and with this group. In seeking to gain market share, try above all to sell more to your existing core customers. This is not, generally, a matter of sheer selling skills. Nor is it largely a matter of selling more of existing products to them, although frequent-buyer programs nearly always give a high return and raise both short- and long-term profits. But much more important still is developing improvements to existing products, or developing totally new products, that are wanted by, and if possible developed in liaison with, your core customers. Innovation should be grounded in the relationship with this group.

Finally, you should aim to keep your core customers forever. Your core customers are money in the bank. If any of them drops out, your profitability will suffer. It follows that quite extraordinary efforts to keep your core customers, that look as though they are depressing profitability, are bound to enhance it substantially over any meaningful time period. Exceptional service may even help short-term profits, by encouraging core customers to buy more. But profitability is only a scorecard providing an after-the-fact measure of a business's health. The real measure of a healthy business lies in the strength, depth, and length of its relationship with its core customers. Customer loyalty is the basic fact that drives profitability in any case. If you start to lose core customers, the business is crumbling beneath your feet, whatever you do to dress up short-term earnings. If core customers are deserting, sell the business as fast as you can, or fire the management—fire yourself if you are the boss—and take whatever drastic steps are necessary to win the core customers back or at least stop the attrition. Conversely, if the core customers are happy, the long-term expansion of the business is assured.

Serving the core 20 percent of customers must be a company-wide obsession

Only a focus on the key 20 percent of customers can make marketing a firm's central process. We started this section by looking at the shift from being production led to being marketing led. We then observed that the so-called excesses of the marketing approach were a result of focusing on 100 percent rather than 20 percent of customers. For the key 20 percent of customers, no excess can possibly be excessive enough. You can spend up to the limits of your cash and your energy and know that you will obtain an excellent return.

Your organization cannot be centered on 100 percent of its customers: it can be centered on 20 percent. To be centered on these is the main job of any marketing person. But this type of marketing is also the main job of everyone in the firm. The customer will see and judge by the efforts of everyone in the firm, seen and unseen. In this sense, the 80/20 Principle breaks new ground. It is central to marketing, it makes marketing central to the firm, but it also makes marketing the job of everyone in any organization. And marketing, for all the organization's members, must mean providing ever higher levels of delight for the key 20 percent of its customers.

SELLING

Sales is marketing's close cousin: the front-line activity to communicate to and, at least as important, to listen to customers. 80/20 Thinking, as we will see next, is just as crucial for sales as for marketing.

The key to superior sales performance is to stop thinking averages and start thinking 80/20. Average sales performance is very misleading. Some sales people earn over $100,000 per annum while a large minority barely beat the minimum wage. Average performance means little to these people or to their employers.

Take any salesforce and perform an 80/20 Analysis. It is odds on that you will find an unbalanced relationship between sales and salespeople. Most studies find that the top 20 percent of salespeople generate between 70 and 80 percent of sales.[11] For those who do not realize the prevalence of 80/20 relationships in life, this is a pretty remarkable result. But for anyone in business, it holds an important key to raising profits in short order. In the short term, profits are tied to sales more closely than to any other variable. Why does the 80/20 Principle apply to sales and what can we do about it?

There are two sets of reasons why sales per salesperson vary so much. The first set relates to pure salesforce performance issues; the second to structural issues of customer focus.

Salesperson performance

Suppose that your analysis duplicates one recent example and you find that 20 percent of your sales personnel are generating 73 percent of your sales. What should you do about it?

One obvious but often neglected imperative is to *hang on to the high performers*. You shouldn't follow the old adage: if it ain't broke don't fix it. If it ain't broke, make damn sure it doesn't break. The next best thing to staying close to your customers is to stay close to the top salespeople. Keep them happy; this cannot be done solely with cash.

Next, *hire more of the same type of salesperson*. This does not necessarily mean people with the same qualifications. Personality and attitude can be much more important. Put your sales superstars in a room together and work out what they have in common. Better still, ask them to help you hire more people like them.

Third, *try to identify when the top salespeople sell the most and what they did differently then*. The 80/20 Principle applies to time as well as to people: 80 percent of sales by each of your salespeople were probably generated in 20 percent of their worktime. Try to identify so-called lucky streaks and why they happened. One commentator makes the point well:

> If you're in sales, think back to the best streak you ever had. What did you do differently that week? I don't know if ball players or salespeo-

ple are more superstitious . . . but the successful ones in each field tend to look at the conditions that were present when they were on a hot streak and try, try, try not to change them. Unlike a ball player, however, if you're in sales, and you're on a hot streak, change your underwear.[12]

Fourth, *get everyone to adopt the methods that have the highest ratio of output to input.* Sometimes it's advertising, sometimes personal sales visits, sometimes focused mail shots, sometimes it's making telephone calls. Do more of what makes best use of time and money. You could decide to analyze this, but it may be quicker and cheaper simply to observe how the top salespeople spend their time.

Fifth, *switch a successful team from one area with an unsuccessful team from another area.* Do this as a genuine experiment: you will soon find out whether the good team can beat the structural difficulties or vice versa. If the good team cracks the problem in the previously difficult area but the other team is foundering, ask the former team what to do: the answer may lie in splitting the teams so that some are left in each area. Recently a client of mine had terrific success in international sales but the domestic team was demotivated and losing market share. I suggested switching teams. The CEO demurred, because the export team had language talents that would be wasted in domestic sales. Eventually he agreed to release one of the international team, fired the sales director of domestic, and put the young man from international in charge. Suddenly, the previously unstoppable loss of market share was reversed. Not all such stories will have a happy ending, but in sales it is generally true that nothing fails like failure and vice versa.

Finally, what about *salesforce training?* "Is it worth investing in training the lower 80% of the salesforce to enhance their performance levels, or is it a waste of time because so many of them are destined to wash out regardless of training?"[13] As on any issue, ask yourself what answer the 80/20 Principle implies. My answer:

· Only train those who you are reasonably sure plan to stick around with you for several years.
· Get those who are the best salespeople to train them, rewarding

the sales superstars according to the subsequent performance of their trainees.

· Invest the most training in those who perform best after the first series of training. Take the best 20 percent of the trainees and invest 80 percent of the training effort in them. Stop training the bottom 50 percent, unless it is clear that you are obtaining a good payback even on this effort.

Many salesforce performance differentials do derive from pure selling skill, but many do not. These structural factors can also be looked at in 80/20 terms.

Selling is not just having good sales techniques

80/20 Analysis can identify structural reasons that reach far beyond individual competence. These structural factors are often much easier to address, and even more rewarding, than dealing with individual merit. A great deal often depends on the products being sold and the customers being served:

> Look at the salesforce. We find, for example, that 20 percent of our salespeople are generating 73 percent of our sales; we find that 16 percent of our products are accounting for 80 percent of sales; also, 22 percent of our customers are producing 77 percent of our sales . . .
>
> Looking further at our salesforce, we find that Black has 100 active accounts. 20 of these produce about 80 percent of Black's sales. Green covers 100 counties, and we find that 80 percent of her customers are concentrated in only 24 counties. White sells 30 different products. Six account for 81 percent of her sales.[14]

We have already highlighted the 80/20 Principle's application to products and customers in the section on marketing. Those in charge of salesforces should therefore:

· Focus every salesperson's efforts on the 20 percent of products that generate 80 percent of sales. Make sure that the most profitable products attract four times the credit that an equivalent dollar of less profitable products does. The salesforce should be rewarded for selling the most profitable products, not the least profitable.

- Focus salespeople on the 20 percent of customers who generate 80 percent of sales and 80 percent of profits. Teach the salesforce to rank their customers by sales and profits. Insist that they spend 80 percent of their time on the best 20 percent of customers, even if they have to neglect some of the less important customers.

  Spending more time with the minority of high-volume customers should result in higher sales to them. If opportunities to sell more existing products have been exhausted, the salesforce should concentrate on providing superior service, so that existing business will be protected, and on identifying new products that the core customers want.

- Organize the highest volume and profit accounts under one salesperson or team, regardless of geography. Have more national accounts and fewer regional ones.

  National accounts used to be confined to firms where one buyer had responsibility for purchasing all of one product, regardless of the location to which it went. Here it is plainly sensible to have an important buyer marked by a senior national sales executive. But increasingly, large accounts should be treated as national accounts and served by a dedicated person or team, even where there are many local buying points. Rich Chiarello, senior vice president of U.S. sales at Computer Associates International, comments:

  > Out of the top 20 percent of organizations, I'm going to get 80 percent of my revenue. I'm going to treat those companies as national accounts. I don't care if a rep flies all over the country, he's going to own the account, and we're going to identify everyone in that organization and put a plan in place to sell them our products.

- Lower costs and use the telephone for less important accounts. A frequent complaint of salesforces is that downsizing or spending more time on large accounts can result in some sales territories having twice as many accounts as can reasonably be covered. One solution is to drop some accounts, but this should only be done as a last resort. A better solution, very often, is to centralize the 80 percent of smaller accounts and provide a telephone selling and ordering service. This can provide a more efficient service much more cheaply than is possible by face-to-face selling.

· Finally, get the salesforce to revisit old customers who have provided good business in the past. This can mean knocking on old doors or calling old phone numbers.

This is an amazingly successful sales technique, amazingly neglected. An old, satisfied customer is very likely to buy from you again. Bill Bain, the founder of strategic consultants Bain & Company, used to sell Bibles door to door in the Deep South. He tells of a lean spell, trudging from door to door and making no new sales, before he had a blinding glimpse of the obvious. He went back to the last customer who had bought a Bible and sold her another one! Another man following the same technique is one of the top real estate brokers in the United States, Nicholas Barsan, a Romanian emigrant. He wins over $1 million of personal commissions each year and over a third of these come from repeat customers. Mr. Barsan literally knocks on old doors and ask the homeowners (who were clients of his) if they're ready to sell.

Making use of these 80/20 structural influences can turn mediocre salespeople into good ones and good ones into superstars. The impact of a better salesforce on a firm's bottom line is immediate. Even more important is the longer-term impact on market share and customer delight of a salesforce pulsating with energy and confidence, determined to deliver the best to the core customer group, but still able to listen to what they really want.

THE VITAL FEW CUSTOMERS

Some customers are vital. Most are not. Some sales efforts are wonderfully productive. Most are inefficient. Some will lose you money.

Channel marketing and sales effort where you can offer a minority of potential customers something that is unique, better, or much better value than they can obtain elsewhere, provided that you can make higher profits in the process. Any successful enterprise draws its success from this simple, and simplifying, principle.

THE TOP 10 BUSINESS USES OF THE 80/20 PRINCIPLE

The versatility of the 80/20 Principle is legion: it can be used in almost any area of function to direct strategic and financial improvement. Therefore, my Top 10 applications of the 80/20 Principle, shown in Figure 34, inevitably represent an arbitrary choice. In compiling the list, I took into account the extent to which, historically, the business world has already used the 80/20 Principle and also my own opinion of its potential and underexploited value.

Previous chapters have already covered my top six uses: strategy in Chapters 4 and 5; quality and information technology in Chapter 3; cost reduction and service improvement in Chapter 5; and marketing and sales in Chapter 6. The current chapter provides a summary of the other four applications of the 80/20 Principle in my hit parade.

---

1 Strategy
2 Quality
3 Cost reduction and service improvement
4 Marketing
5 Selling
6 Information technology
7 Decision making and analysis

8   Inventory management
9   Project management
10 Negotiation

Figure 34   The Top 10 business applications of the 80/20 Principle

DECISION MAKING AND ANALYSIS

Business requires decisions: frequent, fast, and often without much idea whether they are right or wrong. Since 1950, business has increasingly been blessed, or if you prefer plagued, by management scientists and analytical managers incubated in business schools, accounting firms and consultancies, who can bring analysis (usually linked to extensive and expensive data gathering) to bear on any issue. Analysis has probably been the greatest U.S. growth industry of all in the past half-century, and analysis has been instrumental in some of the greatest U.S. triumphs, such as the moon landing and the incredible accuracy of bombing in the Gulf War.

Anglo-Saxon big business has taken analysis too far

But analysis has had its darker side: the escalation of corporate staffs that are only now being properly dismantled; the infatuation with the latest fads peddled by highly numerate consultants; the stock market's obsession with ever more sophisticated analysis of near-term earnings, despite the fact that these capture only a small part of what a company is really worth; and the withdrawal of intuitive confidence from the forefront of so much of business. The latter has led not just to the pervasive reality behind the cliché of "analysis paralysis," but also to a change for the worse in those who head the West's great corporations. Analysis has driven out vision, just as analysts have driven out visionaries from the CEO's suite.

In short, you can have too much of a good thing and there is no doubt that the United States and Great Britain exhibit a strange misallocation of analysis: the private sector has far too much and the public sector far too little. Our large corporations need much less, but much more useful, analysis.

The 80/20 Principle is analytical but puts analysis in its place

Remember the main tenets of the 80/20 Principle:

· The doctrine of the vital few and the trivial many: there are only a few things that ever produce important results.
· Most efforts do not realize their intended results.
· What you see is generally not what you get: there are subterranean forces at work.
· It is usually too complicated and too wearisome to work out what is happening and it is also unnecessary: all you need to know is whether something is working or not and change the mix until it is; then keep the mix constant until it stops working.
· Most good events happen because of a small minority of highly productive forces; most bad things happen because of a small minority of highly destructive forces.
· Most activity, en masse and individually, is a waste of time. It will not contribute materially to desired results.

Five rules for decision making with the 80/20 Principle

Rule one says that *not many decisions are very important.* Before deciding anything, picture yourself with two trays in front of you— like the dreaded In and Out trays on a desk—one marked Important Decisions and one Unimportant Decisions. Mentally sort the decisions, remembering that only one in twenty is likely to fall into the Important Decision box. Do not agonize over the unimportant decisions and above all don't conduct expensive and time-consuming analysis. If possible, delegate them all. If you can't, decide which decision has a probability of 51 percent of being correct. If you can't decide that quickly, toss a coin.

Rule two affirms that *the most important decisions are often those made only by default,* because turning points have come and gone without being recognized. For example, your chief money makers leave because you have not been close enough to them to notice their disaffection or correct it. Or your competitors develop a new product (as competitors to IBM did with the PC) that you think is wrongly conceived and will never catch on. Or you lose a leading market-share position without realizing it, because the channels of distribution change. Or you invent a great new product and enjoy a modest success with it, but someone else comes along and makes billions out of a lookalike rolled out like crazy. Or the nerd working for you in R&D ups and founds Microsoft.

When this happens, no amount of data gathering and analysis will help you realize the problem or opportunity. What you need are intuition and insight: to ask the right questions rather than getting the right answers to the wrong questions. The only way to stand a reasonable chance of noticing critical turning points is to stand above all your data and analysis for one day a month and ask questions like:

- What uncharted problems and opportunities, that could potentially have tremendous consequences, are mounting up without my noticing?
- What is working well when it shouldn't or at least was not intended to? What are we unintentionally providing to customers that for some reason they seem to appreciate greatly?
- Is there something going badly astray, where we think we know why but where we might be totally wrong?
- Since something important is always happening underneath the surface, without anyone noticing it, what could it be this time?

The third rule of 80/20 decision making is for important decisions: *gather 80 percent of the data and perform 80 percent of the relevant analyses in the first 20 percent of the time available, then make a decision 100 percent of the time and act decisively as if you were 100 percent confident that the decision is right.* If it helps you to remember, call this the 80/20/100/100 rule of decision making.

Fourth, *if what you have decided isn't working, change your mind early rather than late.* The market in its broadest sense—what works in practice—is a much more reliable indicator than tons of analysis. So don't be afraid to experiment and don't persevere with losing solutions. Do not fight the market.

Finally, *when something is working well, double and redouble your bets.* You may not know why it's working so well, but push as hard as you can while the forces of the universe are bending your way. Venture capitalists know this. Most of the investments in their portfolio fail to meet their expectations, but they are redeemed by a few superstar investments that succeed beyond everyone's wildest dreams. When a business keeps performing below its budgets, you may be sure you have a dog. When a business consistently out-performs expectations, there is at least a good chance that it can be multiplied by ten or a hundred times. In these circumstances, most people settle for modest growth. Those who seize the day become seriously rich.

INVENTORY MANAGEMENT

We saw in Chapter 5 that simplicity requires few products. Managing stock is another key discipline flowing from the 80/20 Principle. Good stock keeping, following the 80/20 Principle, is vital to profits and cash; it is also an excellent check on whether a business is pursuing simplicity or complexity.

Nearly all businesses have far too much stock, partly because they have too many products and partly because they have too many variants of each product. Stock is measured in stock-keeping units (SKUs), with one unit for each variant.

Stock almost invariably follows some sort of 80/20 distribution: that is, around 80 percent of stock only accounts for 20 percent of volume or revenues. This means that slow-moving stock is very expensive and cash guzzling to keep and probably involves product that is inherently unprofitable in any case.

I can cite two recent examples of stock review. In one of them:

> Upon analyzing the data, Pareto's 80/20 rule held close to true: 20 percent of the SKUs picked represented 75 percent of the daily volume. These picks were primarily full cases and typically required multiple cases per SKU. The remaining 80 percent of the SKUs represented only 25 percent of the daily volume. These picks amounted to only a few pieces per SKU per day.[1]

The 20 percent was very profitable and the 80 percent unprofitable. Another case comes from a warehouse introducing an electronic system; before doing so it decided to see if it had the right stock in the first place:

> A preliminary study showed that the 80/20 rule didn't fit. Rather than 20 percent of the SKUs accounting for 80 percent of warehouse activity, only 0.5 percent (just 144 SKUs) account for 70 percent of the activity.[2]

Again, while I know nothing at all about the product, it is a safe bet that the top 0.5 percent of SKUs by volume are a great deal more profitable than the other 99.5 percent.

An example which is very important to me, because correcting it made me a lot of money, is that of Filofax. My partner at the time, Robin Field, takes up the story.

> While Filofax design and features had remained static [in the late 1980s], the product line width had expanded beyond all control. The same basic binder was available in a bewildering variety of sizes and a huge assortment of—mainly exotic—skins. Name a creature and Filofax would have ordered several thousand binders made of its hide and proudly placed them in its catalogue and in stock. I don't know what a Karung is, but I inherited an awful lot of its skin in 1990.
>
> Similarly, name a subject: bridge, chess, photography, bird watching, windsurfing, and Filofax would have commissioned several specialist inserts, had tens of thousands of them printed and put them in inventory . . .
>
> The result was, of course, not only a huge overhang of worthless stock, not only an administrative burden of vast complexity, but total confusion among our retailers.[3]

Although good stock management is vital, there are only four key points to it. The most strategic point—cut down radically on your unprofitable product—has already been covered in Chapter 3.

For any given number of products, you should cut down on the number of variants, starting with the slowest movers. Simply cut them out of the product range, as Filofax did. Do not listen to anyone who tells you that the slow movers are really needed. If this was so, they'd move much faster.

Try to export the problem and cost of inventory management to other parts of the value-added chain—to your suppliers or to your customers. The ideal solution is for your stock never to come near your facilities. With modern information technology this is increasingly possible and can raise service standards while simultaneously cutting costs.

Finally, if you must hold a certain amount of stock, there are many tactical ways to use the 80/20 Principle to cut costs and speed up picking and packing:

> The 80/20 rule is reliable in many applications, meaning that about 80 percent of the activity involves only about 20 percent of the inventory. The areas divided by size and weight . . . can now also be divided by part number into areas of high or low activity. In general, fast-moving items should be located as close to the shoulder–hip zone as possible, to minimize operator movement and reduce fatigue.[4]

Inventory management in the future

Despite its historical overtones of the brown coat and the dusty store, inventory management is a fast-moving and exciting area. "Virtual inventory," with on-line order processing, is becoming widespread, lowering costs but also improving service to distributors and customers. Innovators such as Baxter International's hospital supply business are having great success with "customer-intimate" inventory systems. In all cases, progress is being driven by focus: focus on the most important customers, focus on a simple product line, simply tracked and simply delivered.

The 80/20 Principle is also alive and well in another increasingly important component of corporate value creation: project management.

PROJECT MANAGEMENT

Management structures are being exposed as inadequate and worse. They usually destroy more value than they add. One way of destroying or circumventing structures, so as to create value for valuable customers, is the project. Many of the most energetic people in business, from chief executives down, do not really have a job: rather, they pursue a number of projects.

Project management is an odd task. On the one hand, a project involves a team: it is a cooperative and not a hierarchical arrangement. But on the other hand, the team members usually do not know fully what to do, because the project requires innovation and ad hoc arrangements. The art of the project manager is to focus all team members on the few things that really matter.

Simplify the objective

First, simplify the task. A project is not a project: almost invariably, a project is several projects. There may be a central theme in the project and a series of satellite concerns. Alternatively, there may be three or four themes wrapped up in the same project. Think of any project with which you are familiar and you will see the point.

Projects obey the law of organizational complexity. The greater the number of a project's aims, the effort to accomplish the project satisfactorily increases, not in proportion, but geometrically.

Eighty percent of the value of any project will come from 20 percent of its activities, and the other 80 percent will arise because of needless complexity. Therefore do not start your project until you have stripped it down to one simple aim. Jettison the baggage.

Impose an impossible time scale

This will ensure that the project team does only the really high-value tasks:

Faced with an impossible time scale, [project members] will identify and implement the 20 percent of the requirement that delivers 80 percent of the benefit. Again, it is the inclusion of the "nice to have" features that turn potentially sound projects into looming catastrophes.[5]

Impose stretch targets. Desperate situations inspire creative solutions. Ask for a prototype in four weeks. Demand a live pilot in three months. This will force the development team to apply the 80/20 rule and really make it work. Take calculated risks.[6]

Plan before you act

The shorter the time allowed for a project, the greater proportion of time that should be allowed for its detailed planning and thinking through. When I was a partner at management consultants Bain & Company, we proved conclusively that the best-managed projects we undertook—those that had the highest client and consultant satisfaction, the least wasted time, and the highest margins—were those where there was the greatest ratio of planning time to execution time.

In the planning phase, write down all the critical issues that you are trying to resolve. (If there are more than seven of these, bump off the least important.) Construct hypotheses on what the answers are, even if these are pure guesswork (but take your best guesses). Work out what information needs to be gathered or processes need to be completed to resolve whether you are right or not with your guesses. Decide who is to do what and when. Replan after short intervals, based on your new knowledge and any divergences from your previous guesses.

Design before you implement

Particularly if the project involves designing a product or service, ensure you have the best possible answer in the design phase before you start implementation. Another 80/20 rule says that 20 percent of the problems with any design project cause 80 percent of the costs or overruns; and that 80 percent of these critical problems arise in the design phase and are hugely expensive to correct later, requiring massive rework and in some cases retooling.

NEGOTIATION

Negotiation completes my Top 10 applications of the 80/20 Principle in business. Not surprisingly, negotiation has been much studied. The 80/20 Principle adds just two points, but they can be crucial.

Few points in a negotiation really matter

Twenty percent or fewer of the points at issue will comprise over 80 percent of the value of the disputed territory. You may think this will be obvious to both sides, but people like to win points, even completely unimportant ones. Similarly, they respond to concessions, even trivial ones.

Therefore, build up a long list of spurious concerns and requirements early in a negotiation, making them seem as important to you as possible. These points must, however, be inherently unreasonable, or at least incapable of concession by the other party without real hurt (otherwise they will gain credit for being flexible and conceding the points). Then, in the closing stages of the negotiation, you can concede the points that are unimportant to you in exchange for more than a fair share of the really important points.

For instance, imagine that you are negotiating with a sole supplier for the prices on 100 parts of a key product you make. Eighty percent of the cost of any product rests in 20 percent of the parts. You should only really be concerned about the prices of these 20 parts. But if you concede the asking price on the other 80 parts too early in the negotiation, you lose valuable bargaining chips. You should therefore construct reasons for the prices on some of the unimportant 80 parts being important to you, perhaps by exaggerating the number of units you are likely to consume.

Don't peak too early

Second, it has often been observed that most negotiations go through a phony war and only get going in earnest when the deadline looms:

> It also seems true that on account of the incredible pressure that time can put on a negotiation, 80 percent of the concessions . . . will occur in the last 20 percent of the time available. If demands are presented early on, neither side may be willing to yield, and the entire transaction can fall apart. But if additional demands or problems surface in the final 20 percent of the time available for the negotiation, both sides will be more flexible.[7]

Impatient people don't make good negotiators.

How to secure a pay raise

Orten Skinner gives an intriguing example of how to exploit the 80/20 Principle:

> 80 percent of concessions will be made in the last 20 percent of negotiating time. If your appointment to ask for a long-overdue raise is scheduled for 9:00 a.m. and you know your supervisor has another appointment at 10:00, expect the critical moments to occur around 9:50. Pace yourself accordingly. Don't make your request too early to permit a gracious compromise on your supervisor's part.[8]

BEYOND THE TOP 10

By now you will have realized that the 80/20 Principle cuts across whatever boxes we create. The insights derive from the living reality behind people, behind business, and behind the world in which business operates. The 80/20 Principle is so pervasive because it is a reflection of deeper forces ruling our existence. It is time to draw these strands together.

8

THE VITAL FEW
GIVE SUCCESS TO YOU

The 80/20 Principle comprises radar and autopilot. The radar gives us insight: it helps us spot opportunities and dangers. The autopilot allows us to stroll around our business arena and talk to customers and anyone else who might matter, knowing that we are still in control of our destiny. The logic of the 80/20 Principle requires us to grasp and internalize a few simple points; we can then easily "think 80/20" and "act 80/20" whatever we are doing.

A few things are always much more important than most things

This is invariably true, yet difficult at first to credit. Unless we have numbers or 80/20 Thinking to guide us, most things always appear more important than the few things that are actually more important. Even if we accept the point in our minds, it is difficult to make the next hop to focused action. Keep the "vital few" in the forefront of your brain. And keep reviewing whether you are spending more time and effort on the vital few rather than the trivial many.

Progress means moving resources from low-value to high-value uses

Like individual entrepreneurs, the free markets shift resources out of areas of lower productivity into areas of higher productivity and yield. But neither markets nor entrepreneurs, let alone today's overcomplex corporate or government bureaucracies, do this well enough. There is always a tail of waste, usually a very long tail, where 80 percent of resources are producing only 20 percent of value. This always creates arbitrage opportunities for genuine entrepreneurs. The scope for entrepreneurial arbitrage is always underestimated.

A few people add most of the value

The best people—meaning the people best fitted to what they are doing and doing the things that make the most money—generate enormous surpluses, usually far beyond what they are allowed to take out. Normally there are very few such people. The majority add little more than they take out. A large minority (still often the majority) take out more than they contribute. This misallocation of resources is greatest in larger and more diversified corporations.

Any large, managed corporation is an organized conspiracy to misallocate rewards. The larger and more complex the firm, the greater the extent and success of the conspiracy. Those who work in corporations, or have extensive dealings with them, know that a few employees are priceless. They add value far beyond their cost. Many employees are passengers adding much less value than they cost. Some, perhaps 10–20 percent, subtract value, even ignoring their compensation.

There are many reasons for this happening: the difficulty of measuring true performance; the political skill or otherwise of executives; the difficult-to-eradicate tendency to favor those whom we like; the ridiculous but prevalent idea that job role should count for as much or more than individual performance; and the sheer human tendency toward egalitarianism, often buttressed by the legitimate wish to foster team working. Waste and idleness gravitate to where complexity and democracy meet.

I recently advised the head of an investment bank on how to divide up his extremely large annual bonus pool. My client is an extremely rich self-made businessman whose delight and source of success lie in spotting and exploiting market imperfections. He believes passionately in the market. He also knows that two people out of the hundreds in the bonus pool made more than 50 percent of the money in his division last year; in his line of business it is easy to measure. But when I suggested giving more than half the total pool to these two, he was aghast. Later on, we came to the case of one executive who we both knew was subtracting more value than he added (but who was both likable and an extremely astute politician within the bank). Why not cut his bonus to zero, I suggested. Again, my friend hadn't thought of that: "Gee, Richard, I've already cut it to a quarter of what it was last year and I daren't go any further." Yet in this case, the executive should have been paying the bank to work there. Happily, the nettle was grasped. The bonus was set at zero. The executive has now moved to a job where he's adding some value.

Accounting systems are the enemy of fair rewards, because they are absolutely brilliant at obscuring where the money is really being made. This is why, human frailty apart, the imbalance between performance and reward is greater in large and complex firms than in small businesses. The entrepreneur with four employees knows who is making the organization money, and how much, without needing a divisional P&L. The CEO of a large corporation needs to rely on misleading accounting data and the filter provided by the head of human resources (dread phrase!); it is not surprising that in large firms the top performers get less than they should and the mass of mediocre managers end up with more than they deserve.

Margins vary wildly

Margins—between value and cost, between effort and reward—are always highly variable. High-margin activities constitute a small part of total activities but a majority of total margins. If we didn't interfere with the natural allocation of resources, these imbalances would become even more marked. But we bury our heads in the sand (accounting systems conveniently provide endless beaches specifically for this purpose) and refuse to acknowledge the reality that the majority of what we and our firms do is worth much less than the minority of high-margin activities.

Resources are always misallocated

We give too many resources to low-margin activities and too few to high-margin activities. Yet despite our best endeavors, the high-margin activities continue to flourish and the subsidized activities fail to generate their own momentum. If resources are available, because of the slack created by the high-margin activities, the low-margin activities will consume more and more resources while continuing to contribute little, zero or negative surpluses for reinvestment.

We are continually surprised at how well the best activities are doing and at how long it is taking for the problem areas to turn around. Usually, the latter never do. We nearly always take too long to realize this and only the intervention of a new boss, a crisis, or a management consultant makes us do what we should have done long ago.

Success is underrated and underrecognized

Success is undervalued, undercelebrated, and underexploited. Often it is dismissed as a lucky streak. But luck, like accidents, doesn't happen as often as we think. "Luck" is our word for success which we cannot fathom. Behind luck there is always a highly effective mechanism, generating surpluses regardless of our failure to notice it. Because we cannot believe our "luck," we fail to multiply and benefit from value-creating virtuous circles.

Equilibrium is illusory

Nothing lasts forever and nothing is ever in equilibrium. Innovation is the only constant. Innovation is always resisted and often retarded, but rarely extinguished. Successful innovation is hugely more productive than the status quo; it has to be, to overcome it. Beyond a certain point, the momentum of effective innovation becomes irresistible. Personal, corporate, and national success resides not in invention, or even in creating the marketable innovation, but in spotting the point at which the innovation is about to become irresistible and then riding it for all it is worth.

Change is necessary for survival. Constructive change requires insight into what is most effective and a focus on that winning way.

The biggest wins all start small

Finally, something big always comes from something which is small to start with. Small causes, small products, small firms, small markets, small systems: all of these are often the start of something big. Yet they are rarely recognized as such. Our attention is usually on the mass of what already exists, not on the trend evident in small phenomena. We usually only notice something after it has already become big, when the growth is already decelerating. Fortunes are made by the very few who latch on to growth when it is still small and accelerating. Even those who are experiencing the growth rarely realize its significance or potential to make a fortune.

STOP THINKING 50/50

We need massive reeducation to stop thinking 50/50 and start thinking 80/20. Below are some hints.

- Think skewness. Expect 20 percent to equal 80 percent. Expect 80 percent to equal 20 percent.
- Expect the unexpected. Expect 20 percent to lead to 80 percent and 80 percent to result in 20 percent.
- Expect everything—your time, your organization, your market, and every person or business entity you come across—to have quality 20 percent: its essence, its power, its value, a small part with substantially all the goodness hidden away by the mass of mediocrity. Look for the powerful 20 percent.
- Look for the invisible 20 percent and the subterranean 20 percent. It's there—find it. Unexpected successes are one give-away. If a business activity succeeds beyond expectations, that is a 20 percent activity—and it will have much further to run.
- Expect tomorrow's 20 percent to be different to today's 20 per-

cent. Where is the germ, the seed, of tomorrow's 20 percent? Where are the 1 percents that will grow to 20 percents and be worth 80 percent? Where are the 3 percents that last year were 1 percents?

· Develop the facility for mentally blocking out the 80 percents— the easy answer, the obvious reality, the evident mass, the current incumbent, the conventional wisdom, the prevailing consensus. None of these is what it seems or worth its weight in the basest of base metals. These 80 percents are huge blots on the landscape, stopping you seeing the 20 percents beyond. Look round these ugly blots, look over them, look beneath them, look through them. However you do it, ignore them, pretend they don't exist. Free up your vision for the elusive 20 percents.

Psychologists tell us, however, that thought and attitudes can be changed by appropriate action, as well as the other way round. The best way to start thinking 80/20 is to start acting 80/20, just as the best way to start acting 80/20 is to start thinking 80/20. You have to try them out in tandem. The bullets below contain hints on how to act 80/20.

· Whenever you spot a 20 percent activity, run to it, surround your-self with it, immerse yourself in it, patent it, make yourself its expert, worshipper, high priest, partner, creator, propagandist, and indispensable ally. Make the most of it. If the most appears to be more than you can imagine, multiply your imagination.

· Use whatever resources you have at your disposal—talent, money, friends, business allies, powers of persuasion, your credit, your organization, whatever you have or can purloin—to seize, magnify and exploit any 20 percent you come across.

· Use alliances with other people extensively, but only ally yourself to 20 percent people and to the 20 percent of them that are powerful allies. Then seek to ally your alliance to other 20 percenters and 20 percentages.

· Exploit 80/20 arbitrage. Whenever you can, move resources from 80 percent activities to 20 percent activities. The profit from this is enormous because it is highly leveraged arbitrage. You use what is not very valuable to make something that is enormously valuable, winning at both ends of the exchange.

There are two principal media of 80/20 arbitrage: people and money, or assets that are proxies for money or can be turned into money.

Move 20 percent people (including yourself) away from 80 percent activities toward 20 percent activities.

Move money from 80 percent activities to 20 percent activities. If possible and not too risky, use leverage (gearing) in the process. If you really are moving 80 percent to 20 percent activities, the risk is much lower than generally perceived. There are two forms of money leverage. One is borrowing. The other is using other people's money (OPM) as equity rather than debt. OPM used for 80 percent activities is addictive, dangerous, and risky. It ends in tears. OPM used for 20 percent activities creates winners all round and, quite fairly, allows you to be the biggest winner.

· Innovate new 20 percent activities. Steal 20 percent ideas from elsewhere: other people, other products, other industries, other intellectual spheres, other countries. Apply them in your own 20 percent backyard.

· Ruthlessly prune 80 percent activities. Eighty percent time drives out 20 percent time. Eighty percent allies hog space that should go to 20 percent allies. Eighty percent assets deprive 20 percent activities of funds. Eighty percent business relationships displace 20 percent ones. Being in 80 percent organizations or places stops you spending time in 20 percent ones. Living in an 80 percent place prevents you moving to a 20 percent one. Mental energy expended on 80 percent activities takes away from 20 percent projects.

So there we have it. Think 80/20 and act 80/20. Those who ignore the 80/20 Principle are doomed to average returns. Those who use it must bear the burden of exceptional achievement.

ON TO PART THREE

The 80/20 Principle has proved its worth in business and in helping business to startling success in the West and in Asia. Even those who do not love business, or know of the 80/20 Principle, have been touched by the progress made by the minority who do.

Yet the 80/20 Principle is a principle of life, not of business. It originated in academic economics. It works in business because it reflects the way the world works, not because there is something about business that particularly fits the 80/20 Principle. In any situation, the 80/20 Principle is either true or not true; whenever it has been tested, inside or outside the business arena, it works equally well. It is just that the principle has been tested far more often within the confines of business enterprise.

It is high time to liberate the power of the 80/20 Principle and use it beyond business. Business and the capitalist system are exciting and important parts of life, but they are basically procedures, the envelope of life, but not its contents. The most precious part of life lies in the inner and outer lives of individuals, in personal relationships and in the interactions and values of society.

Part Three attempts to relate the 80/20 Principle to our own lives, to achievement, and to happiness. Part Four explores how the 80/20 Principle is intrinsic to the advance of civilization, to progress in society. Parts Three and Four are more speculative and less proven than what we have covered thus far, but are potentially even more important. The reader is asked to collaborate in the expedition to the unknown that we are about to begin.

PART
THREE

WORK LESS, EARN

AND ENJOY

MORE

9

BEING FREE

The 80/20 Principle, like the truth, can make you free. You can work less. At the same time, you can earn and enjoy more. The only price is that you need to do some serious 80/20 Thinking. This will yield a few key insights that, if you act on them, could change your life.

And this can happen without the baggage of religion, ideology, or any other externally imposed view. The beauty of 80/20 Thinking is that it is pragmatic and internally generated, centered around the individual.

There is a slight catch. *You* must do the thinking. You must "editionize" and elaborate what is written here for your own purposes. But this shouldn't be too difficult.

The insights from 80/20 Thinking are few in number but very powerful. Not all of them will apply to every reader, so if you find your experience different, skip along until you meet the next insight that does resonate with your own position.

BECOME AN 80/20 THINKER, STARTING WITH YOUR OWN LIFE

My ambition is not just to serve up insights from 80/20 Thinking and have you tailor them to your own life. I am actually much more ambitious than that. I want you to lock on to the nature of 80/20 Thinking so that you can develop your own insights, both particular and general, which have not crossed my mind. I want to enlist you in the army of 80/20 thinkers, multiplying the amount of 80/20 Thinking let loose in the world.

The common attributes of 80/20 Thinking are that it is reflective, unconventional, hedonistic, strategic, and nonlinear; and that it combines extreme ambition (in the sense of wanting to change things for the better) with a relaxed and confident manner. It is also on the constant lookout for 80/20-type hypotheses and insights. Some explanation of these areas will provide a pointer to how to conduct 80/20 Thinking so you will know when you are on the right track.

80/20 THINKING IS REFLECTIVE

The objective of 80/20 Thinking is to generate action which will make sharp improvements in your life and that of others. Action of the type desired requires unusual insight. Insight requires reflection and introspection. Insight sometimes requires data gathering, and we will indulge gently in a little of this as it relates to your own life. Often, insight can be generated purely by reflection, without the explicit need for information. The brain already has much more information than we can imagine.

80/20 Thinking is different from the type of thinking which prevails today. The latter is usually rushed, opportunistic, linear (for example, x is good or bad, what caused it?), and incrementalist. The predominant type of thinking in today's world is very closely allied to immediate action and consequently is greatly impoverished. Action drives out thought. Our objective, as 80/20 thinkers, is to leave action behind, do some quiet thinking, mine a few small pieces of precious insight, and then act: selectively, on a few objectives and a narrow front, decisively and impressively, to produce terrific results with as little energy and as few resources as possible.

80/20 THINKING IS UNCONVENTIONAL

80/20 Thinking discovers where conventional wisdom is wrong, as it generally is. Progress springs from identifying the waste and suboptimality inherent in life, starting with our daily lives, and then doing something about it. Conventional wisdom is no help here, except as a counter indicator. It is conventional wisdom that leads to the waste and suboptimality in the first place. The power of the 80/20 Principle lies in doing things differently based on unconventional wisdom. This requires you to work out why most other people are doing things wrongly or to a fraction of their potential. If your insights are not unconventional, you are not thinking 80/20.

80/20 THINKING IS HEDONISTIC

80/20 Thinking seeks pleasure. It believes that life is meant to be enjoyed. It believes that most achievement is a by-product of interest, joy, and the desire for future happiness. This may not seem controversial, but most people do not do the simple things that would be conducive to their happiness, even when they know what they are.

Most people fall into one or more of the following traps. They spend a lot of time with people they do not much like. They do jobs they are not enthusiastic about. They use up most of their "free time" (incidentally an anti-hedonistic concept) on activities they do not greatly enjoy. The reverse is also true. They do not spend most time with the people they like most; they do not pursue the career they would most like; and they do not use most of their free time on the activities they enjoy most. They are not optimists, and even those who are optimists do not plan carefully to make their future lives better.

All this is curious. One could say that it is the triumph of experience over hope, except that "experience" is a self-created construct that usually owes more to our perception of external reality than to objective external reality itself. It would be better to say that it is the triumph of guilt over joy, of genetics over intelligence, or predestination over choice, and, in a very real sense, of death over life.

"Hedonism" is often held to imply selfishness, a disregard for others, and a lack of ambition. All this is a smear. Hedonism is in fact a necessary condition for helping others and for achievement. It is very difficult, and always wasteful, to achieve something worthwhile without enjoying it. If more people were hedonistic, the world would be a better and, in all senses, a richer place.

80/20 THINKING BELIEVES IN PROGRESS

There has been no consensus for the past 3,000 years on whether progress exists, whether the history of the universe and of mankind demonstrates a jagged upward path or something less hopeful. Against the idea of progress are Hesiod (around 800 B.C.), Plato (428–348 B.C.), Aristotle (384–322 B.C.), Seneca (4 B.C.–A.D. 54), Horace (A.D. 65–8), St Augustine (A.D. 354–430), and most living philosophers and scientists. In favor of the idea of progress stand nearly all of the Enlightenment figures of the late seventeenth century and eighteenth century, such as Fontenelle and Condorcet, and a majority of nineteenth-century thinkers and scientists, including Darwin and Marx. Team captain for progress must be Edward Gibbon (1737–94), the oddball historian, who wrote in *The Decline and Fall of the Roman Empire:*

> We cannot be certain to what height the human species may aspire in their advance toward perfection . . . We may therefore safely acquiesce in the pleasing conclusion that every age of the world has increased, and still increases, the real wealth, the happiness, the knowledge, and perhaps the virtue, of the human race.

Nowadays, of course, the evidence against progress is much stronger than in Gibbon's day. But so too is the evidence for progress. The debate can never be resolved empirically. Belief in progress has to be an act of faith. Progress is a duty.[1] If we did not believe in the possibility of progress, we could never change the world for the better. Business understands this. On the whole, business, in alliance with science, has provided the greatest evidence for progress. Just as we have discovered that natural resources are not inexhaustible, business and science have come along and supplied new dimensions of unnatural inexhaustibility: economic space, the microchip, new enabling technologies.[2] But to be of greatest benefit, progress should not be confined to the worlds of science, technology, and business. We need to apply progress to the quality of our own lives, individually and collectively.

80/20 Thinking is inherently optimistic because, paradoxically, it reveals a state of affairs that is seriously below what it should be. Only 20 percent of resources really matter in terms of achievement. The rest, the large majority, are marking time, making token contributions to the overall effort. Therefore, give more power to the 20 percent, get the 80 percent up to a reasonable level, and you can multiply the output. Progress takes you to a new and much higher level. But, even at this level, there will still typically be an 80/20 distribution of outputs/inputs. So you can progress again to a much higher level.

The progress of business and science vindicates the 80/20 Principle. Construct a huge computer that can make calculations several times faster than any previous machine. Demand that the computer be made smaller, faster, and cheaper, several times smaller, faster, and cheaper. Repeat the process. Repeat it again. There is no end in sight to such progress. Now apply the same principle to other provinces of life. If we believe in progress, the 80/20 Principle can help us to realize it. We may even end up proving Edward Gibbon right: real wealth, happiness, knowledge, and perhaps virtue can be constantly increased.

80/20 THINKING IS STRATEGIC

To be strategic is to concentrate on what is important, on those few objectives that can give us a comparative advantage, on what is important to us rather than others; and to plan and execute the resulting plan with determination and steadfastness.

80/20 THINKING IS NONLINEAR

Traditional thinking is encased within a powerful but sometimes in-accurate and destructive mental model. It is linear. It believes that x leads to y, that y causes z, and that b is the inevitable consequence of a. You made me unhappy because you were late. My poor schooling led to my dead-end job. I have been successful because I am very clever. Hitler caused the Second World War. My firm cannot grow because the industry is declining. Unemployment is the price we pay for low inflation. High taxes are necessary if we want to look after the poor, the sick, and the old. And so on.

All of these are examples of linear thinking. Linear thinking is attractive because it is simple, cut and dried. The trouble is that it is a poor description of the world and an even worse preparation for changing it. Scientists and historians have long ago abandoned linear thinking. Why should you cling to it?

80/20 Thinking offers you a life raft. Nothing flows from one sim-ple cause. Nothing is inevitable. Nothing is ever in equilibrium or unchangeable. No undesired state of affairs need endure. Nothing desirable need be unobtainable. Few people understand what is really causing anything, good or bad. Causes may be very influential without being particularly noticeable or even (yet) very extensive. The balance of circumstances can be shifted in a major way by a minor action. Only a few decisions really matter. Those that do, matter a great deal. Choice can always be exercised.

80/20 Thinking escapes from the linear-logic trap by appealing to experience, introspection, and imagination. If you are unhappy, do not worry about the proximate cause. Think about the times you have been happy and maneuver yourself into similar situations. If your career is going nowhere, do not tinker around at the edges seeking incremental improvements: a bigger office, a more expensive car, a grander-sounding title, fewer working hours, a more understanding boss. Think about the few, most important achievements that are yours in your whole life and seek more of the same, if necessary switching jobs or even careers. Do not look for causes, especially not for causes of failure. Imagine and then create the circumstances that will make you both happy and productive.

80/20 THINKING COMBINES EXTREME AMBITION WITH A RELAXED AND CONFIDENT MANNER

We have been conditioned to think that high ambition must go with thrusting hyperactivity, long hours, ruthlessness, the sacrifice both of self and others to the cause, and extreme busyness. In short, the rat race. We pay dearly for this association of ideas. The combination is neither desirable nor necessary.

A much more attractive, and at least equally attainable, combination is that of extreme ambition with confidence, relaxation, and a civilized manner. This is the 80/20 ideal, but it rests on solid empirical foundations. Most great achievements are made through a combination of steady application and sudden insight. Think of Archimedes in his bath or Newton sitting under a tree being struck by an apple. The immensely important insights thus generated would not have happened if Archimedes had not been thinking about displacement or Newton about gravity, but neither would have occurred if Archimedes had been chained to his desk or Newton frenetically directing teams of scientists.

Most of what any of us achieve in life, of any serious degree of value to ourselves and others, occurs in a very small proportion of our working lives. 80/20 Thinking and observation make this perfectly clear. We have more than enough time. We demean ourselves, both by lack of ambition and by assuming that ambition is served by bustle and busyness. Achievement is driven by insight and selective action. The still, small voice of calm has a bigger place in our lives than we acknowledge. Insight comes when we are feeling relaxed and good about ourselves. Insight requires time—and time, despite conventional wisdom, is there in abundance.

80/20 INSIGHTS FOR INDIVIDUALS

The rest of Part Three will explore 80/20 insights for your personal life, some of which can be sampled here as a taster. It only takes action on a few insights to improve greatly the quality of your life.

· 80 percent of achievement and happiness takes place in 20 percent of our time—and these peaks can be expanded greatly.
· Our lives are profoundly affected, for good and ill, by a few events and a few decisions. The few decisions are often taken by default rather than conscious choice: we let life happen to us rather than shaping our own lives. We can improve our lives dramatically by recognizing the turning points and making the decisions that will make us happy and productive.
· There are always a few key inputs to what happens and they are often not the obvious ones. If the key causes can be identified and isolated, we can very often exert more influence on them than we think possible.
· Everyone can achieve something significant. The key is not effort, but finding the right thing to achieve. You are hugely more productive at some things than at others, but dilute the effectiveness of this by doing too many things where your comparative skill is nowhere near as great.
· There are always winners and losers—and always more of the latter. You can be a winner by choosing the right competition, the right team and the right methods to win. You are more likely to win by rigging the odds in your favor (legitimately and fairly) than by striving to improve your performance. You are more likely to win again where you have won before. You are more likely to win when you are selective about the races you enter.
· Most of our failures are in races for which others enter us. Most of our successes come from races we ourselves want to enter. We fail to win most races because we enter too many of the wrong ones: their races, not ours.
· Few people take objectives really seriously. They put average effort into too many things, rather than superior thought and effort

into a few important things. People who achieve the most are selective as well as determined.

· Most people spend most of their time on activities that are of low value to themselves and others. The 80/20 thinker escapes this trap and can achieve much more of the few higher-value objectives without noticeably more effort.

· One of the most important decisions someone can make in life is their choice of allies. Almost nothing can be achieved without allies. Most people do not choose their allies carefully or even at all. The allies somehow arrive. This is a serious case of letting life happen to you. Most people have the wrong allies. Most also have too many and do not use them properly. 80/20 thinkers choose a few allies carefully and build the alliances carefully to achieve their specific objectives.

· An extreme case of carelessness with allies is picking the wrong "significant other" or life partner. Most people have too many friends and do not enjoy an appropriately selected and reinforced inner circle. Many people have the wrong life partners—and even more do not nurture the right life partner properly.

· Money used rightly can be a source of opportunity to shift to a better lifestyle. Few people know how to multiply money, but 80/20 thinkers should be able to do so. As long as money is subordinated to lifestyle and happiness, there is no harm in this ability.

· Few people spend enough time and thought cultivating their own happiness. They seek indirect goals, like money and promotion, that may be difficult to attain and will prove when they are attained to be extremely inefficient sources of happiness. Not only is happiness not money, it is not even like money. Money not spent can be saved and invested and, through the magic of compound interest, multiplied. But happiness not spent today does not lead to happiness tomorrow. Happiness, like the mind, will atrophy if not exercised. 80/20 thinkers know what generates their happiness and pursue it consciously, cheerfully, and intelligently, using happiness today to build and multiply happiness tomorrow.

TIME IS WAITING IN THE WINGS

The best place to start 80/20 Thinking about achievement and happiness is the subject of time. Our society's appreciation of the quality and role of time is very poor. Many people intuitively understand this and several hundred thousand busy executives have sought redemption in the form of time management. But these executives are just tinkering around the edges. Our whole attitude toward time needs to be transformed. We don't need time management—we need a time revolution.

10

TIME REVOLUTION

But at my back I always hear
Time's wingèd chariot hurrying near;
And yonder all before us lie
Deserts of vast eternity.

ANDREW MARVELL[1]

Almost everyone, whether ultra-busy or ultra-idle, needs a time revolution. It is not that we are short of time or even that we have too much of it. It is the way we treat time, even the way we think about it, that is the problem—and the opportunity. For those who have not experienced a time revolution, it is the fastest way to make a giant leap in both happiness and effectiveness.

THE 80/20 PRINCIPLE AND TIME REVOLUTION

The 80/20 Principle, when applied to our use of time, advances the following hypotheses:

- Most of any individual's significant achievements—most of the value someone adds in professional, intellectual, artistic, cultural, or athletic terms—is achieved in a minority of their time. There is a profound imbalance between what is created and the time taken to create it, whether the time is measured in days, weeks, months, years, or a lifetime.
- Similarly, most of an individual's happiness occurs during quite bounded periods of time. If happiness could be accurately measured, a large majority of it would register in a fairly small proportion of the total time and this would apply during most periods, whether the period measured was a day, a week, a month, a year, or a lifetime.

We could rephrase these two ideas with spurious precision, but greater snappiness, using 80/20 shorthand:

- 80 percent of achievement is attained in 20 percent of the time taken; conversely, 80 percent of time spent leads to only 20 percent of output value.
- 80 percent of happiness is experienced in 20 percent of life; and 80 percent of time contributes only 20 percent of happiness.

Remember that these are hypotheses to be tested against your experience, not self-evident truths or the results of exhaustive research.

Where the hypotheses are true (as they are in a majority of cases I have tested), they have four rather startling implications:

- Most of what we do is of low value.
- Some small fragments of our time are much more valuable than all the rest.
- If we can do anything about this, we should do something radical: there is no point tinkering around the edges or making our use of time a little more efficient.
- If we make good use of only 20 percent of our time, there is no shortage of it!

Spend a few minutes or hours reflecting on whether the 80/20 Principle operates for you in each of these spheres. It doesn't matter what the exact percentages are and in any case it is almost impossible to measure them precisely. The key question is whether there is a major imbalance between the time spent on the one hand and achievement or happiness on the other. Does the most productive fifth of your time lead to four-fifths of valuable results? Are four-fifths of your happiest times concentrated into one-fifth of your life?

These are important questions and should not be answered glibly. It might be an idea to set this book aside and go for a walk. Don't come back until you have decided whether your use of time is unbalanced.

THE POINT IS *NOT* TO MANAGE YOUR TIME BETTER!

If your use of time is unbalanced, a time revolution is required. You don't need to organize yourself better or alter your time allocation at the margins; you need to transform how you spend your time. You probably also need to change the way you think about time itself.

What you need should not, however, be confused with time management. Time management originated in Denmark as a training device to help busy executives organize their time more effectively. It has now become a $1 billion industry operating throughout the world.

The key characteristic of the time management industry now is not so much the training, but more the sale of "time managers," executive personal organizers, both of the traditional paper-based type and now increasingly electronic. Time management also often comes with a strong evangelical pitch: the fastest-growing corporation in the industry, Franklin, has deep Mormon roots.[2]

Time management is not a fad, since its users are usually highly appreciative of the systems used, and they generally say that their productivity has risen by 15–25 percent as a result. But time management aims to fit a quart into a pint jar. It is about speeding up. It is specifically aimed at business people pressured by too many demands on their time. The idea is that better planning of each tiny segment of the day will help executives act more efficiently. Time management also advocates the establishment of clear priorities, to escape the tyranny of daily events that, although very urgent, may not be all that important.

Time management implicitly assumes that we know what is and is not a good use of our time. If the 80/20 Principle holds, this is not a safe assumption. In any case, if we knew what was important, we'd be doing it already.

Time management often advises people to categorize their list of "to do" activities into A, B, C, or D priorities. In practice, most people end up classifying 60–70 percent of their activities as A or B priorities. They conclude that what they are really short of is time. This is why they were interested in time management to start with. So they end up with better planning, longer working hours, greater earnestness, and usually greater frustration too. They become addicted to time management, but it doesn't fundamentally change what they do, or significantly lower their level of guilt that they are not doing enough.

The name time management gives the game away. It implies that time can be managed more efficiently, that it is a valuable and scarce resource and that we must dance to its tune. We must be parsimonious with time. Given half a chance, it will escape from us. Time lost, the time management evangelists say, can never be regained.

We now live in an age of busyness. The long-predicted age of leisure is taking an age to arrive, except for the unemployed. We now have the absurd situation noted by Charles Handy[3] that working hours for executives are growing—60 hours a week are not unusual—at the same time as there is a worsening shortage of work to go round.

Society is divided into those who have money but no time to enjoy it and those who have time but no money. The popularity of time management coexists with unprecedented anxiety about using time properly and having enough time to do one's job satisfactorily.

80/20 TIME HERESY

The 80/20 Principle overturns conventional wisdom about time. The implications of 80/20 time analysis are quite different and, to those suffering from the conventional view of time, startlingly liberating. The 80/20 Principle asserts the following:

- Our current use of time is not rational. There is therefore no point in seeking marginal improvements in how we spend our time. We need to go back to the drawing board and overturn all our assumptions about time.
- There is no shortage of time. In fact, we are positively awash with it. We only make good use of 20 percent of our time. And for the most talented individuals, it is often tiny amounts of time that make all the difference. The 80/20 Principle says that if we doubled our time on the top 20 percent of activities, we could work a two-day week and achieve 60 percent more than now. This is light years away from the frenetic world of time management.
- The 80/20 Principle treats time as a friend, not an enemy. Time gone is not time lost. Time will always come round again. This is why there are seven days in a week, twelve months in a year, why the seasons come round again. Insight and value are likely to come from placing ourselves in a comfortable, relaxed, and collaborative position toward time. It is our use of time, and not time itself, that is the enemy.
- The 80/20 Principle says that we should act less. Action drives out thought. It is because we have so much time that we squander it. The most productive time on a project is usually the last 20 percent, simply because the work has to be completed before a deadline. Productivity on most projects could be doubled simply by halving the amount of time for their completion. This is not evidence that time is in short supply.

TIME IS THE BENIGN LINK BETWEEN THE PAST, PRESENT, AND FUTURE

It is not shortage of time that should worry us, but the tendency for the majority of time to be spent in low-quality ways. Speeding up or being more "efficient" with our use of time will not help us; indeed, such ways of thinking are more the problem than the solution.

80/20 Thinking directs us to a more "eastern" view of time. Time should not be seen as a sequence, running from left to right as in nearly all graphical representations that the culture of business has imposed on us. It is better to view time as a synchronizing and cyclical device, just as the inventors of the clock intended. Time keeps coming round, bringing with it the opportunity to learn, to deepen a few valued relationships, to produce a better product or outcome, and to add more value to life. We do not exist just in the present; we spring from the past and have a treasure trove of past associations; and our future, like our past, is already immanent in the present. A far better graphical representation of time in our lives than the left-to-right graph is a series of interlocked and ever larger and higher triangles, as shown in Figure 35.

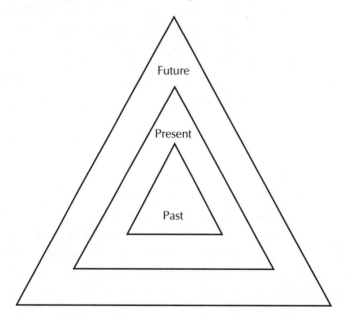

Figure 35   The time triad

The effect of thinking about time in this way is that it highlights the need to carry with us, through our lives, the most precious and valued 20 percent of what we have—our personality, abilities, friendships, and even our physical assets—and ensure that they are nurtured, developed, extended, and deepened, to increase our effectiveness, value, and happiness. This can only be done by having consistent and continuous relationships, founded on optimism that the future will be better than the present, because we can take and extend the best 20 percent from the past and the present to create that better future. Viewed in this way, the future is not a random movie that we are halfway through, aware of (and terrified by) time whizzing past. Rather, the future is a dimension of the present and the past, giving us the opportunity to create something better. 80/20 Thinking insists that this is always possible. All we have to do is to give freer rein and better direction to our most positive 20 percent.

A PRIMER FOR TIME REVOLUTIONARIES

Here are seven steps to detonating a time revolution.

Make the difficult mental leap of dissociating effort and reward

The Protestant work ethic is so deeply engrained in everyone, of all religions and none, that we need to make a conscious effort to extirpate it. The trouble is that we do enjoy hard work, or at least the feeling of virtue that comes from having done it. What we must do is to plant firmly in our minds that hard work, especially for somebody else, is not an efficient way to achieve what we want. Hard work leads to low returns. Insight and doing what we ourselves want lead to high returns.

Decide on your own patron saints of productive laziness. Mine are Ronald Reagan and Warren Buffett. Reagan made an effortless progression from B-film actor to darling of the Republican Right, governor of California, and extremely successful president.

What did Reagan have going for him? Good looks, a wonderfully mellifluous voice which he deployed instinctively on all the right occasions (the high point of which undoubtedly consisted in his words to Nancy when shot, "Honey, I forgot to duck"), some very astute campaign managers, old-fashioned grace, and a Disneyesque view of America and the world. Reagan's ability to apply himself was limited at best, his grasp of conventional reality ever more tenuous, his ability to inspire the United States and destroy communism ever more awesome. To maul Churchill's dictum, never was so much achieved by so few with so little effort.

Warren Buffett became (for a time) the richest man in the United States, not by working but by investing. Starting with very little capital, he has compounded it over many years at rates far above stock market average appreciation. He has done this with a limited degree of analysis (he started before sliderules were invented) but basically with a few insights which he has applied consistently.

Buffett started his riches rollercoaster with one Big Idea: that U.S. local newspapers had a local monopoly that constituted the most perfect business franchise. This simple idea made him his first fortune, and much of his subsequent money has been made in shares in the media: an industry he understands.

If not lazy, Buffett is very economical with his energy. Whereas most fund managers buy lots of stocks and churn them frequently, Buffett buys few and holds them for ages. This means that there is very little work to do. He pours scorn on the conventional view of investment portfolio diversification, which he has dubbed the Noah's Ark method: "one buys two of everything and ends up with a zoo." His own investment philosophy "borders on lethargy."

Whenever I am tempted to do too much, I remember Ronald Reagan and Warren Buffett. You should think of your own examples, of people you know personally or those in the public eye, who exemplify productive inertia. Think about them often.

Give up guilt

Giving up guilt is clearly related to the dangers of excessively hard work. But it is also related to doing the things you enjoy. There is nothing wrong with that. There is no value in doing things you don't enjoy.

Do the things that you like doing. Make them your job. Make your job them. Nearly everyone who has become rich has had the added bonus of becoming rich doing things they enjoy. This might be taken as yet another example of the universe's 80/20 perversity.

Twenty percent of people not only enjoy 80 percent of wealth but also monopolize 80 percent of the enjoyment to be had from work: and they are the same 20 percent!

That curmudgeonly old Puritan John Kenneth Galbraith has drawn attention to a fundamental unfairness in the world of work. The middle classes not only get paid more for their work, but they have more interesting work and enjoy it more. They have secretaries, assistants, first-class travel, luxurious hotels, and more interesting working lives too. In fact, you would need to have a large private fortune to afford all the perquisites that senior industrialists now routinely award themselves.

Galbraith has advanced the revolutionary view that those who have less interesting jobs should be paid more than those with jobs that are more fun. What a spoilsport! Such views are thought provoking, but no good will come of them. As with so many 80/20 phenomena, if you look beneath the surface you can detect a deeper logic behind the apparent inequity.

In this case the logic is very simple. Those who achieve the most have to enjoy what they do. It is only by fulfilling oneself that anything of extraordinary value can be created. Think, for example, of any great artist in any sphere. The quality and quantity of the output are stunning. Van Gogh never stopped. Picasso ran an art factory long before Andy Warhol, because he loved what he did.

Revel in Michelangelo's prodigious, sexually driven, sublime output. Even the fragments that I can remember—his *David, The Dying Slave,* the Laurentian Library, the New Sacristy, the Sistine chapel ceiling, the Pietà in Saint Peter's—are miraculous for one individual. Michelangelo did it all, not because it was his job, or because he feared the irascible Pope Julius II or even to make money, but because he loved his creations and young men.

You may not have quite the same drives, but you will not create anything of enduring value unless you love creating it. This applies as much to purely personal as to business matters.

I am not advocating perpetual laziness. Work is a natural activity that satisfies an intrinsic need, as the unemployed, retired, and those who make overnight fortunes rapidly discover. Everyone has their own natural balance, rhythm, and optimal work/play mix and most people can sense innately when they are being too lazy or industrious. 80/20 Thinking is most valuable in encouraging people to pursue high-value/satisfaction activities in both work and play periods, rather than in stimulating an exchange of work for play. But I suspect that most people try too hard at the wrong things. The modern world would greatly benefit if a lower quantity of work led to a greater profusion of creativity and intelligence. If much greater work would benefit the most idle 20 percent of our people, much less work would benefit the hardest-working 20 percent; and such arbitrage would benefit society both ways. The quantity of work is much less important than its quality, and its quality depends on self-direction.

Free yourself from obligations imposed by others

It is a fair bet that when 80 percent of time yields 20 percent of results, that 80 percent is undertaken at the behest of others.

It is increasingly apparent that the whole idea of working directly for someone else, of having a job with security but limited discretion, has just been a transient phase (albeit one lasting two centuries) in the history of work.[4] Even if you work for a large corporation, you should think of yourself as an independent business, working for yourself, despite being on Monolith Inc.'s payroll.

The 80/20 Principle shows time and time again that the 20 percent who achieve the most either work for themselves or behave as if they do.

The same idea applies outside work. It is very difficult to make good use of your time if you don't control it. (It is actually quite difficult even if you do, since your mind is prisoner to guilt, convention, and other externally imposed views of what you should do—but at least you stand a chance of cutting these down to size.)

It is impossible, and even undesirable, to take my advice too far. You will always have some obligations to others and these can be extremely useful from your perspective. Even the entrepreneur is not really a lone wolf, answerable to no one. He or she has partners, employees, alliances, and a network of contacts, from whom nothing can be expected if nothing is given. The point is to choose your partners and obligations extremely selectively and with great care.

Be unconventional and eccentric in your use of time

You are unlikely to spend the most valuable 20 percent of your time in being a good soldier, in doing what is expected of you, in attending the meetings that everyone assumes you will, in doing what most of your peers do, or in otherwise observing the social conventions of your role. In fact, you should question whether any of these things is necessary.

You will not escape from the tyranny of 80/20—the likelihood that 80 percent of your time is spent on low-priority activities—by adopting conventional behavior or solutions.

A good exercise is to work out the most unconventional or eccentric ways in which you could spend your time: how far you could deviate from the norm without being thrown out of your world. Not all eccentric ways of spending time will multiply your effectiveness, but some or at least one of them could. Draw up several scenarios and adopt the one that allows you the most time on high-value activities that you enjoy.

Who among your acquaintances is both effective and eccentric? Find out how they spend their time and how it deviates from the norm. You may want to copy some of the things they do and don't do.

Identify the 20 percent that gives you 80 percent

About a fifth of your time is likely to give you four-fifths of your achievement or results and four-fifths of your happiness. Since this may not be the same fifth (although there is usually considerable overlap), the first thing to do is to be clear about whether your objective, for the purposes of each run through, is achievement or happiness. I recommend that you look at them both separately.

For happiness, identify your *happiness islands:* the small amounts of time, or the few years, that have contributed a quite disproportionate amount of your happiness. Take a clean sheet of paper, write "Happiness Islands" at the top and list as many of them as you can remember. Then try to deduce what is common between all or some of the happiness islands.

Repeat the procedures for your *unhappiness islands.* These will not generally comprise the other 80 percent of your time, since (for most people) there is a large no-man's-land of moderate happiness between the happiness and unhappiness islands. Yet it is important to identify the most significant causes of unhappiness and any common denominators between them.

Repeat this whole procedure for achievement. Identify your *achievement islands:* the short periods when you have achieved a much higher ratio of value to time than during the rest of your week, month, year, or life. Head a clean sheet of paper with "Achievement Islands" and list as many as you can, if possible taken over the whole of your life.

Try to identify the achievement islands' common characteristics. Before leaving your analysis, you might want to glance at the list of the Top 10 highest-value uses of time on page 176. This is a general list compiled from many people's experience and may nudge your memory.

List separately your *achievement desert islands.* These are the periods of greatest sterility and lowest productivity. The list of the Top 10 low-value uses of time on page 176 may help you. Again, what do they tend to have in common?

Now act accordingly.

Multiply the 20 percent of your time that gives you 80 percent

When you have identified your happiness and achievement islands, you are likely to want to spend more time on these and similar activities.

When I explain this idea some people say there is a flaw in my logic, because spending more time on the top 20 percent may lead to diminishing returns setting in. Twice as much time on the top 20 percent may not lead to another 80 percent of output, perhaps only to another 40, 50, 60, or 70 percent.

I have two replies to this point. First, since it is impossible (at the moment) to measure happiness or effectiveness with anything approaching precision, the critics may well be right in some cases. But who cares? There will still be a marked increase in the supply of what is best.

But my second answer is that I don't think the critics are generally right. My recommendation is not that you duplicate *exactly* what it is that you are doing today that is in the 20 percent yielding 80 percent. The point of examining the common characteristics of your happiness and achievement islands is to isolate something far more basic

than what has happened: to isolate what you are uniquely programmed to do best.

But my second answer is that I don't think the critics are generally
right. My recommendation is not that you duplicate *exactly* what it is
that you are doing today that is in the 20 percent yielding 80 percent.
The point of examining the common characteristics of your happiness and achievement islands is to isolate something far more basic
than what has happened: to isolate what you are uniquely programmed to do best.

It may well be that there are things you should be doing (to realize
your full potential achievement or happiness) that you have only
started doing imperfectly, to some degree, or even that you have not
started to do at all. For example, Dick Francis was a superb National
Hunt jockey, but did not publish his first racing mystery until he was
nearly 40. Now his success, money earned, and possibly personal
satisfaction from the latter activity far exceed those from the former.
Richard Adams was an unfulfilled, middle-aged, middle-level civil
servant before he wrote the bestseller *Watership Down*.

It is not at all uncommon for analysis of happiness or achievement
islands to yield insight into what individuals are best at, and what is
best for them, which then enables them to spend time on totally new
activities that have a higher ratio of reward to time than anything
they were doing before. There can, therefore, be increasing returns
as well as the possibility of diminishing returns. In fact, one thing you
should specifically consider is a change of career and/or lifestyle.

Your basic objective, when you have identified both the specific
activities and the general type of activity that take 20 percent of your
time but yield 80 percent of happiness or achievement, should be to
increase the 20 percent of time spent on those and similar activities
by as much as possible.

A short-term objective, usually feasible, is to decide to take the 20
percent of time spent on the high-value activities up to 40 percent
within a year. This one act will tend to raise your "productivity" by
between 60 and 80 percent. (You will now have two lots of 80 percent
of output, from two lots of 20 percent of time, so your total output
would go from 100 to 160 even if you forfeited all the previous 20
from low-value activities in reallocating some of the time to the high-
value activities!)

The ideal position is to move the time spent on high-value activities up from 20 to 100 percent. This may only be possible by changing career and lifestyle. If so, make a plan, with deadlines, for how you are going to make these changes.

Eliminate or reduce the low-value activities

For the 80 percent of activities that give you only 20 percent of results, the ideal is to eliminate them. You may need to do this before allocating more time to the high-value activities (although people often find that firing themselves up to spend more time on the high-value activities is a more efficient way of forcing them to set aside the low-value time sinks).

First reactions are often that there is little scope for escaping from low-value activities. They are said to be inevitable parts of family, social, or work obligations. If you find yourself thinking this, think again.

There is normally great scope to do things differently within your existing circumstances. Remember the advice above: be unconventional and eccentric in how you use your time. Do not follow the herd.

Try your new policy and see what happens. Since there is little value in the activities you want to displace, people may not actually notice if you stop doing them. Even if they do notice, they may not care enough to force you to do them if they can see that this would take major effort on their part.

But even if dropping the low-value activities does require a radical change in circumstances—a new job, a new career, new friends, even a new lifestyle or partner—form a plan to make the desired changes. The alternative is that your potential for achievement and happiness will never be attained.

FOUR ILLUSTRATIONS OF ECCENTRIC AND EFFECTIVE TIME USE

My first illustration is William Ewart Gladstone, the dominant liberal statesman of Victorian England who was elected prime minister four times. Gladstone was eccentric in many ways, not least his spectacularly unsuccessful attempts to rescue "fallen women" from prostitution and his not totally unrelated bouts of self-flagellation; but his use of time is the eccentricity on which we shall focus here.[5]

Gladstone was not constrained by his political duties, or, rather, was effective at them because he spent his time pretty much as he pleased in an amazing variety of ways. He was an inveterate tourist, both in the British Isles and overseas, often slipping over to France, Italy, or Germany on private business while prime minister.

He loved the theater, pursued several (almost certainly nonphysical) affairs with women, read avidly (20,000 books in his lifetime), made incredibly long speeches in the House of Commons (which despite their length were apparently compulsive listening), and virtually invented the sport of modern electioneering, which he pursued with enormous gusto and enjoyment. Whenever he felt even slightly ill, he would go to bed for at least a whole day, where he would read and think. His enormous political energy and effectiveness derived from his eccentric use of time.

Of subsequent British prime ministers, only Lloyd George, Churchill, and Thatcher came anywhere near to rivalling Gladstone's eccentric use of time; and all three were unusually effective.

Three highly eccentric management consultants

The other examples of unconventional time management come from the staid world of management consulting. Consultants are notorious for long hours and frenetic activity. My three characters, all of whom I knew quite well, broke all the conventions. They were also all spectacularly successful.

The first, whom I will call Fred, made tens of millions of dollars from being a consultant. He never bothered to go to business school, but managed to set up a very large and successful firm of consultants where almost everyone else worked 70 or more hours a week. Fred visited the office occasionally and chaired partners' meetings once a month, which partners from all over the globe were compelled to attend, but preferred to spend his time playing tennis and thinking. He ruled the firm with an iron fist but never raised his voice. Fred

controlled everything through an alliance with his five main subordi-
nates.

The second, alias Randy, was one of these lieutenants. Apart from
its founder, he was virtually the only exception to the workaholic
culture of the firm. He had himself posted to a far-distant country,
where he ran a thriving and rapidly growing office, also staffed by
people working unbelievably hard, largely from his home. Nobody
knew how Randy spent his time or how few hours he worked, but he
was incredibly laid back. Randy would only attend the most important client meetings, delegating everything else to junior partners
and if necessary inventing the most bizarre reasons why he could not
be there.

Although head of the office, Randy paid zero attention to any
administrative matters. His whole energy was spent working out how
to increase revenues with the most important clients and then putting mechanisms in place to do this with the least personal effort.
Randy never had more than three priorities and often only one;
everything else went by the board. Randy was impossibly frustrating
to work for, but wonderfully effective.

My third and final eccentric time user was a friend and partner:
let's call him Jim. My abiding memory of Jim is of when we shared a
small office, together with a handful of other colleagues. It was
cramped and full of wild activity: people talking on the phone, rush-
ing round to get presentations done, shouting from one end of the
office to the other.

But there was Jim, an oasis of calm inactivity, staring thoughtfully
at his calendar, working out what to do. Occasionally, he would take a
few colleagues aside to the one quiet room and explain what he
wanted everyone to do: not once, not twice, but three times, in life-
threateningly tedious detail. Jim would then make everyone repeat
back to him what they were going to do. Jim was slow, languid, and
half-deaf. But he was a terrific leader. He spent all his time working
out which tasks were high value and who should do them and then
ensuring that they got done.

THE TOP 10 LOW-VALUE USES OF TIME

You can only spend time on high-value activities (whether for achievement or enjoyment) if you have abandoned low-value activities. I invited you above to identify your low-value time sinks. To check that you have not missed some, a list below gives the 10 that are most common.

Be ruthless in cutting out these activities. Under no circumstances give everyone a fair share of your time. Above all, don't do something just because people ask, or because you receive a phone call or a fax. Follow Nancy Reagan's advice (in another context) and Just Say No!—or treat the matter with what Lord George Brown called "a complete ignoral."

The Top 10 low-value uses of time

1 Things other people want you to do
2 Things that have always been done this way
3 Things you're not unusually good at doing
4 Things you don't enjoy doing
5 Things that are always interrupted
6 Things few other people are interested in
7 Things that have already taken twice as long as you originally expected
8 Things where your collaborators are unreliable or low quality
9 Things that have a predictable cycle
10 Answering the telephone

THE TOP 10 HIGHEST-VALUE USES OF TIME

A second list gives the other side of the coin.

The Top 10 highest-value uses of time

1 Things that advance your overall purpose in life
2 Things you have always wanted to do

3   Things already in the 20/80 relationship of time to results
4   Innovative ways of doing things that promise to slash the time
    required and/or multiply the quality of results
5   Things other people tell you can't be done
6   Things other people have done successfully in a different arena
7   Things that use your own creativity
8   Things that you can get other people to do for you with relatively
    little effort on your part
9   Anything with high-quality collaborators who have already tran-
    scended the 80/20 rule of time, who use time eccentrically and
    effectively
10 Things for which it is now or never

When thinking about any potential use of time, ask two questions:

· Is it unconventional?
· Does it promise to multiply effectiveness?

It is unlikely to be a good use of time unless the answer to both
questions is yes.

IS A TIME REVOLUTION FEASIBLE?

Many of you may feel that much of my advice is rather revolutionary
and pie in the sky for your circumstances. Comments and criticisms
that have been made to me include the following:

· I can't choose how to spend my time. My bosses won't allow it.
· I would need to change jobs to follow your advice and I can't
  afford the risk.
· This advice is all very well for the rich, but I just don't have that
  degree of freedom.
· I'd have to divorce my spouse!
· My ambition is to improve my effectiveness 25 percent, not 250
  percent. I just don't believe the latter can be done.
· If it were as easy as you say, everyone would do it.

If you find yourself saying any of these things, time revolution may not be for you.

Don't start a time revolution unless you are willing to be a revolutionary

I could encapsulate (or at least caricature) these responses as follows: "I'm not a radical, let alone a revolutionary, so leave me alone. I'm basically happy with my existing horizons." Fair enough. Revolution is revolution. It is uncomfortable, wrenching, and dangerous. Before you start a revolution, realize that it will involve major risks and will lead you into uncharted territory.

Those who want a time revolution need to link together their past, present, and future, as suggested above by Figure 35. Behind the issue of how we allocate time lurks the even more fundamental issue of what we want to get out of our lives.

11

YOU CAN ALWAYS GET
WHAT YOU WANT

Things that matter most
Must never be at the mercy of things that matter least.

JOHANN WOLFGANG VON GOETHE

Work out what you want from life. In the 1980s phrase, aim to "have it all." Everything you want should be yours: the type of work you want; the relationships you need; the social, mental, and aesthetic stimulation that will make you happy and fulfilled; the money you require for the lifestyle that is appropriate to you; and any require-ment that you may (or may not) have for achievement or service to others. If you don't aim for it all, you'll never get it all. To aim for it requires that you know what you want.

Most of us don't work out what we want. And most of us end up with lopsided lives as a result. We may get work right and relation-ships wrong or the other way round. We may strive after money or achievement, but find after we achieve our goal that the victory is hollow.

The 80/20 Principle records this sorry state. Twenty percent of what we do leads to 80 percent of the results; but 80 percent of what we do leads to only 20 percent. We are wasting 80 percent of our effort on low-value outcomes. Twenty percent of our time leads to 80 percent of what we value; 80 percent of our time disappears on things that have little value to us. Twenty percent of our time leads to 80 percent of happiness; but 80 percent of our time yields very little happiness.

But the 80/20 Principle does not always apply and need not apply. It is there as a diagnostic, to point out an unsatisfactory and wasteful state of affairs. We should aim to frustrate the 80/20 Principle or at least translate it to a higher plane where we can be much happier and more effective. Remember the promise of the 80/20 Principle: if we take note of what it tells us, we can work less, earn more, enjoy more, and achieve more.

To do this, we must start with a rounded view of everything we want. That is what this chapter deals with. Chapters 12, 13, and 14 then deal in more detail with some of the components—with relationships, careers, and money respectively—before we revert in Chapter 15 to the ultimate goal: happiness.

START WITH LIFESTYLE

Do you enjoy your life? Not part of it, but most of it: at least 80 percent of it? And whether you do or not, is there a lifestyle that could suit you better? Ask yourself:

· Am I living with the right person or people?
· Am I living in the right place?
· Am I working the right hours and do they match my ideal work/ play rhythm, and suit my family and social needs?
· Do I feel in control?
· Can I exercise or meditate when I want?
· Am I nearly always relaxed and comfortable with my surroundings?
· Does my lifestyle make it easy for me to be creative and fulfill my potential?

- Do I have enough money and are my affairs organized so that I don't have to worry about them?
- Does the lifestyle facilitate whatever contribution I want to make to enriching the lives of people I want to help?
- Do I see my close friends enough?
- Is the extent of travel in my life just right, not too much, or too little?
- Is the lifestyle right for my partner and family too?
- Do I have everything that I need right here: do I have it all?

WHAT ABOUT WORK?

Work is a key part of life, one which should be neither overdone nor underdone. Almost everyone needs to work, whether it is paid or not. Almost no one should allow work to take over their lives, however much they claim to enjoy it. Hours of work should not be dictated by social convention. The 80/20 Principle can provide a good measure here and a good way to say whether you should work more or less. It is the idea of arbitrage: if on average you are happier outside work than at work, you should work less and/or change your job. If you are on average happier at work than outside work, you should work more and/or change your nonwork life. You haven't got it right until you are equally happy at work and outside work, and until you are happy at least 80 percent of the time at work and 80 percent of the time outside work.

Career alienation

Many people don't like their work much. They don't feel it's them. But they feel that they "must" do it because it provides their livelihood. You may also know people who, while it would be wrong to say that they dislike their jobs, still have an ambivalent view of them: sometimes, or some parts, they enjoy; on other occasions, or other parts, they definitely do not. Many, perhaps most, of the people you know would rather be doing something else, if they could be paid the same for doing that as for their current job.

Career is not a separate box

The career that you and/or your partner pursue should be viewed in terms of the total quality of the life implied by that career: where you live, the time you spend together and with friends, and the satisfaction that you get from actually working, as well as whether your after-tax incomes can support that lifestyle.

You probably have more choices than you think. Your present career may be the right one and you can use it as a benchmark. But think creatively about whether you might not prefer a different career and lifestyle. Construct various different options for your current and future lifestyle.

Start from the premise that there does not have to be any conflict between your work life and the things you enjoy outside work. "Work" can be many things, especially as leisure industries now make up a large slice of the economy. You may be able to work in an area that is your hobby or even turn your hobby into a business. Remember that enthusiasm can lead to success. It is often easier to make an enthusiasm into a career than to become enthusiastic about a career dictated by others.

Whatever you do, be clear about the optimum point you are trying to reach and view it within your life's total context. This is easier said than done: old habits die hard and the importance of lifestyle is easily relegated to the demands of conventional career thinking.

For instance, when two colleagues and I set up our own management consulting business in 1983, we were aware of the negative effects on our lives of the long hours and extensive traveling previously required by our bosses. So we decided that we would institute a "total lifestyle approach" in our new business and stress the quality of life as much as the earnings. But when work started flooding in, we ended up working the usual 80-hour week, and, what was worse, we required our professional staff to do the same (I couldn't understand, at first, what he meant when an anguished consultant accused me and my partners of "ruining people's lives"). In the pursuit of money, the total lifestyle approach had quickly gone out of the window.

Which type of career will make you happiest?

Am I advocating here that you "drop out" of the rat race? Not necessarily. It may be that you will be happiest in the rat race; perhaps, like me, you are basically a rat.

You should certainly be clear about what you enjoy doing and try to include this in your career. But "what" you do is only one element in the equation. You also need to consider the work context within which you should operate and the importance to you of professional achievement. These may be at least as important in determining your professional happiness.

You should be clear where you stand on two dimensions:

- Do you have a high drive for achievement and career success?
- Would you be happiest working for an organization, as a self-employed and self-contained individual (a "sole trader"), or employing other people?

Figure 36 shows this choice. Which box describes you best?

Figure 36   Desired career and lifestyle

Box 1 people are highly ambitious but prefer to work in a context organized and provided by others. The archetypal "organization man" (and woman) of the twentieth century falls in this box. The number of these roles is falling, as large organizations employ fewer people and also as large organizations lose market share to smaller ones (the former trend will continue, the latter may not). But if the supply of these posts is falling, so too is the demand for them. If you want this type of role, you should recognize the fact and pursue your ambition, however unfashionable it may become. Large organizations still provide structure and status even if they can no longer provide security.

Box 2 people are typically professionals who have a drive for recognition by their peers or who want to be the best in their field. They want to be independent and do not fit well into organizations, unless the latter (like most universities) are extremely permissive. These people should ensure that they become self-employed as quickly as possible. Once they are, they should resist the temptation to employ other people, even if this offers high financial rewards. Box 2 people are sole traders, who want to avoid professional dependence on others as far as possible.

Box 3 people have high drive and ambition, hate being employed but do not want the lonely life of the sole trader. They may be unconventional, but they are builders: they want to build a web or a structure around themselves. They are tomorrow's entrepreneurs.

Bill Gates, one of the two richest men in America, was a college dropout who was obsessed with personal computer software. But Bill Gates is not a sole trader. He needs to have other people, large numbers of them, working for him. Many people are like this. The ideology of empowerment has obscured this need and made the desire to build businesses slightly unfashionable. If you want to work with other people, but not for them, you are a Box 3 person. You had better recognize this fact and do something about it. Many frustrated professionals are Box 3 people who like what they do but are operating in Box 1 or 2. They do not recognize that the source of their frustration is not professional but organizational.

Box 4 people do not have a high drive for career achievement but do enjoy working with others. They should ensure that they spend many hours a week doing so, either in a conventional job or in a voluntary role.

Box 5 people are not ambitious but do have a strong desire for autonomy in their work. Rather than set up their own firm, the best role for Box 5 people is as freelancers, working on particular projects for other firms to suit their own convenience.

Box 6 people are individuals whose need for career achievement is low but who enjoy the process of organizing and developing others. Many teachers, social workers, and charity workers are Box 6 people and are well suited to their roles. For Box 6 people the journey is everything; there is no need to arrive.

Many people gravitate towards their "right" box, but where alienation at work exists it is often because the person is in the wrong box.

WHAT ABOUT MONEY?

What indeed! Most people have got peculiar views about money. They think it's more important than it is. But they also think it's more difficult to get than it is. Since most people want to have more money than they currently have, let's deal with the second point first.

My view is that money is not difficult to obtain, and, once you have even a little of it to spare, it is not difficult to multiply.

How do you obtain money in the first place? The best answer, one that works surprisingly often, is to do something that you enjoy.

The logic runs as follows. If you enjoy something, you are likely to be good at it. You are likely to be better at that than at things you don't enjoy (this is not always true, but the exceptions are rare). If you are good at something, you can create something that will satisfy others. If you satisfy others, they will generally pay you well for it. And since most people do not do things they enjoy, and will not be as productive as you are, you will be able to earn above the going rate in your vocation.

But the logic is not foolproof. There are some professions, such as acting, where supply vastly exceeds demand. What do you do in these circumstances?

What you shouldn't do is to give up. Instead, find a profession where supply and demand are more equally matched, but which is close in its requirements to your preferred vocation. Such adjacent professions usually exist, although they may not be immediately apparent. Think creatively. For example, the requirements of politicians are very close to those of actors. The most effective politicians, like Ronald Reagan, John F. Kennedy, Winston Churchill, Harold Macmillan, or Margaret Thatcher, either were or could have been successful actors. Charlie Chaplin was a dead ringer for Adolf Hitler and this was not accidental; sadly, Hitler was one of the century's best and most charismatic actors. This may all seem pretty obvious. But few would-be actors seriously contemplate a career in politics, despite the weaker competition and superior rewards.

What if what you enjoy most has a poor employment market and you can't find an adjacent profession that has good prospects? Then go to your next most preferred vocation and repeat the process until you find one that you like and that pays well.

Once in your profession, if making money is really important to you and if you are any good at what you do, you should aim to become self-employed as soon as possible and, after that, to start to employ others.

I arrive at this conclusion from the 80/20 Principle's argument about arbitrage. Eighty percent of the value in any organization or profession comes from 20 percent of the professionals. The workers who are above average will tend to be paid more than those who are below average, but nowhere near enough to reflect the differential in performance. It follows that the best people are always underpaid and the worst people always overpaid. As an above-average employee, you cannot escape from this trap. Your boss may think you are good, but will never credit your true value relative to others. The only way out is to set up in business yourself and, if you are so inclined, to employ other above-average workers. Don't take either of these steps, however, if you aren't comfortable with being self-employed or a boss (see Figure 40).

Money is easy to multiply

The other thing to remember is that once you have a little spare cash, it can easily be multiplied. Save and invest. This is what capitalism is all about. To multiply money, you don't need to be in business. You can simply invest in the stock market, using the 80/20 Principle as your guide. Chapter 14 will elaborate.

Money is overrated

I would like you to have a lot more money, but don't go overboard on this. Money can help you gain the lifestyle you want, but beware: all those nasty fables about Midas and the like are rooted in truth. Money can buy you happiness, but only to the extent that you use money to do what is really right for you in the first place. Also, money can bite back.

Remember that the more money you have, the less value an extra dollop of wealth creates. In economist speak, the marginal utility of money declines sharply. Once you have adjusted to a higher standard of living, it may give you little or no extra happiness. It can even turn negative, if the extra cost of maintaining the new lifestyle causes anxiety or piles on extra pressure to earn money in nonsatisfying ways.

More wealth also requires more management. Looking after my money irritates me. (Don't offer to relieve me of it; it irritates me less than giving it away would!)

The tax authorities also make money inefficient. Earn more, pay disproportionately more tax. Earn more, work more. Work more and you have to spend more: on living close to work in an expensive metropolitan area or alternatively on commuting, on labor-saving devices, on contracting out housework, and on ever-more expensive leisure compensations. Spend more and you have to work more. You can end up with an expensive lifestyle that controls you rather than vice versa. You might get much better value and happiness out of a simpler and cheaper lifestyle.

WHAT ABOUT ACHIEVEMENT?

There are people who want to achieve—and then there are sane people. All motivational writers fall into the trap of telling you that you need direction and purpose in life. Then they tell you that you don't have it. Then they put you through the agony of deciding what it should be. Finally, they tell you what they think you ought to do.

So if you don't want to achieve anything specific and are happy enough going through life having it all (minus achievement), count yourself lucky (and skip to the end of this chapter).

But if, like me, you feel guilty and insecure without achievement and want to increase it, the 80/20 Principle can help with your affliction.

Achievement should be easy. It shouldn't be "99 percent perspiration and 1 percent inspiration." Instead, see if it's true that 80 percent of your achievement to date—measured by what you yourself value—has come from 20 percent of your inputs. If true or nearly true, then think carefully about this top 20 percent. Could you simply repeat the achievements? Upgrade them? Reproduce similar ones on a grander scale? Combine two previous achievements to compound the satisfaction?

- Think about your past achievements that have had the most positive "market" response from others, those that have led to the greatest critical acclaim: the 20 percent of your work and play that has led to 80 percent of the praise others have given you. How much real satisfaction did this give you?
- What methods worked best for you in the past? Which collaborators? Which audiences? Again, think 80/20. Anything that just yielded an average degree of satisfaction for the time or effort should be discarded. Think of the exceptional highs achieved exceptionally easily. Do not constrain yourself to your work history. Think of your time as a student, a tourist, or with friends.
- Looking forward, what could you achieve that would make you proud, that no one else could do with the same ease? If there were 100 people around you trying to do something, what could you do in 20 percent of the time that it would take 80 of them to finish? Where would you be in the top 20? Even more stringently, what could you do better than 80 percent but in only 20 percent of the time? These questions may initially seem like riddles but, believe me, there are answers! People's abilities in different spheres are incredibly diverse.
- If you could measure the enjoyment derived from anything, what would you enjoy more than 95 percent of your peers? What would you do better than 95 out of 100? Which achievements would fulfill both conditions?

It is important to focus on what you find easy. This is where most motivational writers go wrong. They assume you should try things that are difficult for you; on the same grounds, one suspects, that grandparents used to urge the consumption of cod liver oil before capsules were invented. The inspirationalists quote such worthies as T. J. Watson, who said that "success lies on the far side of failure." My view is that normally failure lies on the far side of failure. Also, success lies on the near side of failure. You are already very successful at some things, and it matters not a whit if those things are very few in number.

The 80/20 Principle is clear. Pursue those few things where you are amazingly better than others and that you enjoy most.

WHAT ELSE DO YOU NEED TO HAVE IT ALL?

We've dealt with work, with lifestyle, with money, and with achievement. To have it all, you also need a few satisfying relationships. This requires a separate chapter.

12

WITH A LITTLE HELP FROM OUR FRIENDS

Relationships help us to define who we are and what we can become. Most of us can trace our successes to pivotal relationships.

DONALD O. CLIFTON AND
PAULA NELSON[1]

Without relationships we are either dead to the world—or dead. Although banal, this is true: our friendships are at the heart of our lives. It is also true that our professional relationships are at the heart of our success. This is a chapter about both personal and professional relationships. We start with personal relationships, with friends, lovers, and loved ones. Then we consider professional relationships in their own right.

What on earth has this got to do with the 80/20 Principle? The answer is quite a lot. There is a trade-off between quality and quantity and we consistently undercultivate what is most important.

The 80/20 Principle provides three provocative hypotheses:

- Eighty percent of the value of our relationships comes from 20 percent of the relationships.
- Eighty percent of the value of our relationships comes from the 20 percent of close relationships that we form first in our lives.
- We devote much less than 80 percent of our attention to the 20 percent of relationships that create 80 percent of the value.

COMPILE YOUR TOP 20 PERSONAL RELATIONSHIPS CHART

At this stage, write down the names of your Top 20 friends and loved ones, those with whom you have the most important relationships, ranked from most important to least important to you. "Important" means the depth and closeness of the personal relationship, the extent to which the relationship helps you in life and the extent to which the relationship enhances your sense of who you are and what you can become. Do this now, before reading on.

As a matter of interest, where did your lover/partner come on the list? Above or below your parents or children? Be honest (but you should probably destroy the list when you are through with this chapter!).

Next, allocate a total of 100 points between the relationships in terms of their importance to you. For example, if the first person on the list is exactly as important as the next 19 down the list combined, allocate 50 points to him or her. You may need to have more than one run at the numbers to make them add up to 100 by the time you're finished.

I don't know what your list looks like, but a typical pattern in line with the 80/20 Principle would have two characteristics: the top four relationships (20 percent of the total) would score most of the points (maybe 80 percent); and there would tend to be a constant relationship between each number and the next one down. For example, number two may be two-thirds or half as important as number one; number three may similarly be two-thirds or half as important as number two; and so on. It is interesting to note that if the number one relationship is twice as important as number two and so on, relationship number six is only about 3 percent as important as number one!

Complete this exercise by noting against each name the proportion of time that you actively spend with the person, talking or doing something together (exclude time spent with someone where they are not the main focus of attention, for example when watching television or a movie). Take the total amount of time spent with the 20 people as 100 units and then allocate these. Typically, you will find that you spend much less than 80 percent of the time with the few people who comprise 80 percent of "relationship value" to you.

The action implications should be plain. Go for quality rather than quantity. Spend your time and emotional energy reinforcing and deepening the relationships that are most important.

But there is another wrinkle, to do with the chronology of the relationships in our life. It turns out that our capacity for close relationships is far from infinite. There is another trade-off between quality and quantity of which we should be aware.

THE VILLAGE THEORY

Anthropologists stress that the number of exhilarating and important personal relationships that people can establish is limited.[2] Apparently, the common pattern of people in any society is to have two important childhood friends, two significant adult friends, and two doctors. Typically, there are two powerful sexual partners who eclipse the others. Most commonly, you fall in love only once, and there is one member of your family whom you love above all others. The number of significant personal relationships is remarkably similar for everyone, regardless of their location, sophistication, or culture.

This has led to the anthropologists' "village theory." In an African village, all these relationships happen within a few hundred meters and are often formed within a short period of time. For us, these relationships may be spread all over the planet and over a whole lifetime. They nonetheless constitute a village which we each have in our heads. And once these slots are filled, they're filled forever.

The anthropologists say that if you have too much experience, too early, you exhaust your capacity for further deep relationships. This may explain the superficiality often observed in those whose profession or circumstances force them to have a great number of relationships, such as salespeople, prostitutes, or those who move very frequently.

J. G. Ballard quotes a case example of a rehabilitation project in California for young women who mixed with criminals. The women were young, 20 or 21, and the program aimed to introduce them to new social backgrounds, basically to middle-class volunteers, who befriended them and invited them to their homes.

Many of these girls had been married at an incredibly early age. Many had had their first children at 13 or 14. Some had been married three times by the time they were 20. They had often had hundreds of lovers and sometimes had close relationships or children by men who were then shot or jailed. They'd been through everything—relationships, motherhood, break-ups, bereavements—and experienced the whole gamut of human experience while still in their teens.

The project was a total failure. The explanation was that the women were incapable of forming any deep new relationships. They were all used up. Their relationship slots had been filled, forever.

This sad story is salutory. It also fits in with the 80/20 Principle: a small number of relationships will account for a large proportion of emotional value. Fill your relationship slots with extreme care and not too early!

PROFESSIONAL RELATIONSHIPS AND ALLIANCES

We now turn to your relationships and alliances related to your work. Here the importance of a few close allies can hardly be overstated.

Individuals may appear to do amazing things—and they do. But exceptional individual performance requires allies.

You alone cannot make yourself successful. Only others can do that for you. What you can do is to select the best relationships and alliances for your purposes.

You badly need allies. You must treat them well, as an extension of yourself, as you treat yourself (or should). Do not assume your friends and allies are all of roughly equal importance. Focus your attention on nurturing the key alliances of your life. If this seems obvious or banal, ask yourself how many of your friends follow these lines. Then ask yourself whether you do.

All spiritual leaders had many allies. If they needed them, so do you. To take one example: Jesus Christ depended on John the Baptist to draw him to public attention; then on the 12 disciples; then on other apostles, notably St. Paul, arguably the greatest marketing genius in history.[3]

Nothing is more important than your choice of alliances and how you build them. Without them you are nothing. With them, you can transform your life, often the lives of those around you, and occasionally, in small or large ways, the course of history.

We can best appreciate the importance of alliances by a brief historical excursion.

History is driven by individuals who form effective alliances

Vilfredo Pareto, the "bourgeois Karl Marx," claimed that history was essentially a history of the succession of élites.[4] The objective of energetic individuals or families was therefore devoted to rise into the élite or to be part of one élite that displaced another (or, if already in the élite, to stay there and keep the élite in place).

If you turn a Paretian or Marxian, class-based view of history on its head, you can conclude that alliances within élites or would-be élites are the driving forces of progress. The individual is nothing except as part of a class, certainly; but equally, the individual allied with other individuals of the same class (or possibly, with individuals from another class) is everything.

The importance of individuals, allied to others, is apparent from some of history's turning points. Would there have been a Russian Revolution in 1917 without the pivotal role of Lenin? Probably not at all; and certainly not one that diverted the course of world history for the next 72 years. Would the Russian Revolution of 1989 that reversed the one of 1917 have succeeded without the presence of mind and bravery of Boris Yeltsin? If he had not climbed on a tank outside the Russian White House, the Communist gerontocrats would probably have cemented their shaky coup.

We can play the game of historical what-ifs repeatedly to demonstrate the importance of individuals. There would have been no Holocaust and no Second World War without Hitler. Without Roosevelt and Churchill, Hitler would probably have united Europe rather earlier and more thoroughly and in a considerably more vexacious way than his successors have done. And so on. But the key point often overlooked is that none of these individuals could have turned the course of history without relationships and alliances.

In almost any sphere of achievement,[5] you can identify a small number of key collaborators, without whom individuals could not have succeeded but with whom individuals have had massive impact. In government, in mass ideological movements, in business, in medicine, in the sciences, in philanthropy, or in sport, the pattern is the same. History is not composed of blind, nonhuman forces. History is not run by classes or élites operating according to some preprogrammed economic or sociological formula. History is determined and changed by dedicated individuals who form effective alliances with a small number of close collaborators.

YOU NEED A FEW KEY ALLIES

If you have had any success in life, you will (unless you are a blind egotist headed for a fall) recognize the crucial important of allies in your achievements. But you will also detect the hand of the 80/20 Principle here. The key allies are few in number.

It is generally a safe assertion that at least 80 percent of the value of your allies comes from fewer than 20 percent of their number. For anyone who has done anything, the list of allies, when you come to think of it, is incredibly long. But of the hundreds or more involved, the value is highly skewed. Usually half a dozen key allies are far more important than all the rest.

You don't need many allies but you need the right ones, with the right relationships between you and each of them and between themselves. You need them at the right time, in the right place and with a common interest in advancing your interests. Above all, the allies must trust you and you must be able to trust them.

Make a list of your Top 20 business relationships, of people that you consider to be important allies, and compare it with an estimation of the total number of contacts with whom you would be on first-name terms—if you have a Rolodex, a Filofax, or a telephone list, this is the total number of active contacts on that list. Eighty percent of the value to you of alliances is likely to be comprised in 20 percent of the relationships. If this is not the case, the alliances (or some of them) are likely to be of poor quality.

ACHIEVEMENT ALLIANCES

If you are well into your career, make a list of the people who have helped you the most to date. Rank them from top to bottom and then assign 100 points between the top 10.

In general, the people who have helped you the most in the past will also be the people who can do so in the future. Sometimes, however, a good friend who is some way down the list becomes a much more important potential ally: perhaps because he or she has gained a new and highly influential post, has made a killing through an investment, or secured valuable recognition. Go through the exercise again, ranking your allies from one to ten and allocating another 100 points to them, this time on the basis of their future ability to help you.

People help you because there is a strong relationship between you. The best relationships are built on five attributes: mutual enjoyment of each other's company, respect, shared experience, reciprocity, and trust. In successful business relationships these attributes become entwined and are impossible to untangle, but we can think of them separately.

Mutual enjoyment

The first of our five attributes is the most obvious. If you do not enjoy talking to someone, in their office, a restaurant, at a social occasion, or on the phone, you will not build a strong relationship. They have to enjoy your company too.

If this seems terribly obvious, reflect for a moment on the people with whom you mix socially, but basically for professional purposes. How many of them do you really like? A surprising number of people spend a lot of time with people they don't like. This is a complete and utter waste of time. It's not enjoyable, it's tiring, it's often expensive, it prevents you doing better things, and it will get you absolutely nowhere. Stop doing it! Spend more time with the contacts you enjoy, particularly if they can also be useful to you.

Respect

There are people whose company I enjoy immensely, but whom I do not greatly respect professionally; and vice versa. I would never advance someone's career if I didn't respect their professional abilities.

If someone is to help you professionally, they must be impressed by you! Yet very often we hide our light under a bushel. A good friend, Paul, who was in a position to advance my career considerably, once remarked in a board meeting where we were both outside directors that he was prepared to believe that I was competent professionally, although he had never seen the slightest evidence of it! I resolved to find a context where I could show some evidence. I did— and Paul moved sharply up my list of business allies.

Shared experience

Just as in the primitive village, we have a limited number of slots for important professional experiences. Shared experience, especially if it involves struggle or suffering, is very bonding. One of my greatest relationships, both as business ally and friend, came from being a new recruit in my first job alongside another recruit in the same situation. I am sure we would not have developed such rapport if we had not both hated our jobs in the oil refinery so much.

The implication is that if you are in a difficult job, develop one ally whom you like and respect. Make it a deep and fruitful alliance. If you don't, you are missing a big opportunity!

Even if you are not suffering, find one person who has a great deal of shared experience and make him or her a key ally.

Reciprocity

For alliances to work, each ally must do a great deal for the other party—repeatedly, consistently, over a long period of time.

Reciprocity requires that the relationship is not one sided. Equally, reciprocity should come naturally and not be too finely calculated. The important thing is that you do whatever you possibly can, consistent with high ethical standards, to help the other person. This requires time and thought! You should not wait until they ask a favor.

What surprises me in reviewing business relationships is how infrequently true reciprocity is built up. Even if all the other ingredients—friendship, respect, shared experience, and trust—are present, people very often neglect to be proactive in helping their allies. This, again, is a massive wasted opportunity to deepen the relationship and store up future help.

The Beatles told us that "in the end, the love you take is equal to the love you make." Similarly, in the end, the professional help you receive is equal to that you provide.

Trust

Trust cements relationships. Lack of trust can unwind them very quickly. Trust requires total honesty at all times. If there is even a suspicion that you are not saying what you think, even for the most high-minded reasons or to remain diplomatic, trust can be undermined.

If you do not trust someone totally, don't try to build up an alliance. It shouldn't work and it won't.

But if you do have total trust, it makes business relationships so much faster and more efficient. A lot of time and cost can be eliminated. Never forfeit trust by being capricious, cowardly, or cunning.

IF YOU ARE IN THE EARLY STAGES OF YOUR CAREER, FILL YOUR ALLY SLOTS CAREFULLY

A good rule of thumb is that you should develop up to six or seven absolutely gilt-edged business alliances, composed as follows:

- one or two relationships with mentors, people more senior than you
- two or three relationships with peers
- one or two relationships where you are the mentor.

Relationships with mentors

Choose your one or two mentors carefully. Do not let them choose you: they might deprive a much better mentor of the slot. The mentors you choose should have the following two characteristics:

- You must be able to build up the "five-ingredient" relationship comprising mutual enjoyment, respect, shared experience, reciprocity, and trust.
- The mentor should be as senior as possible or, even better, relatively junior but clearly destined for the top. The best mentors are extremely able and ambitious.

It may seem strange to say that relationships with mentors should be reciprocal, since inevitably the mentor will have more to offer than the mentee. But mentors must be rewarded or else they will lose interest. The mentee must provide fresh ideas, mental stimulation, enthusiasm, hard work, knowledge of new technologies, or some other attribute of value to the mentor. Wise mentors very often use younger allies to keep them up to date with emerging trends and potential opportunities or threats that may not be apparent from the top.

Relationships with peers

With peers, you are very often spoilt for choice. There are many potential allies. But remember that you have only two or three slots to fill. Be very selective. Make a list of all potential allies who have the "five ingredients" or potential for them. Pick the two or three from the list who you believe will be the most successful. Then work hard at making them allies.

Relationships where you are the mentor

Do not neglect these. You are likely to get the most out of your one or two mentees if they work for you, preferably for quite a long period of time.

MULTIPLE ALLIANCES

Alliances very often build up into webs or networks, where many of the same people have relationships with each other. These networks can become very powerful, or at least seem so from the outside. They are often great fun.

But do not get carried away, smug in the knowledge that you are "in with the in crowd." You may just be a fringe player. Don't forget that all true and valuable relationships are bilateral. If you have a strong alliance with both X and Y and they have one between each other, that is excellent. Lenin said that a chain is as strong as its weakest link. However strong the relationships between X and Y, the ones that really matter for you are yours with X and yours with Y.

CONCLUSION

For both personal and professional relationships, fewer and deeper is better than more and less deep. One relationship is not as good as another. Seriously flawed relationships, when you spend a lot of time together but the result is unsatisfying, should be terminated as soon as possible. Bad relationships drive out good. There is a limited number of slots for relationships; don't use up the slots too early or on low-quality relationships.

Choose with care. Then build with commitment.

A FORK IN THE BOOK

We have now reached an optional fork in this book's progress. The next two chapters (13 and 14) are, respectively, for those who want to know how to advance their careers or multiply their money. Readers for whom these are not important concerns should advance to Chapter 15, where the seven habits of happiness await.

13

INTELLIGENT AND LAZY

There are only four types of officer. First, there are the lazy, stupid ones. Leave them alone, they do no harm . . . Second, there are the hard-working intelligent ones. They make excellent staff officers, ensuring that every detail is properly considered. Third, there are the hard-working, stupid ones. These people are a menace and must be fired at once. They create irrelevant work for everybody. Finally, there are the intelligent lazy ones. They are suited for the highest office.

GENERAL VON MANSTEIN
on the German Officer Corps

This is a chapter for the truly ambitious. If you do not suffer from the insecurity that fuels the desire to be rich or famous, move on to Chapter 15. But if you want to win the rat race, here is some advice that may surprise you.

General Von Manstein captures the essence of this chapter, which is the 80/20 Principle's guidance on how to have a successful career. If the general had been a management consultant, he would have made a fortune out of the matrix shown in Figure 37.

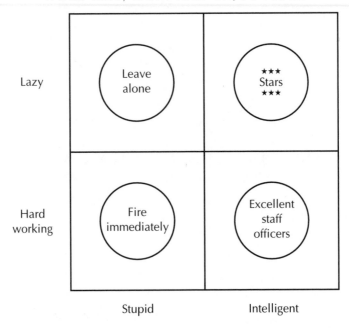

Figure 37   The Von Manstein matrix

This advice is what to do about other people. But what about yourself? It might be thought that intelligence and propensity to work are fixed properties, in which case the Von Manstein matrix, although interesting, is useless. But the position advanced in this chapter is slightly different. Even if you are hard working, you can learn to become lazy. And even if you or other people think you are stupid, you are intelligent at something. The key to becoming a star is to simulate, manufacture, and deploy lazy intelligence. As we will see, lazy intelligence can be worked at. The key to earning more and working less is to pick the right thing to do and to do only those things that add the highest value.

First, however, it is instructive to see how the 80/20 Principle distributes rewards to those who work. Rewards are both unbalanced and unfair. We can either complain about this or align ourselves to take advantage of the Von Manstein matrix.

IMBALANCE IS RAMPANT IN PROFESSIONAL SUCCESS AND RETURNS

The 80/20 Principle is nowhere more evident today than in the very high and increasing returns enjoyed by very small numbers of élite professionals.

We live in a world where the returns for top talent, in all spheres of life, have never been higher. A small percentage of professionals obtain a disproportionate amount of recognition and fame and usually also a high percentage of the spoils available.

Take any sphere of contemporary human endeavor, in any country or globally. Whether the sphere be athletics, baseball, basketball, football, golf, rugby, tennis, or any other popular sport; or architecture, sculpture, painting, or any other visual art; or music of any category; the movies or the theater; novels, cookery books, or autobiography; or even hosting TV chat shows, reading the news, politics, or any other well-defined area, there will be a small number of preeminent professionals whose names spring to mind.

Considering how many people there are in each country, it is a remarkably small number of names, and usually a small percentage—typically well under 5 percent—of the professionals active in the relevant sphere. The fraction of any profession who are recognized "names" is very small, but they hog the limelight. They are always in demand and always in the news. They are the human equivalent of consumer goods brands, obtaining instant recognition as known quantities.

The same concentration operates with regard to popularity and financial rewards. More than 80 percent of novels sold are from fewer than 20 percent of novel titles in print. The same is true of any other category of publishing: of pop CDs and concerts, of movies, even of books about business. The same applies to actors, TV celebrities, or any branch of sports. Eighty percent of prize money in golf goes to fewer than 20 percent of professional golfers; the equivalent is true in tennis; and in horseracing, more than 80 percent of winnings go to fewer than 20 percent of owners, jockeys, and trainers.

Name	Profession	Earnings $m, 1994
Steven Spielberg	Film director	165
Joseph Jamail	Trial lawyer	90
Oprah Winfrey	Television presenter	72
Michael Jordan	Baseball/basketball player	30
David Copperfield	Magician	29
Sylvester Stallone	Film actor/director	24
Andrew Lloyd Webber	Composer	24
Michael Jackson	Singer	22
Andre Agassi	Tennis player	22
Stephen King	Writer	21
Shaquille O'Neal	Basketball player	17
Jack Nicklaus	Golfer	15
Gerhard Berger	Racing driver	14
Roberto Baggio	Soccer player	5
Allen Grubman	Corporate lawyer	5

Source: Forbes

Figure 38   Superstar earnings for top professionals

There is a big gap between the top and the rest

We live in an increasingly marketized world. The top names can command enormous fees—but those who are not quite as good or well known make relatively little.

As an illustration, Lady Thatcher's memoirs have to date sold over 2 million copies and a huge number of cassettes and videos: she personally received $5.4 million. A typical memoir from one of the most interesting of her senior ministers, Nicholas Ridley, has sold some 5,000 copies, a quarter of 1 percent of Lady Thatcher's total. Many other Thatcher Cabinet members have written their memoirs and some have attained minor success, but the best estimate is that, although Lady Thatcher comprised less than 2 percent of the people serving in her Cabinets and only 5 percent of those who have published memoirs, her sales account for more than 95 percent of the total.

There is a big difference between being at the top, and well known to all, and being almost at the top, and well known only to a few enthusiasts. The best-known baseball, basketball, or football stars can make millions; those just below the top rank, only a comfortable living.

Why do the winners take all?

The distribution of incomes for superstars is even more unbalanced than for the population as a whole and provides excellent illustrations of the 80/20 Principle (or in most cases, 90/10 or 95/5). Various writers have sought economic or sociological explanations of the superreturns to superstars.[1]

The most persuasive explanation is that two conditions facilitate superstar returns. One is that it is possible for the superstar to be accessible to many people at once. Modern communications enable this to happen. The incremental cost of "distributing" Michael Jackson, Steven Spielberg, Stephen King, Luciano Pavarotti, or Andre Agassi to additional consumers can be almost nothing, since the additional cost of broadcasting, making a CD, or printing a book is a very small part of the total cost structure.

The additional cost of making these superstars available is certainly no more than for a second-rate substitute, except in so far as the superstars themselves take a higher fee. Although the fee may be many millions or tens of millions, the incremental cost per consumer is very low indeed, often a matter of cents or fractions of a cent.

The second condition for superstar returns is that mediocrity must not be a substitute for talent. It must be important to obtain the best. If one house cleaner is half as quick as another, the market will clear by paying her half as much. But who wants someone who is half as good as Michael Jackson or Pavarotti? In this case, the non-superstar, even working for nothing, would have vastly inferior economics to the superstar. The non-superstar would attract a smaller audience and, for a tiny decrease in the total cost, bring in very much lower revenues.

Winner takes all is a modern phenomenon

What is intriguing is that this disparity between top returns and the rest has not always existed. The best basketball or football champions of the 1940s and 1950s, for example, did not make much money. It used to be possible to find a prominent politician who died fairly poor. And the further back we go, the less true it was that the winner took all.

For instance, William Shakespeare was absolutely preeminent in terms of talent among his contemporaries. So was Leonardo da Vinci. By rights or, rather, by today's standards, they should have been able to exploit their brilliance, creativity, and fame to become the richest men of their times. Instead, they made do with the sort of income that is enjoyed today by millions of moderately talented professionals.

The imbalance of financial rewards for talent is becoming more and more pronounced over time. Today, income is more closely linked to merit and marketability, so that the 80/20 connection, because it can be clearly demonstrated in money terms, becomes easily apparent. Our society is clearly more meritocratic than that of a century, or even a generation, ago. This is particularly so in Europe generally and Great Britain in particular.

If top footballers like Bobby Moore had made fortunes in the 1940s or 1950s, it would have provoked fury among the British Establishment; it would have been unseemly. When the leader writers of the 1960s discovered that the Beatles were millionaires, it caused astonishment. Today the fact that George Michael or Michael Jackson are among the world's richest people causes no surprise. Nowadays we have less respect for rank and more for markets.

The other new element is, as mentioned above, the technological revolution in broadcasting, telecommunications, and consumer products like the CD and CD-Rom. The key consideration now is to maximize revenue, which superstars can do. The extra cost of hiring them may be a huge amount of money for an individual, but the cost per consumer is trivial.

ACHIEVEMENT HAS ALWAYS OBEYED THE 80/20 PRINCIPLE

If we set money aside and deal in the more enduring and important matters (at least for everyone except the superstars themselves), we can see that the concentration of achievement and fame in very few people, whatever the profession, has always been true. Constraints that seem odd to our eyes—such as class or the absence of telecommunications—stopped Shakespeare and Leonardo da Vinci becoming millionaires. But lack of wealth did not diminish their achievements or the fact that a huge proportion of impact came from a tiny proportion of creators.

80/20 RETURNS ALSO APPLY
TO NONMEDIA PROFESSIONALS

Although it is most noticeable and exaggerated with respect to media superstars, it is significant that 80/20 returns are not confined to the world of entertainment. Increasingly, the top professionals in any recognized profession take the lion's share of the loot. Note that in Figure 42 the second highest-paid professional listed is Joseph Jamail, hardly a household name to rank alongside Andre Agassi. Jamail is a trial lawyer and, as yet, does not feature on TV talk shows or make blockbuster movies. Yet he made $90 million in 1994, over four times what Agassi earned.

Further down the table of top earners come corporate lawyers, top surgeons, sought-after corporate executives, investment bankers, tax experts, and a host of other professionals. Increasingly, in each of these fields, the winner-takes-all philosophy is spreading. The top individuals, and the top specialist firms, in each of these areas can command fees that are many times that of slightly less eminent practitioners. If there is a corporate takeover fight, for example, two or more protagonists may compete for the services of the top one or two firms or individuals, bidding a price far above the normal rate. Wherever large amounts of money are at stake and top individuals can influence the odds, or are perceived to, the returns to individual professionals can reach astronomic levels.

Talent has probably always followed an 80/20 pattern. The effect of technology may be, roughly, to move talent to a curve approximating 90/10 or 95/5. Rewards used to follow, perhaps, a 70/30 curve, but for the most famous they must surely now be close to 95/5 or an even more unbalanced curve.

WHAT DOES ALL THIS MEAN
FOR THE AMBITIOUS?

What are the rules for success in this 80/20 world? You may want to give up and refuse to compete in a world where the odds against megasuccess are so long. But I believe this is the wrong conclusion. Even if you do not aim to become a world-beating millionaire (but especially if you do), there are 10 golden rules for successful careers in an increasingly 80/20 world (see below).

Although these principles are more valuable the more ambitious you are, they apply to any level of career and ambition. As we elaborate, put on your 80/20 thinker cap to editionize the text to your own career. Recall the Von Manstein matrix: find the place where your name is already inscribed, where you can be intelligent, lazy, and highly rewarded.

10 golden rules for career success

1   Specialize in a very small niche; develop a core skill
2   Choose a niche that you enjoy, where you can excel and stand a chance of becoming an acknowledged leader
3   Realize that knowledge is power
4   Identify your market and your core customers and serve them best
5   Identify where 20 percent of effort gives 80 percent of returns
6   Learn from the best
7   Become self-employed early in your career
8   Employ as many net value creators as possible
9   Use outside contractors for everything but your core skill
10 Exploit capital leverage

Specialize in a very small niche

Specialization is one of the great, universal laws of life. This is how life itself evolved, with each species seeking out new ecological niches and developing unique characteristics. A small business that does not specialize will die. An individual who does not specialize will be doomed to life as a wage slave.

In the natural world the number of species is unknown, but it is almost certainly an astonishingly large number. The number of niches in the business world is very much larger than generally appreciated; hence many small businesses, apparently in competition in a broad market, can actually all be leaders in their own niches and avoid head-to-head competition.[2]

For the individual, too, it is better to know a few things well, or preferably one thing exceptionally well, than it is to know many things superficially.

Specialization is intrinsic to the 80/20 Principle. The reason that it operates—that 20 percent of inputs can result in 80 percent of outputs—is that the productive fifth is much more specialized and suited to the task at hand than are the unproductive four-fifths.

Whenever we observe the 80/20 Principle working, this is evidence both of a waste of resources (on the part of the unproductive four-fifths) and of the need for further specialization. If the unproductive 80 percent specialized in what they are good at, they could become the productive 20 percent in another sphere. This in turn would produce another 80/20 relationship, but at a higher level. What used to be the unproductive 80 percent, or some of it, will now be the productive 20 percent in another distribution.

This process, what the German nineteenth-century philosopher G. W. F. Hegel called a "dialectic,"[3] can go on and on, constituting the engine of progress. Indeed, there is evidence that this is precisely what has happened over time, both in the natural world and in society. Higher living standards have been driven by greater and greater specialization.

The computer evolved from a new specialization within electronics; the personal computer from a further specialization; modern user-friendly software from further specializations; the CD-Rom from yet another stage of the same process. Biotechnology, which will revolutionize food production, has evolved in a similar way, with each new advance requiring and feeding on ever more progressive specialization.

Your career ought to evolve in a similar way. Knowledge is the key. One of the most marked tendencies in the world of work over the

past generation has been the increasing power and status of technicians, formerly often blue-collar workers but now empowered by
specialist knowledge in league with ever more specialized information technology.[4] These experts are now often more powerful and
well paid than the technologically more primitive managers who pur-
ported to add value by organizing the technicians.[5]

At the most basic level, specialization requires qualifications. More
than 80 percent of qualifications in most societies are held by 20
percent of the workforce. Increasingly, the most important class distinction in advanced societies is not ownership of land or even of
wealth, but ownership of information. Eighty percent of information
is the property of 20 percent of people.

The American economist and statesman Robert Reich has divided
the U.S. workforce into four groups. The top group he calls "sym-
bolic analysts," people who deal with numbers, ideas, problems, and
words. They include financial analysts, consultants, architects, lawyers, doctors, and journalists, indeed all workers whose intelligence
and knowledge are the source of power and influence. Interestingly,
he calls this group the "fortunate fifth"—in our terms the top 20
percent—who he says hold 80 percent of information and 80 percent
of wealth.

Anyone who has any recent experience of intellectual disciplines
knows that knowledge is undergoing a profound and progressive
fragmentation. In some ways this is worrying, since there is almost
nobody in the intelligentzia or society as a whole who can integrate
different advances in knowledge and tell us what it all means. But in
other ways, the fragmentation is further evidence of the need for and
value of specialization.

And for the individual, observing the increasing trend of rewards
going to the top dogs, this is an extremely hopeful process. You may
have no hope of becoming Albert Einstein or even Bill Gates, but
there are literally hundreds of thousands, if not millions, of niches
where you can choose to specialize. You could even, like Gates,
invent your own niche.

Find your niche. It may take you a long time, but it is the only way
you will gain access to exceptional returns.

Choose a niche that you enjoy and in which you can excel

Specialization requires very careful thought. The narrower an area, the more important it is to choose it with extreme care.

Specialize in an area in which you are already interested and which you enjoy. You will not become an acknowledged leader in anything that cannot command your enthusiasm and passion.

This is not as demanding a requirement as you may think. Everyone is excited by something; if not, they are dead or dying. And almost every hobby, every enthusiasm, every vocation can these days be turned into a business activity.

You can also look at it from the other end. Almost anyone who has made it to the top has done so with great enthusiasm for what they are doing. Enthusiasm drives personal achievement and also infects others with enthusiasm, creating a multiplier effect. You cannot feign or manufacture enthusiasm.

If you are not enthusiastic about your current career, and are ambitious, you should stop doing it. But before you take this step, work out a better career. Write down all the things about which you are enthusiastic. Then work out which of these could be made into a career niche. Then choose the one about which you are most enthusiastic.

Realize that knowledge is power

The key to making a career out of an enthusiasm is knowledge. Know more about an area than anybody else does. Then work out a way to marketize it, to create a market and a set of loyal customers.

It is not enough to know a lot about a little. You have to know more than anybody else, at least about something. Do not stop improving your expertise until you are sure you know more, and are better in your niche, than anybody else. Then reinforce your lead by constant practice and inveterate curiosity. Do not expect to become a leader unless you really are more knowledgeable than anyone else.

Marketization is a creative process: you will need to work out for yourself how to do this. Perhaps you can follow the example of others who have marketized their knowledge in an adjacent area. But if this option is not available, follow the guidelines below.

Identify your market and your core customers and serve them best

Your market is those people who might pay for your knowledge. The core customers are those who would value your services most.

The market is the arena within which you will operate. This requires you to define how the knowledge you have can be sold. Are you going to work for an established firm or an individual as an employee, to work for a number of corporations or individuals as a freelancer, or to set up business marketing services (derived from the labor of yourself and others) to individuals or to firms?

Are you going to supply raw knowledge, to process it for specific situations, or to use the knowledge to create a product? Are you going to invent the product, to add value to someone else's semifinished product, or to be a retailer of finished products?

Your core customer or customers are the specific individuals or corporations that may place the highest value on your activity and that may provide a stream of well-paid work.

Whether you are employed, self-employed, a small or large employer, or even the head of state, you have core customers on whom your continued success depends. This is true whatever the level of your past achievement.

It is surprising, incidentally, how often leaders forfeit their position by neglecting or even abusing their core customer group. Tennis star John McEnroe forgot that his customers were the spectators and even the professional tennis organizers. Mrs. Thatcher (as she then was) forgot that her most important customers were her own Conservative Members of Parliament. Richard Nixon forgot that his core customer group was Middle America, with its requirement for integrity.

Serving customers is key, but they must be the right customers for you, those whom with relatively little effort you can make extremely happy.

Identify where 20 percent of effort gives 80 percent of returns

There is no fun in work unless you can achieve a lot with a little. If you have to work 60 or 70 hours a week in order to cope, if you feel that you are always behind, if you are struggling to keep up with work's requirements: then you are in the wrong job or doing it completely the wrong way! You are certainly not benefiting from the 80/20 Principle or from the Von Manstein matrix.

Keep reminding yourself of some of the golden 80/20 insights. In any sphere of activity, 80 percent of people are only achieving 20 percent of results; and 20 percent of people are achieving 80 percent of results. What are the majority doing wrong and the minority doing right? Come to that, who are the minority? Could you do what they do? Could you take what they do and do it in an even more extreme form? Could you invent an even more clever and efficient way to do it?

Is there a good fit between yourself and your "customers?" Are you in the right corporation? The right department? The right job? Where could you impress your "customers" with relatively little effort? Do you enjoy what you do and are you enthusiastic about it? If not, begin planning today to switch to a job where you can be.

If you like your job and your "customers" but are not coasting to glory, you are probably spending your time in the wrong way. What is the 20 percent of your time when you achieve 80 percent of your results? Do more of it! What is the 80 percent of your time when you achieve little? Do less of it! The answer can be as simple as that, although implementing the change will require you to break all your normal habits and conventions.

In every market, for every customer, in every firm, in all professions, there is a way to do things more efficiently and effectively: not just a bit better, but a step-function better. Look beneath the surface for 80/20 truths in your profession or industry.

In my own profession, that of management consulting, the answers are clear. Big clients, good. Big assignments, good. Large case teams with many cheap junior members, good. Close client relationships—between individuals—good. Relationships with the top person, the

CEO, very good. Long client relationships, very good. Long and close client relationships with the top people in large corporations, with large budgets, and the use of many junior consultants—laughing all the way to the bank!

What are the 80/20 truths in your line of business? Where do corporations make supranormal, even obscene, profits? Which of your colleagues is riding high while always seeming relaxed, with time to indulge themselves in their favorite hobbies? What are they doing that's so cute? Think, think, think. The answer is there somewhere. All you have to do is find it. But don't ask the industry Establishment what the answer is, don't do a survey of your colleagues, and don't try to find the answer in print. All you will find is the conventional wisdom, repeated a zillion ways. The answer will lie with the industry heretics, the professional mavericks, and the eccentric individuals.

Learn from the best

The winners in any field have, almost by definition, found ways to make 20 percent of effort yield 80 percent of results. This does not mean that the leaders are lazy or lacking in dedication. Leaders usually work very hard. But their output, for no more time than is put in by the merely competent in their field, is several times more valuable than the output of the merely competent. The leaders produce results which, in both quality and quantity, knock spots off the competition.

Put another way, leaders do things differently. Leaders are usually outsiders; they think and feel differently. Those who are best in any sphere do not think and act in similar ways to the average performers. The leaders may not be conscious of what they do differently. Very rarely do they think about it and articulate it. But, if leaders do not generally explain the secrets of their success, these can often be deduced by observation.

Previous generations understood this well. The disciple sitting at the feet of the master, the apprentice learning a trade from a craftsman, the student learning by assisting a professor with research, the artist serving time with an accomplished artist: all learnt by observing the best in their field at work, by assisting and by imitating.

Be willing to pay a high price to work for the best. Find any excuse to spend time with them. Work out what their characteristic ways of operating are. You will find that they see things differently, spend time differently, and interact with other people differently. Unless you can do what they do, or something even more different from the average modus vivendi in the profession, you will never rise to the top.

Sometimes, it is not just a matter of working for the best individuals. Key know-how can be located within the collective culture of the best firms. The key is in the differences. Arguably, you should work for one of the average firms, then for one of the very best, and observe the differences. For instance, I worked for Shell and wrote lots of memos. I then went to work for one of the Mars companies and learned to talk to people face to face until I got the desired answers. The latter was a 20/80 practice: 20 percent of effort leading to 80 percent of results. Leaders have many such 20/80 practices.

Observe, learn, and practice.

Become self-employed early in your career

Leverage your own time so that you focus on the things where you add five times more value than elsewhere. The second step is to ensure that you capture as much of this value for yourself. The ideal position, one that you should aim to reach early in your career, is to capture all of the value of your work for yourself.

Karl Marx's theory of surplus value states that the workers produce all value and excess value is appropriated by the capitalists who employ the workers. Put crudely, profits are the excess value stolen from the workers.

The theory is nonsense, but can usefully be stood on its head. The ordinary employee who produces average results may actually be exploiting the corporation more than he or she is exploited: corporations typically have far too many managers and the net value added by a majority of them is actually negative. Yet the employee who uses the 80/20 Principle properly will probably be many times more effective than the average. The 80/20 employee is most unlikely to be paid several times what his or her peers are. The 80/20 employee will therefore probably obtain a better deal by becoming self-employed.

When you are self-employed, you get paid by results. For those who use the 80/20 Principle, this is good news.

The one circumstance in which it may not be appropriate to become self-employed yet is when you are still in the rapid learning stage. If a corporation or professional firm is teaching you a great deal, the value of this learning may exceed the differential between the value you add and what you are paid. This is typically the case during the first two or three years of a professional career. It can also be the case when more experienced professionals join a new firm that has higher standards than the ones in which they have previously worked. In this case, the period of superlearning usually lasts for a few months only, or a year at the most.

When these periods are over, become self-employed. Do not worry overmuch about security. Your professional expertise and use of 80/20 precepts constitute your security. In any case, firms can no longer deliver security.

Employ as many net value creators as possible

If the first stage of leverage is the best use of your time and the second stage is to ensure that you capture for yourself the value you create, the third stage is to leverage the power of other people.

There is only one you, but there are a very large number of people whom you could potentially employ. A minority of these people—but the minority from which the 80/20 practitioner will choose to hire—add a great deal more value than they cost.

It follows that the greatest source of leverage is other people. To some extent, you can and should leverage off other people whom you do not employ: your allies. But you can obtain the most direct and complete leverage from the people you employ.

A simple numerical illustration may help to focus the mind on the enormous value of employment leverage. Let us assume that by using the 80/20 Principle you become five times more effective than the average professional in your line of business. Let us also assume that you are self-employed and so capture all of this value. The best that you will do, therefore, is to get results 500 percent of the average. Your "surplus" over the average is therefore 400 units.

But let us now assume that you can identify 10 other professionals, each of whom is, or can be trained to become, three times better than the average. They are not as good as you are, but they still add much more value than they cost. Let us also assume that in order to attract and retain these people, you pay them 50 percent more than the going rate. Each one of them will produce 300 units of value and cost 150 units. You therefore make a "profit," or capitalistic surplus, of 150 units for each employee. By hiring the 10, you therefore have another 1,500 surplus units to add to the 400 extra units that you yourself are creating. Your total surplus is now 1,900 units, nearly five times as much as before you started hiring.

Naturally, you do not have to stop at 10 employees. The only constraints are your ability to find employees who add surplus value and your ability (and theirs) to find customers. The latter constraint should not normally operate in the absence of the former, since professionals who add excess value should normally find a ready market for their services.

Clearly, it is crucial to hire only net value creators: those whose value comfortably exceeds their cost. But it would be wrong to say you should only hire the best. The most excess value is created by employing as many excess value creators as possible, even if some of them are only twice as good as the average whereas others may be five times (or even more) as effective. Within your own workforce, there is still likely to be an 80/20 or 70/30 distribution of effectiveness. The greatest absolute surplus value may coexist with a fairly skewed distribution of talent. The only requirement is that your least supereffective employee still adds more value than he or she costs.

Use outside contractors for everything but your core skill

The 80/20 Principle is a principle of selectivity. You achieve maximum effectiveness by concentrating on the fifth of activities at which you are the best. This principle applies not just to individuals but to firms as well.

The most successful professional firms and corporations are those that outsource everything but what they are best at. If their skill is marketing, they do not manufacture. If their real advantage is in research and development, they use third parties not just for making the goods, but for marketing and selling them. If they are best at volume manufacture of standardized products, they do not make "specials" or up-market varieties. If they are best at high-margin specials, they do not try their hand in the mass market. And so on.

The fourth stage of leverage is to use outside contractors as much as possible. Keep your own firm as simple as possible and purely focused on those areas where it is several times better than the competition.

Exploit capital leverage

So far we have advocated labor leverage, but you can also benefit from capital leverage.

Capital leverage is using money to capture additional surplus value. At its most basic, it means buying machines to replace labor whenever the machines are more cost effective. Today the most interesting examples of capital leverage involve the use of money to "roll out" good ideas that have already proven themselves in particular local circumstances. In effect, the capital is used to multiply frozen know-how captured in a particular formula. Examples include all forms of software distribution, the rollout of fast-food (and increasingly not-so-fast-food) restaurant formulae such as McDonald's and the globalization of soft drinks supply.

SUMMARY

Rewards increasingly demonstrate the 80/20 Principle: the winners take all. Those who are truly ambitious must aim for the top in their field.

Choose your field narrowly. Specialize. Choose the niche that is made for you. You will not excel unless you also enjoy what you are doing.

Success requires knowledge. But success also requires insight into what delivers the greatest customer satisfaction with the least use of resources. Identify where 20 percent of resources can be made to deliver 80 percent of returns.

Early in your career, learn all there is to be learned. You can only do this by working for the best firms and the best individuals within them, "best" being defined with reference to your own narrow niche.

Obtain the four forms of labor leverage. First, leverage your own time. Second, capture 100 percent of its value by becoming self-employed. Third, employ as many net value creators as possible. Fourth, contract out everything that you and your colleagues are not several times better at doing.

If you do all this, you will have built your career into a firm, your own firm. At this stage, use capital leverage to multiply its wealth.

MULTIPLYING MONEY

If you are interested in a successful career, you are probably also interested in multiplying your money. As we shall see in Chapters 14 and 15 respectively, this is both easier, and less worthwhile, than is commonly thought.

14

MONEY, MONEY, MONEY

To every one who has will more be given, and he will have abundance;
but from him who has not, even what he has will be taken away.

MATTHEW 25:29

This is another optional chapter, designed for those who have some
money and wish to know how to multiply it.

If the future is at all like the past, it is quite easy to multiply
money. All you need to do is put it in the right place and then leave it
there.[1]

MONEY OBEYS THE 80/20 PRINCIPLE

It is no accident that Vilfredo Pareto discovered what we now know
as the 80/20 Principle when he was researching the distribution of
incomes and wealth. He found that there was a predictable and

highly unbalanced distribution of money. Money, it seems, dislikes being equally distributed:

- Unless redistributed by progressive taxation, incomes tend to be unequally distributed, with a minority gaining most of aggregate income.
- Even with progressive taxation, wealth follows an even more unequal pattern than incomes; it is even harder to make wealth equal than to make incomes equal.
- This is because the majority of wealth is created from investment rather than from income; and because investment returns tend to be even more unbalanced than income returns.
- Investment creates high amounts of wealth because of the phenomenon of compounding. For example, the value of shares may increase by 12.5 percent per annum, on average. This means that $100 invested in 1950 would be worth around $22,740 today. In general, real investment returns (after taking out the effects of inflation) are highly positive, except when inflation is rampant.
- The compounding returns of investment are highly differential: some investments are much better than others. This helps to explain why wealth becomes so unequally distributed. It makes a huge amount of difference whether you compound wealth at annual rates of, say, 5, 10, 20 or 40 percent. $1,000 compounded over 10 years at these rates would produce, respectively, $1,629, $2,593, $6,191 or $28,925! For eight times the annual return, compounding at 40 percent produces a return nearly 18 times higher than compounding at 5 percent; and the results become even more skewed the longer we go on.

Oddly enough, certain categories of investment, and certain investment strategies, are predictably much better than others at creating wealth.

80/20 INSIGHTS INTO MAKING MONEY

- You are more likely to become wealthy, or to obtain the greatest increase in wealth, from investment income rather than from employment income. This means that there is a premium on accumulating enough money early on to fund investment. Accumulating your stake for entry to the investment world usually requires hard work and low spending: for a period, net income must be higher than spending.

The only exceptions to this rule are acquisition of money from legacies or other gifts, marrying into a wealthy family, windfalls from lotteries or other forms of gambling, and crime. The first cannot easily be predicted, the third is so unlikely that it should be totally discounted, the fourth is not recommended, so only the second can be consciously planned and even then the outcome is uncertain.

- Because of the compounding effects of investment, you can become rich either by starting to invest early in life, or by living a long time, or both. Starting early is the most controllable strategy.
- As early as possible, develop a consistent, long-term investment strategy, based on principles that have worked well in the past.

How, then, do we obtain 80 percent of investment returns with 20 percent of the money? The answer is to follow Koch's 10 commandments of investment:

Make your investment philosophy reflect your personality

A key to successful personal investing is to match your personality and skills to one of a number of proven techniques. Most private investors fail because they use techniques that, while perfectly valid, are not suited to them as individuals. The investor should choose from a menu of perhaps 10 successful strategies, to suit his or her own temperament and knowledge.

Koch's 10 commandments of investment

1   Make your investment philosophy reflect your personality
2   Be proactive and unbalanced
3   Invest mainly in the stock market
4   Invest for the long term
5   Invest most when the market is low

6   If you can't beat the market, track it
7   Build your investments on your expertise
8   Consider the merits of emerging markets
9   Cull your loss makers
10 Run your gains

For example:

- If you like playing with numbers and are analytical, you should become a devotee of one of the analytical methods of investment. Of these, the ones that I like best are value investing (but see the next point), detecting earnings acceleration, and specialist investments such as warrants.
- If you veer more toward optimism than pessimism, avoid an excessively analytical approach such as those above. The optimist often makes a poor investor, so be sure that your investments really are beating the index; if not, sell them and hand the money over to an index-tracking fund.

  Sometimes optimists, who in this case deserve the epithet "visionaries," make great investors, because they select two or three shares that they know have enormous potential. But if you are an optimist, try to restrain your enthusiasm and write down as carefully as possible why the shares you like are so attractive. Try to be rational before you buy. And be sure to sell any loss-making shares even if you are emotionally committed to them.
- If you are neither analytical nor "visionary" but a practical sort of person, you should either specialize in an area about which you know a great deal or follow successful investors who have a clear track record of beating the index.

Be proactive and unbalanced

Being proactive means that you take charge of your investment decisions yourself. The danger of advisers and money managers is not so much that they cream off a lot of the profit, but even more that they are unlikely to recommend or implement the sort of unbalanced portfolio that is the route to superior returns. Risk, it is said, is minimized by having a broad spread of investments in a wide range of different media, such as bonds, stocks, cash, real estate, gold, and collectibles. But risk minimization is overrated. If you want to become rich enough to change your future lifestyle, you need to attain above-average returns. The chances of doing this are much higher if you adopt an unbalanced portfolio. This means that you should have few investments: those that you are convinced will give high returns. And it also means that you should invest in one medium.

Invest mainly in the stock market

Unless you happen to be an expert in a very esoteric investment medium, such as nineteenth-century Chinese silk screens or toy soldiers, the best investment medium is the stock market.

Over the long haul, investing in stocks (also called shares or equities) has produced returns stunningly higher than putting the money in a bank or investing in interest-bearing instruments like government or corporate bonds. For example, I calculated in Great Britain that if you had invested £100 in a building society in 1950, you could have taken out £813 by 1992; but the same £100 invested in the stock market would have returned £14,198, more than 17 times as much.[2] Similar calculations can be made for the United States and nearly every other major stock market.

Anne Scheiber, a private American investor with no particular expertise in the stock market, put $5,000 into blue-chip stocks just after the Second World War. She then sat on them. By 1995 the $5,000 had turned into $22 million: 440,000 percent of the original!

The stock market, happily, is a relatively easy investment medium for the nonexpert.

Invest for the long term

Do not move in and out of individual stocks, or your share portfolio as a whole, very often. Unless they are clear losers, keep your stocks for many years. Buying and selling stocks is expensive as well as time consuming. If you possibly can, take a 10-year view or, even better, a 20-, 30-, or 50-year view. If you put money into stocks for the short term, you are really gambling rather than investing. If you are tempted to take the money out and spend it, you are deferring expenditure rather than investing.

At some stage, of course, you may want to enjoy your wealth rather than wait for your heirs to do so. The best use of wealth is usually to create a new lifestyle where you can choose how to spend your time, to pursue a career or work activity that you would most enjoy. Then the investment period is over. But until you have enough money to make this shift, continue to accumulate.

Invest most when the stock market is low

Although its value goes up over time, the stock market is cyclical, partly as a function of the economic cycle but mainly because moods fluctuate. It is amazing, but irrational concerns driven by fashion, animal spirits, hope, and fear can drive prices up or down. Pareto himself observed this phenomenon:

> There is a rhythm of sentiment which we can observe in ethics, in religion, and in politics as waves resembling the business cycle . . .
>
> Whereas during the upward trend every argument produced in order to demonstrate that an enterprise will produce money is received with favour; whereas such an argument will be absolutely rejected during the downward trend . . . A man who during the downward trend refuses to underwrite certain stocks believes himself to be guided exclusively by reason and does not know that, unconsciously, he yields to the thousand small impressions which he receives from the daily economic news. When, later, during the upward trend, he will underwrite those same stocks, or similar shares offering no better chance of success, he will again think that he is following only the dictates of reason and will remain unaware of the fact that his transition from distrust to trust depends on sentiments generated by the atmosphere around him . . .
>
> It is well known at the Stock Exchange that the public at large buys only in a rising market and sells in a declining market. The financiers who, because of their greater practice in this business, use their reason to a greater extent, although they sometimes allow themselves to be swayed by sentiment, do the opposite, and this is the main source of their gains. During a boom period any mediocre argument to the

effect that this boom must continue has great persuasive power; and if you tried to tell man that, after all, prices cannot continue to go up indefinitely, be sure he would not listen to you.[3]

A whole school, that of value investing, has grown up around this philosophy: buy when the stock market as a whole, or an individual share, is low and sell when it is high. One of the most successful investors of all time, Benjamin Graham, wrote the rule book for value investing, and his rules have been vindicated time and time again.[4]

There are many rules to guide you in value investing. Simplifying greatly, but capturing perhaps 80 percent of their value in well under 20 percent of the space, here are three rules to help you:

· Do not buy when everyone else is and when everyone is convinced that the stock market can only go up. Instead, buy when everyone else is pessimistic.
· Use the price/earnings ratio (P/E) as the best single benchmark for deciding whether shares are expensive or cheap. The P/E of a share is its price divided by its after-tax earnings. For example, if a share is 250 cents and its earnings per share are 25 cents, the share is on a P/E of 10. If the share price goes up, in a period of optimism, to 500 cents, but the earnings per share are still 25 cents, the P/E is now 20.
· In general, a P/E of over 17 for the stock market as a whole is a danger signal. Do not invest heavily when the market is this high. A P/E of under 12 is a buy signal; one of under 10 a definite buy signal. Your stockbroker or a good financial newspaper should tell you what the current market average P/E is. If asked which P/E you mean, say learnedly "the historic P/E, bozo."[5]

If you can't beat the market, track it

It is quite possible to develop an investment approach that is superior to the stock market average by following certain precepts and developing an approach tailored to your own personality and skills. These possibilities are explored below. But it is more likely that selecting your own investments will lead you to performance inferior to that of the stock market indices.

In the latter case, or if you don't even wish to experiment with your own approach in the hope of beating the market, you should "track the index."

Index tracking, also called market tracking, means buying the shares that are in the stock market index. You then only sell shares when they drop out of the index (this happens to underperforming shares), and you only buy new shares when they are first included in the index.

You can track the index yourself, at the cost of some effort in following the financial press. Alternatively, you can put your money into a "tracker fund" run by fund managers who, for a small annual fee, will do it for you.

You can choose different funds depending on which market you choose to track. Generally, it is safest to choose your home market and to go for a fund tracking the index comprised of the largest and best-quality shares (called "blue chips").

Index tracking is fairly low risk and yet, over the long term, should deliver high returns. If you decide to follow this approach, you need read no further than these first six commandments. It can be more fun and more rewarding, although at higher risk, to make your own selections. The next four commandments apply in that case. Remember, however, that this commandment requires you to go back to index tracking unless your own investment strategy generally beats the index. If it doesn't, cut your losses and track the index.

Build your investments on your expertise

The whole essence of the 80/20 philosophy is to know a few things well: to specialize.

This law applies particularly to investment. If you are deciding yourself which shares to buy, specialize in an area in which you are a relative expert.

The great thing about specialization is that the possibilities are almost endless. You could, for example, specialize in shares of the industry in which you work, or of your hobby, your local area, or anything else in which you are interested. If you like shopping, for example, you might decide to specialize in the shares of retailers. Then if you notice a new chain springing up, where each new store seems to be full of keen shoppers, you might want to invest in those shares.

Even if you do not start out as an expert, it may pay to specialize in a few shares, for example those in a particular industry, so that you can learn as much as possible about that area.

Consider the merits of emerging markets

Emerging markets are stock markets outside the developed countries: in countries where the economy is growing fast and where the stock market is still developing. Emerging markets include most of Asia (but not Japan), Africa, the Indian subcontinent, South America, the ex-communist countries of Central and Eastern Europe, and the fringes of Europe such as Portugal, Greece, and Turkey.

The basic theory is very simple. Stock market performance is highly correlated with the growth of an economy as a whole. Therefore, invest in countries that have the fastest current and expected GNP growth—the emerging markets.

There are other reasons emerging markets can be very good investments. They have the lion's share of future privatizations and these are generally good homes for money. The strange and sudden death of Communism around 1990 forced many emerging countries to adopt more free-market economic policies, which are likely to work their way through, after the inevitable initial social disruption, into higher returns for investors. And emerging-country shares are often very good value, because they tend to have quite low P/E ratios. As the market develops and matures, and individual companies become larger, the P/Es are likely to go up, boosting the share prices considerably.

But investing in emerging markets is definitely riskier than investing at home. The companies are younger and less stable, the whole country's stock market could fall as a result of political changes or reductions in commodity prices, the currency could depreciate (and with it the value of your shares), and you may find it much more difficult to take your money out than you did to put it in. Also, the cost of investing in terms of spreads and commissions is much higher than in developed markets. The chances of getting ripped off by a market maker are much higher.

Three policies must be followed by an investor in emerging markets. One is to invest only a small part of your total portfolio, up to 20 percent, in emerging markets. The second is to invest most of your emerging market funds only when the market is relatively low and the average P/E for the countries you are investing in is under 12. The third is to invest for the long term and only pull money out when the P/Es are relatively high.

But, with these caveats, emerging markets are, over the long haul, likely to outperform and it can be wise as well as fun to have some investment in them.

Cull your loss makers

If any share falls by 15 percent (of the price you paid), sell it. Follow this rule rigorously and consistently.

If you want to buy it back later at a lower price, wait until the price has stopped falling, for at least a number of days (and preferably weeks), before you reinvest.

Apply the same 15 percent rule to the new investment: stop the loss after 15 percent.

The only acceptable exception to this commandment is if you are a very long-term investor who does not want to be bothered with the swings in markets and does not have the time to monitor investments. Those who stayed in stocks during and after the 1929–32, 1974–5, and 1987 crashes will have done well over the long term. Those who sold after the first 15 percent declines (where this was possible) and returned after the market had risen 15 percent from its lows would have done even better.

The key point about the 15 percent rule has to do with individual stocks, not with the market. If an individual stock falls by 15 percent, which is much more common than the market falling by the same amount, it should be sold. Whereas few, if any, fortunes have been lost by sticking to the stock market (or a broad portfolio of stocks) over the long term, a large number of fortunes have been lost by mistaken loyalty to one or a few declining stocks. For individual stocks, the best indication of the future trend is the current one.

Run your gains

Cut your losses, but do not cut your gains. The best long-term indicator of a great investment is a short-term gain, repeated over and over again! Resist the temptation to take profits too early. This is where many private investors make their worst mistakes: they take nice profits, but forfeit much fatter ones. Nobody ever went broke by taking a profit, but many people never got rich by following the same procedure!

There are two further 80/20 rules of investment that we have not yet explored:

- Comparing a large number of investment portfolios held over a long period of time, it is usually true that 20 percent of the portfolios contain 80 percent of the gains.
- For an individual holding a portfolio over a long period of time, 80 percent of the gains will usually come from 20 percent of the investments. In a portfolio composed exclusively of equities, 80 percent of the gains will come from 20 percent of the shares held.

The reason these rules hold true is that a few investments are usually stunningly good performers, while the majority are not. These few superstar shares can give phenomenal returns. It is absolutely crucial, therefore, to let the superstars stay within the portfolio throughout the process: to let the profits ride. In the dying words of a character from one of Anita Brookner's novels: "never sell Glaxo."

It would have been easy to lock in a 100 percent gain on IBM, McDonald's, Xerox, or Marks & Spencer in the 1950s or 1960s, on Shell, GE, Lonrho, BTR, or the Swedish pharmaceuticals firm Astra in the 1970s, on American Express, Body Shop, or Cadbury Schweppes early in the 1980s, or on Microsoft later that decade. Investors who took these gains would have missed out on several times that appreciation later.

Good businesses tend to produce a virtuous cycle of consistent out-performance. Only when this momentum is reversed, which may take several decades, should you consider selling. Again, one good rule of thumb is not to sell unless the price falls by 15 percent from its recent high price.

To do this, set a "lock-gain" price at which you will sell, 15 percent below the high. A 15 percent reduction may indicate a change in the trend. Otherwise, continue to hold until circumstances force you to sell.

CONCLUSION

Money begets money. But some methods of breeding have much more prolific results. Samuel Johnson said that a man was never so innocently employed as when making money. His observation pitches the accumulation of wealth, whether through investment or a successful professional career or both, at the right moral level. Neither pursuit is to be denigrated but, equally, neither is a guaranteed passport to serving society or personal happiness. And both money making and professional success carry the dangers that they become ends in themselves.

A success hangover is quite possible. Wealth creates the need to administer it, to deal with lawyers, tax advisers, bankers, and other profoundly stimulating contacts. The logic of professional success outlined in the preceding chapter leads almost inexorably to ever-greater professional demands. To succeed, you must aim for the top. To get there, you must turn yourself into a business. To obtain maximum leverage, you must employ a large number of people. To maximize the value of your business, you must use other people's money and exploit capital leverage—to become even larger and more profitable. Your circle of contacts expands and the time for friends and relationships contracts. On the giddy roundabout of success, it is easy to lose focus, perspective, and personal values. It is a perfectly rational response to say, at any stage, stop success: I want to get off!

This is why it is sensible to stand back from careers and money making and consider the most important subject of all: happiness.

15

THE SEVEN HABITS
OF HAPPINESS

Temperament is not destiny.

DANIEL GOLEMAN[1]

Aristotle said that the goal of all human activity should be happiness. Down the ages, we haven't listened much to Aristotle. Perhaps he should have told us how to be happier. He could usefully have started by analyzing the causes of happiness and unhappiness.

Can the 80/20 Principle really apply to happiness? I believe it can. It appears to be true for most people that the majority of perceived happiness occurs in a minority of the time. One 80/20 hypothesis would be that 80 percent of happiness occurs in 20 percent of our time. When I have tried this hypothesis on friends and asked them to divide their weeks into days and parts of days, or their months into weeks, or their years into months, or their lives into years, about two-thirds of the respondents show a marked pattern of imbalance, approximating to the 80/20 pattern.

The hypothesis does not work for everyone. About a third of my friends don't exhibit the 80/20 pattern. Their happiness is much more equally distributed over time. What is fascinating is that this latter group seem to be markedly happier overall than the larger group whose happiness peaks in small amounts of their lives.

This fits in with common sense. Those who are happy with most of their lives are more likely to be happier overall. Those whose happiness is highly concentrated in short bursts are likely to be less happy with life overall.

It also fits in with the idea advanced throughout this book that 80/20 relationships imply waste and great scope for improvement. But, more significantly, it suggests that the 80/20 Principle might help us to be happier.

TWO WAYS TO BE HAPPIER

· Identify the times when you are happiest and expand them as much as possible.
· Identify the times when you are least happy and reduce them as much as possible.

Spend more time on the type of activities that are very effective at making you happy and less time on other activities. Start by cutting off the "valleys of unhappiness," the things that tend to make you actively unhappy. The best way to start being more happy is to stop being unhappy. You have more control over this than you imagine, simply by avoiding situations where experience suggests you are likely to become unhappy.

For activities that are very ineffective at making you happy (or effective at making you unhappy), think systematically of ways that you could enjoy them more. If this works, fine. If it doesn't, think how to avoid these situations.

BUT AREN'T PEOPLE POWERLESS TO
DEAL WITH UNHAPPINESS?

You might object, particularly if you have some experience of people who are chronically unhappy (and are often consigned to the seemingly objective, but terribly slippery and unhelpful, category of the "mentally ill," which has perhaps brought the world more misery than most categorizations), that this analysis is far too simplistic and assumes a degree of control over our own happiness that, for deep-rooted psychological reasons, many or most or all people do not have. Isn't our capacity to be happy largely predestined, by heredity and childhood experience? Do we really have any control over our happiness?

There is no doubt that there are people who are temperamentally more inclined to happiness than others. For some the glass is always half full, for others half empty. Psychologists and psychiatrists believe that capacity for happiness is determined by the interaction between genetics, childhood experiences, brain chemistry, and important life events. Clearly, adults can do nothing about their genes, childhood experiences, or past misfortunes in life. It is all too easy for those inclined to evade responsibility to blame their defeatism on forces outside their control, particularly if they are easily overawed by medical Jeremiahs.

Happily, common sense, observation, and the latest scientific evidence all indicate that, while everyone is dealt a different hand of cards with respect to happiness just as for every other blessing, there is a great deal that can be done to play our hand better and to improve it during the game of life. Adults are differently endowed with athletic ability, as a result of genetics and the extent of training and exercise during childhood, youth, and subsequently. Yet everyone can markedly improve their fitness by sensible, regular exercise. Similarly, we may through hereditary influences and background be thought more or less intelligent, but everyone can train their mind and develop it. We may be more or less inclined, through our genes and environment, to become overweight, but healthy eating and exercise can make most fat people considerably thinner. Why, in principle, should our ability to become happier be any different, whatever our starting point in terms of temperament?

Most of us have seen examples where the lives of acquaintances or friends have been materially changed and happiness permanently enhanced or reduced, as a result of actions freely taken by those individuals. A new partner, a new career, a new place to live, a new lifestyle, or even a conscious decision to adopt a different attitude to life: any of these can make all the difference to an individual's happiness, and all of them are under the individual's control. Predestination is an unconvincing hypothesis if it can be shown that only those who believe in predestination are subject to its sway. Evidence that some people can freely change their destiny ought to be persuasive and encourage us to emulate those exercising free will.

The freedom to be happy is at last supported by science

At last, the field of psychology and psychiatry (which, more than economics, has deserved the epithet of the dismal science), prodded by the findings of other scientific disciplines, is producing a more cheerful picture consistent with our common sense and observations of life. Geneticists used to be excessively deterministic, reducing complex human behavior to the whim of inherited genes. As a more enlightened geneticist, Professor Steve Jones of University College, London, points out: "There have been announcements of the discovery of single genes for manic depression, schizophrenia and alcoholism. All have been withdrawn."[2] Now, we are told by an eminent neuropsychiatrist, "The new field of psychoneuro-immunology is telling us . . . that a human being acts as an integrated whole . . . The evidence suggests that there is a delicate balance between what we think and feel on a daily basis and our physical and mental health."[3] In other words, within limits, you can choose to make yourself happy or unhappy and even to make yourself healthy or unhealthy.

Sensitive dependence on initial conditions

This does not mean that we should discard earlier research about the importance of childhood experiences (or later misfortunes). We saw in Part One that chaos theory highlights "sensitive dependence on initial conditions." This means that early in the life of any phenomenon, chance events and apparently small causes can cause a large deviation in the eventual outcome.

Something analogous appears to happen in childhood, producing beliefs about ourselves—that we are loved or unloved, intelligent or unintelligent, highly valued or of low worth, able to take risks or constrained to obey authority—that are then often played out through life. The initial belief, which may be arrived at with no objective foundation whatever, acquires a life of its own and becomes self-fulfilling. Later events—poor examination results, a lover who leaves, failure to get the job we want, a career that moves sideways, being fired, a setback in health—may blow us off course and reinforce negative views about ourselves.

Putting the clock back to find happiness

So, is this a chilling world where unhappiness is the path laid out for us? I do not think so.

The humanist Pico of Mirandola (1463–93) pointed out that human beings are not entirely like other animals.[4] All other creatures have a definite nature that they cannot change. Humans have been given an indefinite nature and thus the ability to mold themselves. The rest of creation is passive; humans alone have an active nature. They were created; we could create.

When unhappiness strikes, we can recognize what is happening to us and refuse to accept it. We are free to change the way in which we think and act. To invert Jean-Jacques Rousseau, man is everywhere in chains yet everywhere can be free. We can change the way that we think about external events, even where we cannot change them. And we can do something more. We can intelligently change our exposure to events that make us either happy or unhappy.

MAKING OURSELVES HAPPY BY STRENGTHENING EMOTIONAL INTELLIGENCE

Daniel Goleman and other writers have contrasted academic intelligence or IQ with *emotional* intelligence: "abilities such as being able to motivate oneself and delay gratification; to regulate one's moods and to keep distress from swamping the ability to think; to empathize and to hope."[5] Emotional intelligence is more crucial for happiness than intellectual intelligence, yet our society places little emphasis on the development of emotional intelligence. As Goleman aptly remarks:

> Even though a high IQ is no guarantee of prosperity, prestige, or happiness in life, our schools and our culture fixate on academic abilities, ignoring emotional intelligence, a set of traits—some might call it character—that also matters immensely for our personal destiny.[6]

The good news is that emotional intelligence can be cultivated and learned: certainly as a child, but also at any stage in life. In Goleman's wonderful phrase, "Temperament is not destiny": we can change our destiny by changing our temperament. Psychologist Martin Seligman points out that "moods like anxiety, sadness and anger don't just descend on you without your having any control over them . . . you can change the way you feel by what you think."[7] There are proven techniques for exiting feelings of incipient sadness and depression before they become damaging to your health and happiness. Moreover, by cultivating habits of optimism you can help to prevent disease as well as have a happier life. Again, Goleman shows that happiness is related to neurological processes in the brain:

> Among the main biological changes in happiness is an increased activity in a brain center that inhibits negative feelings and fosters an increase in available energy, and a quieting of those that generate worrisome thought . . . there is . . . a quiescence, which makes the body recover more quickly from the biological arousal of upsetting emotions.[8]

Identify personal levers that can magnify positive thoughts and cut off negative ones. In what circumstances are you at your most positive and most negative? Where are you? Who are you with? What are you doing? What is the weather like? Everyone has a wide range of emotional intelligence, depending on the circumstances. You can start to build up your emotional intelligence by giving yourself a break, by skewing the odds in your favor, by doing the things where you feel most in control and most benevolent. You can also avoid or minimize the circumstances where you are at your most emotionally stupid!

MAKING OURSELVES HAPPIER BY CHANGING THE WAY WE THINK ABOUT EVENTS

We have all experienced the trap of self-reinforced depression, when we think in a gloomy and negative way and simply make things worse, so that we can imagine no way out of the box. When we come out of the depression, we see that the way out was always there. We can train ourselves to break the self-reinforcing pattern of depression by simple steps, such as seeking out company, changing our physical setting, or forcing ourselves to exercise.

There are many examples of people exposed to the worst misfortunes, like those in concentration camps or with fatal diseases, who react in a positive way that changes their perspective and strengthens their ability to survive.

According to Dr. Peter Fenwick, a consultant neuropsychiatrist, "The ability to see silver linings in clouds is not simply Pollyannaism; it is a healthy self-protective mechanism with a good biological basis."[9] Optimism, it seems, is a medically approved ingredient for both success and happiness, and the greatest motivator on earth. Hope has been defined specifically by C. R. Snyder, a psychologist at the University of Kansas, as "believing you have both the will and the way to accomplish your goals, whatever they may be."[10]

MAKING OURSELVES HAPPIER BY CHANGING THE WAY WE THINK ABOUT OURSELVES

Do you think of yourself as successful or unsuccessful? If you opt for unsuccessful, you may be sure that there are many people who have achieved less than you have and would be described by most people as less successful than you are. Their perception of self-success contributes both to their success and their happiness. Your feeling of being unsuccessful limits your success and your happiness.

The same applies to whether you think you are happy or unhappy. Richard Nixon ended the Vietnam War by declaring that America's objectives had been achieved. He was economical with the truth, but who cared? The rebuilding of America's self-esteem could begin. Similarly, you can make yourself happy or unhappy just by the way that you decide to feel.

Make the choice that you want to be happy. You owe it to yourself and you owe it to other people too. Unless you are happy, you will make your partner and anyone else with prolonged exposure to you less happy. Therefore you have a positive duty to be happy.

Psychologists tell us that all perceptions about happiness relate to our sense of self-worth. A positive self-image is essential to happiness. A sense of self-worth can and should be cultivated. You know you can do it: give up guilt, forget about your weaknesses, focus and build on your strengths. Remember all the good things you have done, all the small and big achievements to your credit, all the positive feedback you have ever received. There is a lot to be said for yourself. Say it—or at least think it. You will be amazed at the difference it makes to your relationships, your achievements, and your happiness.

You may feel that you are deceiving yourself. But in fact, by having a negative perception of yourself you are at least as guilty of self-deception. All the time we tell ourselves stories about ourselves. We have to: there is no objective truth. You might as well choose positive rather than negative stories. By doing so you will increase the sum of human happiness, starting with yourself and radiating out to others.

Use all the willpower at your disposal to make yourself happy. Construct the right stories about yourself—and believe them!

MAKING OURSELVES HAPPIER BY CHANGING EVENTS

A further route to superior happiness is to change the events you encounter in order to increase your happiness. None of us can ever have complete control over events but we can have much more control than we think.

If the best way to start being happy is to stop being unhappy, the first thing we should do is to avoid situations and people that tend to make us depressed or miserable.

Making ourselves happier by changing the people we see most

There is medical evidence that high levels of stress can be coped with provided that we have a few excellent personal relationships. But relationships of any kind that take up a large part of our time and are part of the daily fabric of our lives, whether at home, at work, or in our social lives, will powerfully influence both our happiness and our health. To quote John Cacioppo, an Ohio State University psychologist:

> It's the most important relationships in your life, the people you see day in and day out, that seem to be crucial for your health. And the more significant the relationship is in your life, the more it matters for your health.[11]

Think about the people you see every day. Do they make you happier or less happy? Could you change the amount of time you spend with them accordingly?

Avoid the snake-pits

There are many situations with which each of us typically copes badly. I have never seen the point in training people not to be scared of snakes. The more sensible action is to avoid the jungle (or the pet shop).

What upsets us, of course, varies from person to person. I cannot stop myself getting angry when confronted with pointless bureaucracy. I can feel stress building up when exposed to lawyers for more than a few minutes. I am anxious in traffic jams. I often become mildly depressed when days go by without seeing the sun. I hate being jammed into the same space with too many of my fellow humans. I cannot abide listening to people making excuses and detailing problems beyond their control. If I were to become a rush-hour commuter, working with lawyers, and living in Sweden, I am sure I would become depressed and quite possibly do myself in. But I have learned to avoid, as far as practicable, such situations. I do not commute, avoid mass transit systems in the rush hour, spend at least a week a month in the sun, pay someone else to deal with bureaucracy, drive around jams even if it takes longer, avoid having anyone of a negative disposition report to me, and find that my telephones mysteriously disconnect five minutes after I am called by lawyers. As a result of all these actions, I am significantly happier.

No doubt you have your own pressure points. Write them down: now! Consciously engineer your life to avoid them; write down how: now! Check each month how far you are succeeding. Congratulate yourself on each small avoidance victory.

In Chapter 10 you identified your unhappiness islands. Analysis or reflection on when you have been least happy very often leads to obvious conclusions. You hate your job! You get depressed by your spouse! Or perhaps more precisely, you hate one-third of your job, you cannot abide being with your spouse's friends or in-laws, you suffer mental torture from your boss, you detest housework. Great! You've finally had a blinding glimpse of the obvious. Now do something about it . . .

DAILY HAPPINESS HABITS

After you have removed—or at least set in motion plans to remove—
the causes of unhappiness, concentrate most energy on the positive
seeking of happiness. For this, there is no time like the present.
Happiness is profoundly existential. Happiness only exists now. Past
happiness may be remembered or future happiness planned, but the
pleasure this gives can only be experienced in the "now."

What we all need is a set of daily happiness habits, similar to (and
in fact partially related to) our daily fitness or healthy eating regime.
My seven daily happiness habits are summarized in Figure 39.

---

1   Exercise
2   Mental stimulation
3   Spiritual/artistic stimulation/meditation
4   Doing a good turn
5   Taking a pleasure break with a friend
6   Giving yourself a treat
7   Congratulating yourself

Figure 39   Seven daily happiness habits

One essential ingredient of a happy day is *physical exercise.* I
always feel good after (even if not during) exercise. Apparently this is
because exertion releases endorphins, natural antidepressants that
are similar to certain exhilarating drugs (but with none of the dangers
or expense!). Daily exercise is an essential habit: if you don't make it
a habit, you will do it far less often than you should. If it is a workday,
I always exercise before going to work, to ensure that my exercise
time is not blown away by unexpected work pressures. If you travel a
lot, ensure that you plan when you will exercise at the same time that
you order the tickets, if necessary changing the schedule to accom-
modate the exercise. If you are a high-powered executive, do not let
your secretary put any meetings in the calendar before 10 A.M., so
that you will have plenty of time to exercise and prepare yourself for
the day ahead.

Another key component of a happy day is *mental stimulation.* You may obtain this at work but, if not, ensure that there is some intellectual or mental exercise each day. There are a huge number of ways to obtain this, depending on your interests: crossword puzzles, certain newspapers and magazines, reading part of a book, talking for at least 20 minutes to an intelligent friend about an abstract topic, writing a short article or journal entry, in fact, doing anything that requires active thought on your part (watching television, even of the high-brow kind, does not qualify).

A third essential daily regime is *spiritual or artistic stimulation.* This need not be as forbidding as it sounds: all that is required is at least half an hour's food for the imagination or spirit. Going to a concert, art gallery, theater, or movie all qualify, as do reading a poem, watching the sun rise or set, looking at the stars, or attendance at any event where you are stimulated and excited (this can even include a ball game, race meeting, political rally, church, or park). Meditation also works well.

Daily happiness habit number four is *doing something for another person or people.* This does not have to be a major work of benevolence; it can be a random act of kindness such as paying for someone else's parking meter or going out of your way to direct someone. Even a brief altruistic act can have a great effect on your spirits.

The fifth habit is to *share a pleasurable break with a friend.* This must be an uninterrupted tête-à-tête lasting at least half an hour, but the form of the occasion is up to you (a cup of coffee, a drink, a meal, or a leisurely walk are all appropriate).

Habit number six is to *give yourself a treat.* To prompt you each day, write down now a list of all the pleasures in which you could indulge yourself (don't worry, you don't have to show the list to anyone!). Ensure that you chalk up at least one of these each day.

The final habit, at the end of each day, is to *congratulate yourself* on having followed your daily happiness habits. Since the point is to make yourself happy rather than unhappy, you can count a score of five or more (including this number seven) as a success. If you haven't notched up five habits, but have still achieved something significant or enjoyed yourself, congratulate yourself anyway on a day's worthwhile living.

MEDIUM-TERM STRATAGEMS FOR HAPPINESS

In addition to your seven happiness habits, Figure 40 distills seven shortcuts to a happy life.

---

1   Maximize your control
2   Set attainable goals
3   Be flexible
4   Have a close relationship with your partner
5   Have a few happy friends
6   Have a few close professional alliances
7   Evolve your ideal lifestyle

Figure 40   Seven shortcuts to a happy life

Shortcut number one is to *maximize control over your life.* Lack of control is the root cause of much unease and uncertainty. I would rather drive a long way round a complex city route, with which I am familiar, than try to navigate a potentially shorter course that I do not know. Bus drivers are more frustrated than bus conductors, and more liable to heart attacks, not just because of the lack of exercise on the job but because they have much more limited control over when the bus moves. Working in the classic large bureaucracy leads to alienation because one's working life cannot be controlled. Self-employed people who can determine their working hours and work scheduling are happier than employed people who cannot.

Maximizing the proportion of your life under your own control requires planning and often risk taking. The happiness dividends, however, should not be underestimated.

Setting reasonable and attainable goals is the second shortcut to happiness. Psychological research has shown that we are likely to achieve most when we have reasonably challenging but not too difficult goals. Objectives that are too easy will lead us to be complacent, accepting mediocre performance. But objectives that are too tough—the sort of objectives set by those of us laden with guilt or burdened with high and punitive expectations—are demoralizing and lead us to self-fulfilling self-perceptions of failure. Remember that you are trying to become happier. If in doubt, when setting yourself goals, err on the soft side. It is better for your happiness to set soft goals and succeed than it is to set tough goals and fail, even if the latter would have led you to objectively superior performance. If there is a trade-off between achievement and happiness, choose happiness.

The third shortcut is to *be flexible when chance events interfere with plans and expectations.* John Lennon once remarked that life is what happens while we're making other plans. Our objective must be to make our plans stick so that we happen to life rather than the other way round, but we must be prepared for life to insert its quota of objections and diversions. Life's interjections should be cheerfully and playfully accepted as a counterpoint to our plans. If possible, life's unplanned contribution should be incorporated into our own plan, so that it can proceed to an even higher level. If imagination fails us here, life's objection should be worked around or quashed. If neither of these tactics works, we should accept what we cannot control with grace and maturity and get on with molding what we can control. On no account should we let life's objections ruffle us or make us angry, self-doubting, or bitter.

Fourth, *develop a close relationship with a happy partner.* We are programmed to develop a close living relationship with one person. This selection of the partner is one of the few decisions in life (one of the 20 percent) that will help determine whether we are happy or not. Sexual attraction is one of the universe's great mysteries and demonstrates an extreme form of the 80/20 Principle: the real chemistry can occur in fleeting seconds, so that you feel 99 percent of the attraction in 1 percent of the time and you know at once that this is the person for you![12] But the 80/20 Principle should put you on your guard: danger and wasted happiness could lie ahead. Bear in mind that there are many people with whom you could, in theory, bond; this rush of blood to the head (or the heart) will happen again.

If you have not yet selected a partner, remember that your happiness will be greatly influenced by the happiness of your partner. For the sake of your happiness, as well as for love, you will want to make your partner happy. But this is a great deal easier if your partner has, to start with, a happy temperament and/or if he or she consciously adopts a prohappiness daily regime (such as my happiness habits).

Team up with an unhappy partner and the odds are that you yourself will end up unhappy. People with low self-esteem and self-confidence are a nightmare to live with, however much mutual love abounds. If you are a very happy person, you might just make an unhappy person happy, but it is a hell of a trick to pull off. Two mildly unhappy people who are deeply in love might just, with strong determination to be happy and a good happiness regimen, manage to attain mutual happiness; but I would not bet on it. Two unhappy people, even in love, will drive each other nuts. If you want to be happy, choose to love a happy partner.

You may, of course, already have a partner who is not happy and, if so, you will probably be seriously subtracting from your own happiness. If so, it should be a major project for both of you to make your partner happy.

The fifth shortcut is to *cultivate close friendships with a few happy friends.* The 80/20 Principle predicts that most of the satisfaction you draw from all of your friends will be concentrated in your relationship with a small number of close friends. The principle also indicates that you are likely to misallocate your time, spending too much with the not-so-good friends and too little with the very good friends (although you may allocate more time per friend to the good friends, there are more of the not-so-good variety in most people's friendship portfolio, so that in aggregate the not-so-good friends take more time than the good ones). The answer is to decide who the good friends are and give them 80 percent of the time allocated to friends (you should probably increase this absolute amount of time as well). You should try to build these good friendships as much as possible, because they will be a great source of mutual happiness.

Shortcut six is similar to five: *develop strong professional alliances with a small number of people whose company you enjoy.* Not all your work or professional colleagues should become your friends; if so, you would spread your friendship too thinly. But a few should become close friends and allies; people whom you will go out of your way to support and who will do the same for you. This will not only enhance your career. It will also immeasurably enrich the pleasure you take at work; it will help to prevent your feeling alienated at work; and it will provide a unifying link between your work and play. This unity, too, is essential for full happiness.

The final shortcut to lasting happiness is to *evolve the lifestyle you and your partner want.* This requires a harmonious balance between your work life, home life, and social life. It means that you live where you want to work, have the quality of life that you want, have time to attend to family and social affairs, and are equally happy at work and outside it.

CONCLUSION

Happiness is a duty. We should choose to be happy. We should work at happiness. And in doing so, we should help those closest to us, and even those who just stumble across us, to share our happiness.

PART FOUR

CRESCENDO

16

PROGRESS REGAINED

If the misery of the poor be caused not by the laws of nature, but by our institutions, great is our sin.

CHARLES DARWIN[1]

Is the 80/20 Principle just a useful piece of knowledge, a cheap and effective diagnostic kit to be kept handy in the home, the office, and the lab? Is it just a piece of mental software, useful but devoid of ethical content, like a computer program? Or is there more to it than that? Can we invest the 80/20 Principle with a purpose and moral force that go beyond the technocratic and that can characterize it as an important force for good?

That the 80/20 Principle can help make corporations more profitable is incontrovertible. This book has argued, I hope persuasively, that people can use the 80/20 Principle to get a great deal more out of their lives, to raise their effectiveness and happiness. Once we stake a claim to enhance happiness, we begin also to lay a claim to moral force, since it is reasonable that something that can enhance happiness is a force for good. But one individual's happiness can sometimes be bought at the expense of that of another person or people. We could only claim ethical value for the 80/20 Principle if we could demonstrate that it could be used for the good of most or all in society. The acid test, therefore, is whether we can use the 80/20 Principle to help create a better society.

I think we can, provided that we take the 80/20 Principle beyond the merely descriptive and extend it to include action steps that are in tune with it. My confidence that this can be done rests largely on the successful and benign use of the 80/20 Principle in business and the belief that this type of use can and should be extended to issues that are more important for society than the success or failure of any individual business enterprise.

WHY SOCIETY SHOULD ADOPT THE 80/20 PRINCIPLE

The 80/20 Principle has been used in business to raise effectiveness, to boost profits and what leads to profits, in quite major ways. But what I want us to concentrate on here is not this fact itself, but rather how such improvements have been generated. Effectiveness has been multiplied by giving further strength and resources to benign forces (the 20 percent that produce 80 percent of profits), by identifying and stopping negative forces (the 20 percent of quality problems that cause 80 percent of the defects), and by raising the effectiveness or changing the role of the majority of weak forces (the 80 percent that are meant to do good things but only end up contributing 20 percent of the value). All of these uses have multiplied wealth for corporations. For individuals, I have suggested using the 80/20 Principle in similar ways, to magnify happiness and effectiveness.

With imagination and practice, there is no earthly reason why we could not do the same for the good of society as a whole, using exactly the same methods. We will examine these possibilities shortly, after clearing away some ideological clutter. For we need to beware. It would not advance the debate about the public good one iota if the 80/20 Principle were to be hijacked to bolster existing ideologies.

IS THE 80/20 PRINCIPLE INHERENTLY
RIGHT WING?

The 80/20 Principle may appear to resonate with the arguments of the radical right. If the universe naturally divides into a minority of powerful forces and a majority of weak ones, and if human lives, society, business, and nature all reflect this phenomenon (as I have argued), it is but a short hop to the crazy world of the extreme right—inequality is natural and the engine of progress; markets are the economic analogue of evolution and must be left untrammeled to find their own way; rule by élites is inevitable and natural; might is right; and social engineering will always come unstuck, because it attempts to frustrate the way the world works.

A short hop indeed, but one that involves a profound misreading of the 80/20 Principle. Let us concede what is right about the right-wing interpretation. It is certainly good to observe what works in nature, in business, in our own lives, and in society: to see the powerful forces that take small elements of energy and produce great returns; to multiply, reproduce, and mimic the 20 percent that yield 80 percent, provided that these 20 percent are forces for good. *But the 20 percent may equally well be forces for bad; and the fact that they are productive forces does not excuse or mitigate the badness.*

The 80/20 Principle asserts that imbalance is natural, but not that what is natural is right, still less that it should be left alone. The principle draws attention to imbalance; but it does not state that the universe, or nature, or business, or society, or the way we lead our lives is unbalanced in any rational or functional way. Nor does it imply that the imbalance is in any way ethical or justified. The 80/20 Principle observes that these processes work and produce powerful results and so should be respected, just as any powerful force, benign or malevolent, should be respected. The whole value and force of the 80/20 Principle, and all of its practical uses in the past 50 years, are that it highlights a state of affairs that is surprising and suboptimal. Once the surprise is appreciated, the principle can guide us to make major improvements on the status quo.

The 80/20 Principle wants to improve on what it observes

At its heart, therefore, the 80/20 Principle is not just descriptive, and it does not glorify what it describes. It is *prescriptive;* it observes a failure to reach anything like an optimal state of affairs, and it points the way to great improvements in the status quo. It is impressive that the powerful minority of resources are so effective—but what about the majority of weak resources? Is nature really so clever, if the majority of natural forces are so ineffective, or when ever larger parts of the universe are put under the domain of humans? Is business so efficient, if 80 percent of business activity (as measured by revenues or assets) produces only 20 percent of profits and cash? Are we making good use of our time if 80 percent of it leads to 20 percent of our output and happiness? And is society making the best use of its talent when 80 percent of its citizens produce only 20 percent of its valued output (measured by money or gross earnings)?

Plainly, no! And equally plainly, this is not just my interpretation of the 80/20 Principle, but precisely the way in which it has been used by practical business people, quality engineers and strategy consultants, and all other users. The essence of the 80/20 Principle is that it wants to improve on what it observes and is a powerful tool for so doing.

Imbalance is not efficient. Although prevalent, imbalance is neither inevitable nor desirable. The 80/20 Principle is not a conservative, Hegelian abstraction; it is a practical tool for making a more sensible world. If you doubt this, look at the practical uses to which business has put the 80/20 Principle. Business leaders who observe the principle at work—and see that 20 percent of products or revenues are producing 80 percent of profits and that 80 percent are contributing only 20 percent of profits—do not shrug their shoulders, mutter something about Pareto, F. A. Hayek, Milton Friedman, and the perfection of capitalism, and pass swiftly on to the next agenda item. No. Sensible and profit-maximizing entrepreneurs do something to correct the imbalance. They make the really productive 20 percent of activities a larger proportion of the total. They either make the unproductive activity more productive or else reduce the call that they make on their enterprise's resources. They use the 80/20 Principle in the pursuit of progress, to improve on reality.

Confronting 80/20 social pessimism

We need to stress the positive and life-enhancing way in which the 80/20 Principle is used in practice, because there has been a sudden upsurge of interest in the social inequality implied in "the 80/20 society," "the winner-take-all society," and related themes. An apocalyptic school of thought has emerged which takes account of some of the characteristics of the 80/20 Principle but which implies that there is little that can be done to retard growing social inequality. It is worth evaluating these pessimistic, often fatalistic arguments that appear to make use of the 80/20 Principle.

In the Overture (pages 1–39) and Chapter 13 (pages 187–205) we referred to the "winner-take-all" phenomenon—rewards for the top people in sport, entertainment, and the professions are becoming higher and higher, so that the gap between the top earners and the rest is widening. This has been documented most persuasively and fully in the United States, but seems to be happening everywhere.

There is mounting evidence that the incomes of the top 10 percent of the working population are rising fast, while those of the bottom 10 percent are rising much more slowly, or are flat. The World Economic Forum in early 1997 at Davos is said to have spent much of its time considering the implications of this trend. One report stated:

> Some US economists see the America of the future as having 20 per cent of well educated professionals earning $75,000 to $500,000 a year to carry out orders from the super-rich, while the remaining 80 per cent that now have a median income of $30,000 a year will do all their dirty work and see their living standards eroded year by year.[2]

A new German bestseller called *The Global Trap*[3] also plays on the idea that rampant inequality will bring about "the 20:80 society," with only the fortunate 20 percent working. The book considers the assessment of a conference of 500 leading politicians, CEOs, and academics in San Francisco in 1995 and claims that, in a global market economy, there will be massive unemployment:

> Twenty per cent of the working age population will be enough to keep the world economy pumping in the next century. "More manpower just isn't needed," contends magnate Washington SyCip. One fifth of all work-seekers will be enough to produce all the goods and perform all the high-value services that the world economy can use. This 20 percent will be able to actively participate in life, work, and recreation . . .
>
> But the rest? Eighty per cent of those willing to work without a job? A new social order will come into being, [the experts] say: rich countries without any middle class to speak of. No one disagrees.

I have some empathy with these seemingly bizarre predictions. In our 1996 book *Managing Without Management*,[4] Ian Godden and I devoted a chapter to the challenge of mass managerial unemployment, in which we commented:

> The post-management corporation will need far fewer people, as a result of a 50 per cent reduction in the number of managerial, clerical and other overhead functions over 10 years . . . If all the eligible private sector firms in any country become post-management corporations, in the absence of countervailing effects this could result in a reduction of total employment of around 15–20 percent. Unemployment would rise from its current US level of just under 6 percent to around 25 percent, and be heavily concentrated within managerial ranks.

Let us summarize the "doom and gloom" case associated with the 80/20 Principle or the 20:80 society. Social inequality, as observed by Vilfredo Pareto, has always been a marked feature of society everywhere. The twentieth century attempted to break the pattern by progressive redistribution of income through taxation and welfare. But, as global markets begin to recover the power that they had in the previous century, the prevalent pattern of social inequality is back. The more power that global markets acquire, the greater the inequality. The greater the productive power of business, the fewer employees are needed. Free global markets will therefore give us two great and related social problems: mass unemployment, including the middle classes which have historically been protected, and greater social inequality, separating the top 20 percent from the bottom 80 percent.

The doomsters divide into two camps: the pessimists and the revolutionaries. The pessimists or fatalists argue that the trends are inevitable and that nothing much can be done about them. But the majority of those calling attention to growing social inequality are revolutionaries. Something, they assert, must be done to break the 80/20 pattern. The most coherent view comes from the German authors of *The Global Trap*. They argue that globalization does more harm than good and that it can and should be arrested: "Globalization is not a law of nature. The time of universal aimlessness has to end."

The doomsters are wrong

What are we to make of this? I believe that both pessimists and revolutionaries are wrong in their conclusions. Much of their analysis is correct and enlightening. But, although they allude (more or less directly) to the 80/20 Principle, they have at best a superficial understanding of it. If they understood the principle properly, they would see how it is possible to have progress without revolution.

Let us deal first with the specific problems of unemployment and inequality, and their relationship to increasingly free and global markets. Yes, there is a danger of mass managerial unemployment, as companies learn how to dispense with unnecessary management, and as international competition then forces companies to lower their costs toward the best demonstrated practice; the alternative, in the face of free markets, is to go bust. That much is right.

But all the evidence of history is that prosperity is not a problem. Every new technology, every new invention, every manpower-saving device, every refinement of productive technique, every lower-cost method of delivering goods and services—in short, every manifestation of industrial progress—has led not just to a remorseless and cumulatively staggering improvement in living standards for all groups in market-based societies, but also to higher total levels of employment. In every generation since the start of the Industrial Revolution, there have been those—the Luddites, the population-explosion prophets of doom, the romantic neofeudalists, the Marxists, the socialists, the fascists, the anticapitalist greens—who have proclaimed the limits to growth and the inability of the market system to deliver required levels of employment. The growth of the population, the entry (or reentry) of women into the working population, the abolition of the peasantry and agriculture as a significant source of employment, and the virtual disappearance of domestic servants—all these apparent harbingers of unemployment have been absorbed into the market system. The history of capitalism is the history of higher living standards and higher levels of employment.

For 250 years the doomsters have consistently been proved wrong. Their argument is that this time it really will be different, and it could be said that they have a case. Global markets *are* becoming freer at an accelerating pace. We *are* now learning that the way we have organized management in the large multibusiness corporation was a mistake. We *can* do without huge numbers of those employed by large companies. There *will* be an upsurge, over the next 10–20 years, in managerial unemployment.

And yet, we can and will adjust. We can retain the global market system—and the increased prosperity that, on the whole, it brings—without having an intractable unemployment problem. Progress, in the form of lower prices for goods already consumed, will release purchasing power for other goods and services. Purchasing power, unless it suddenly collapses because of a slump, will call forth its own new supply of jobs. These will not, in the main, be in large companies. They will be in smaller companies, in personal businesses (the single-person business or the small partnership), and in providing services to individuals that cannot easily (or yet) be "marketized" by large corporations. The progress of the global market will enlarge existing nonglobal markets or create new ones.

To the extent that the private sector does not produce all the jobs needed in the short term—and it may well not do so—we should be capable of shifting people to do useful things in the social sector. There is no shortage of highly and less highly skilled tasks—from education to the enhancement of knowledge in all spheres to improvement of our cities, towns, and villages—that would enrich society. If commercial markets will not pay or pay fully for these tasks to be performed, there is no reason why society should not encourage them to be fulfilled in order to provide both employment and services.

For it is not unemployment per se that is a problem in a wealthy society. If society is rich enough—and freer markets will make it richer and richer—unemployment, in the sense of people who want to work having nothing to do, should never be a problem. People can be employed outside the market economy; they will just not be paid market rates. But, unless we believe that the wealth of society as a whole is going to dip, the failure to pay market rates for noncommercial employment does not in itself create a problem. The problem only arises if the distribution of wealth within society is felt to be unfair.

The really serious issue is not unemployment or poverty, but inequality

Growing social inequality, in societies where the *overall* level of wealth is rising, is the real issue we should all be debating. It is clear that, in the absence of redistribution of wealth, free markets imply unequal wealth and that increasingly free markets create increasing inequality. This is happening fastest in those countries, such as the United States, Great Britain, and parts of Asia, that have made their markets the freest and that have increased this freedom over time. The 80/20 Principle explains *why* it is happening: 80 percent of what is useful and valued (measured democratically by consumers' free purchases) is created by 20 percent of the workforce. If markets are unobstructed, rewards will be unequally distributed because value is unequally created.

This implies that there *is* a trade-off between greater wealth and equality. If we opt for the greatest wealth, there will be greater inequality. The absolute living standards of all can still increase, but the cream will go to the fat cats.

Markets reflect value better than any other mechanism. The right answer to inequality is not to suppress markets and value creation, but rather to ensure that there is more equal and universal participation in markets by all elements in society.

We have not really explored this avenue properly. There are two obvious places to start. One is to bring all elements of society into the market economy: to make everyone a capitalist and an entrepreneur (someone who uses resources in their most productive way). The other is to ensure that everyone in society, but particularly those toward the bottom, know how and want to make the best use of their talents.

Social entrepreneurship

Social inequality occurs in a market economy not so much because the market produces winners and losers, but because not everyone is inside the market economy. Those who are excluded from the market, or who only participate in it to a limited degree, naturally fall behind.

For everyone to be inside the capitalist economy, everyone must have some assets to start with and a reasonable prospect of acquiring more. This is not the place to detail how this can be done, but it is eminently possible and much more cost effective than welfare payments. One way to kickstart capitalism for everyone would be to sell government land and buildings—every government has far more property than it needs—and privatize other state businesses. The proceeds would then be *given* to all citizens in the form of roll-up funds that would be owned by the citizens but could only be used for certain purposes (such as education, purchase of insurance or pensions annuities, or to start a business) after certain periods of time.

Even more important is that education should provide each new citizen with marketable skills in an area of the individual's choice. If necessary, the state should fund this. The 80/20 Principle perhaps has no more important application than in education. Since 20 percent of expenditure or resources produces 80 percent of results, we need to focus on the 20 percent of highly effective educational methods which ensure that all young people are able to work effectively within some part of a market economy. There is no other way of ensuring social cohesion and continued economic progress.

The 80/20 Principle can and must be applied to education

If we want to improve society, the best place to start is by applying the 80/20 Principle to education. There are three key elements to this: identifying the vital few levers that lead to exceptional results, decentralization, and competition.

The 80/20 Principle supplies the hypothesis that there are a few really important reasons that explain superior educational performance and that a few approaches or methods will prove to have exceptional results. If we can isolate the reasons and approaches, and then multiply their incidence, we will be able to make terrific progress.

And we *can* do this. It is not that the research has not been done. Let's look at the insight that can be derived from just two studies.

One Brookings Institute study of 500 U.S. high schools examined the factors influencing student performance.[5] There was perhaps no surprise that the most important influence lay in the aptitude and attitude brought to the school by the student, largely determined by family background. In the medium term, there is a compelling need to ensure that all students come to school with positive attitudes to learning: that they really want to learn. We can only do this by ensuring that all families are included in the wealth-generating, property-owning process. In the short run, however, this is not going to happen, and schools must work with the material they now have.

The study of 500 high schools found that, besides student aptitude and attitude, the next most important influence was the school itself. Some schools were dramatically better than others. And, peeling the onion further, the study sought to explain what was different about the really good schools. The usual explanations were examined: the money spent on the school, teacher salaries, spending per student, class size, graduation requirements. But these usual suspects made no difference. The really important factors were parental control, the clarity of the school's mission, leadership, the school's autonomy, and the freedom and respect enjoyed and earned by the teachers.

Very few school systems are organized to maximize, or even encourage, these desiderata. We could spend *less* public money on education, and obtain greatly improved results, if we gave teachers and parents control of each school.

Then there is the whole question of educational methods within the school. And here I will mention the second study, really a series of studies, contained in a wonderful book by Gordon Dryden and Dr. Jeannette Vos, *The Learning Revolution*.[6] Here are some of the proven methods explained in the book:

- In Flaxmere, New Zealand, backward 11-year-olds, who are up to five years behind their peers, are catching up in under ten weeks, using a tape-assisted reading program.
- In a U.S. army trial, soldiers using techniques explained in the book to learn German achieved 661 percent better results—more than twice the results in one-third of the time.
- Bridley Moor High School in Redditch, England, used accelerated learning techniques to learn a foreign language. Under normal methods, only 11 percent of students scored at least 80 out of 100; under the new methods, 65 percent did. Under normal methods, only 3 percent got 90 out of 100 or better; under the new methods, 38 percent scored 90+. Thus *ten times* as many scored 90+ under the new methods.

Although the Dryden and Vos book does not refer to the 80/20 Principle, it is a glorious celebration of it. The point about the 80/20 Principle is this: *do what works best especially in those parts of life that are themselves supremely important.* There will always be a minority of methods, a minority of practitioners, a minority of reasons and approaches that produce overwhelmingly superior results. Identify these. Then multiply them. Automatically, performance will not just be improved; it will be multiplied.

We *can* solve our educational problems, but we have to be radical. We have to adopt what works best. And this means not only the best proven methods, which engage the phenomenal power of students' brains when switched on, but also the right structures for education. There is overwhelming evidence that this means schools must be in charge of their own destiny. Parents and teachers in each school must be able to experiment and must be in charge, subject only to objective performance audit.

There is one other key to improving our educational systems hugely, and that is competition. Good schools must be able to get larger. They should also be able to take over underperforming schools, if this is the wish of parents and students in the latter. Bad schools must be forced to close.

Some years ago, Peter Drucker pointed out that the United States is the only major developed country with virtually no competition within the school system. This is now changing: East Harlem, Minnesota, Iowa, Arkansas, Ohio, Nebraska, Idaho, Utah, Massachusetts, Vermont, and Maine now all have substantial elements of choice available to students. But most countries, including the United States, do not have a *predominantly* competitive school system. Until this comes, we will be shortchanging our students and our society. When it comes, the leap forward in performance will be startling and continuous.

The underperformance has been so great, and the gap between the few brilliant schools and the mass of mediocre schools so wide, as has that between the few superproductive methods and the mass of normal, unproductive methods, that the systematic application of the 80/20 Principle to education—by using proven methods, giving parents and teachers control and allowing competition to work its magic—will have astonishingly beneficial results. It is a crime against humanity, and most of all against our children, not to release this power.

The 80/20 Principle highlights universal underperformance

I have praised the way in which markets operate and claimed that we can have the additional prosperity that freer markets bring while *also* enjoying prosperity without involuntary unemployment or greater social disharmony. This may seem too good to be true. The reason for my confidence is that the 80/20 Principle continually underlines how poorly we use resources: time, money, energy, personal effort, intelligence. Paradoxically, this poor use of resources is very good news. Because we do things so badly on average, and because we can always find a minority of resources that are *several times* more effective than the majority, we are free to do things very much better. Markets are good because they facilitate the transfer of low-effectiveness resources to high-effectiveness resources. But they do not ensure that this transfer happens. That depends on knowledge, technology, and entrepreneurship. These tend to thrive more under market than nonmarket conditions. Yet markets always need a shove in the right direction. If markets produced the best possible results, continual progress would be impossible. Progress relies on finding a better way to do *everything*. And that includes the way we run our free-market economy. We can always improve on the status quo using the 80/20 Principle.

Free enterprise is not bad at using resources, but not very good either

As the French political economist J-B Say commented around 1800, "The entrepreneur shifts economic resources out of an area of lower productivity into an area of higher productivity and greater yield." This process is at the heart of the 80/20 Principle, which points out how much room for improvement there typically is. Today this process is called "arbitrage." Free markets create the opportunity for arbitrage, but they do not automatically create arbitrage, and it is only in the simplest arenas (such as the value of national currencies) that arbitrage works at all pervasively or effectively.

The modern business corporation, whenever competition is allowed, tends to increase the amount of arbitrage, as J-B Say observed of the entrepreneur. Sadly, however, most corporate chiefs are not entrepreneurs; and the more complex a corporation, the less likely it is to arbitrage effectively. Corporations, particularly those in more than one line of business (multibusiness corporations, which control the great majority of free-market economic resources), are coalitions of many different executives (of widely varying productivity) and many different business segments (of highly different profitability). This is why there is now a widespread and fast-accelerating trend toward breaking up multibusiness corporations, whereby individual divisions of those corporations are "spun off" or "demerged" to create individual corporations focused on just one business arena. These "spun-off" corporations are purer because they have just one line of business and their stock-market performance has been exceptionally favourable, indicating the extent of value subtraction that was going on before the spin-off.[7] The weight of this prior value destruction, and the ease of multiplying profits once the process of arbitrage is made easier by simplification, should be no surprise to those who understand the 80/20 Principle.

The 80/20 Principle says that business does not allocate resources very well

The process of arbitrage, of moving resources to more productive resources, does not happen automatically, even in the freest of free-enterprise societies. It always needs a shove in the right direction. How do you find the direction? And what sort of shove is required?

The 80/20 Principle supplies clear answers. The direction can be defined by isolating the few powerful forces from the many weak forces, by disaggregating (de-averaging) the contribution being made by each relative to the resources being used by each. If the forces are benign (contributing to profits, for example), great leaps forward can be made by taking away resources from the many poorly performing areas and giving more resources to the few highly productive areas (an "area" can be a product, a customer, a channel of distribution, a group of executives, or any combination of these). In some cases, the not-very-productive areas can be made several times more productive, either by training them to mimic the behavior of the productive areas or by redeploying them in new configurations where they can be several times more productive. Finding the direction involves looking very carefully at disaggregating performance; it usually also involves simplification, decentralization, and measurement of performance at a low level of aggregation on a routine basis; and radical surgery is required to reallocate resources to their best use. The shove is toward more micro and radical solutions, where only high productivity is rewarded by the allocation of more resources and low productivity rewarded by depletion of resources.

Business people, like everyone else, are generally reluctant to make such radical and simplifying changes. Radical simplification disturbs vested interests (not least, those of the managers in charge themselves), creates disruptive change, and requires everyone to be both accountable and useful. Most people prefer life to be quiet, stable, and unaccountable. Because markets are not automatic but work via human activity they are always imperfect; and the larger and more complex the organization participating in the markets, the greater the imperfection. Business organizations have performed well, relative to nonbusiness organizations, because there is more scope for arbitrage and because competition enforces at least some low, minimal level of arbitrage. But it is a mistake to believe that business people like competition. The 80/20 Principle proclaims that markets are always imperfect, the use of resources is nearly always seriously suboptimal, and there is always great scope for intelligent arbitrage. The arbitrage will tend to simplify and put a searchlight on the individual performance of each resource.

So what is the message of the 80/20 Principle for the responsible right? The question is, of course, simplistic. The right comprises conservatives, radicals, and liberals, the authoritarian and the socially libertarian. But most of the right are united by respect for economic inequality, admiration (closet or overt) of élites, dislike of interventionist social and economic policies, and adulation of markets and competition.

On economic inequality, the 80/20 Principle observes that it is deep rooted but wasteful. Similarly, the principle helps to explain the prevalence of élites and supports the view that achievement is a minority sport, but it should also focus our attention on the failure to use all human resources effectively. Élites are only justified if they improve the quality of life for everyone, not just for themselves, and if they are serious about reducing social waste. The 80/20 Principle approves of markets and sees arbitrage as the source of great leaps forward in prosperity, but points out that most businesses are far from efficient and that managers are not natural lovers of either competition or arbitrage. We have not yet examined whether the 80/20 Principle should lead us to more or less interventionist policies, in either the social or economic sphere.

IS THERE A LEFT-WING INTERPRETATION
OF THE 80/20 PRINCIPLE?

If markets do not produce the optimal result and business is inherently inefficient, as the 80/20 Principle proclaims, can the principle supply a justification for intervention by the state in economic and social matters, in order to prevent waste and produce the best result for all citizens?

To begin to answer this question, let us initially steer clear of economic issues and deal briefly with social issues. Are there any insights that a generic application of the 80/20 Principle can quickly reveal? And do they tend to support a conservative or interventionist social policy?

The 80/20 Principle helps to beat crime

New York City has, since 1993, seen a sudden and stunning reduction in crime. For example, in Brooklyn North, one of the most notorious areas, the number of homicides has plummeted from 126 in 1993 to 44 in 1995: a 65 per cent reduction![8] The quality of life in the city has been transformed—a transformation which nobody predicted, but which was deliberately engineered. Police commissioner William Bratton identified that most crime was committed by a small proportion of offenders and arose from a small number of typical situations, such as young men drinking on street corners. He initially directed a massive police effort to swamp the greatest problem areas and to deal with the minority of offenders and situations that were causing a majority of the problem. The policy took the form of "zero tolerance" of illegality, even of apparently minor crimes such as drinking in the streets, public urination, and graffiti. A massive but highly targeted effort proved effective. Whether he knew it or not, Commissioner Bratton was applying the 80/20 Principle: concentrating on the 20 percent that caused 80 percent of the problem, determined in this case to eradicate the 20 percent of pivotal offences.

The effort, like a similar one practiced slightly earlier by the Mayor of Marbella in Spain, was much more effective than anyone predicted, not just in attacking the problem of crime in the targeted group, but also in changing the character of the neighbourhoods affected. The concept of the tipping point discussed in Chapter 1 helps to explain why this happened. The idea is that, once a certain point is reached in the development of an innovation or new practice, a small amount of additional effort can reap huge returns. While a certain amount of crime existed in the area, even if in relatively innocuous forms such as public drinking, urination, or graffiti, behavior gravitated toward the lowest common denominator. Cars were vandalized, moderately law-abiding citizens committed misdemeanors, and the elderly and affluent stayed off the streets. But once the police effort reached the point where crime was sufficiently rare and the neighborhood became tolerably civilized, attitudes and behavior suddenly shifted and the area was transformed.

The implication for social policy is absolutely clear. Expenditure to cure social problems that does not reach the tipping point is money down the drain. But if a little extra effort causes the tipping point to be reached, by putting massive effort in to deal with the 20 percent of situations that cause 80 percent of the problems, then the impact of each incremental amount of money or effort is fantastic.

But what, you may ask, has this to do with the left and the right, with conservative versus liberal politics? In fact, quite a lot. I may have cheated slightly by dealing first with crime, one of the few social issues where the right favors an activist approach by the state (in the form of the police). It is clear beyond reasonable doubt that the 80/20 Principle can be used most effectively to decrease crime. Another example is of a recent approach by certain English police forces to target the 20 percent of criminals who cause 80 percent of the crime, by simultaneous raids on the homes of the target group. And if a focused, interventionist approach works in crime, and can be explained by the 80/20 Principle and the tipping point, there is no reason in essence why an interventionist approach could not be successful in any area of social policy.

Two big "buts" in social intervention

There are, however, two big "buts" in saying that interventionist social programs may be justified by the 80/20 Principle.

One "but" is that the 80/20 Principle is likely to come up with unconventional solutions. Remember the core insight of the principle: that any problem or opportunity will have relatively few critical causes which must be identified and dealt with in an extremely focused and determined way. Applying this insight may contradict the stock answers of both the left and the right.

Take the vexed issue of healthcare. The left in most countries wants to extend the scope of healthcare: to build more hospitals, employ more doctors and nurses, and spend a higher proportion of national wealth on this objective, if necessary funded by higher taxation. The right wants to hold or cut taxes and ensure that subsidized healthcare is only available to those most in need. There is little common ground in this debate and no easy way of saying which policy is better.

But if we ask which side the 80/20 Principle would take, the answer is neither. Two decades ago, the U.S. surgeon general very sensibly tried to attribute the causes of illness and concluded that only 10 percent of it was attributable to medical care or its absence and fully 50 percent was related to personal behavior. Yet U.S. budgets, under both Republicans and Democrats, have allocated *20 times* more spending to corrective medical care than to all the programs encouraging better nutrition, health education, self-care medication, and personal fitness.

The 80/20 Principle asserts that 20 percent of expenditure will generate 80 percent of desired results and vice versa. Progress depends on identifying the 20 percent that yields 80 percent and the 80 percent that yields 20 percent. In this case, the 20 that leads to 80 plainly includes health education, particularly that targeted in the early stages when it can have most effect. In the case of healthcare, as in most areas, prevention is better and a great deal cheaper than cure; stopping disease in the early stages is better and cheaper than stopping it later; and creating habits of healthy living among the young, habits that are likely to endure through a long lifetime, will do more good than almost any other form of social expenditure.

It would be sensible to devote truly massive energies to health education in schools, up to the tipping point where it really works, where it really shifts behavior. It would make sense for the state to create, supervise, and monitor programs to ensure major steps forward in healthy eating and exercise, probably by using private-sector marketing firms and paying them by results. We probably need fewer hospitals, fewer doctors, and fewer nurses and more voluntary and home-based health workers, more nutritionists, more gyms, more fitness equipment, more parks, more cycle lanes, and high taxes on unhealthy food.

The other "but" surrounds the relative performance of the state as doer

The 80/20 Principle is relatively optimistic about social engineering. The principle promises that unconventional solutions based on observing the 20 percent that produces 80 percent, and then putting massive effort behind the 20 percent, can deliver more for less; and that by targeting and putting in enough resources to reach the tipping point, we can make major improvements in any social issue. The first caveat was that the solution will be unconventional and pragmatic, based on observing the 20 percent that works really well. Now it's time for our second "but," one that still causes the left major problems: the state's track record as a provider of services is lamentable and far inferior to the track record of private business. With rare exceptions (such as Britain's National Health Service) state-provided services always seem to be in the 80 percent of activity delivering 20 percent of the value.

Why all versions of the twentieth-century megastate have failed

The 80/20 Principle can not only observe the poor performance of the megastate, it can also go some way toward explaining it. Earlier, we criticized most private enterprise for inefficiency, since the 80/20 Principle demonstrates how inclined most corporations, especially complex and multibusiness corporations, are to cross-subsidize activities and to obfuscate true levels of performance, at the level of each product, customer, division, or executive. Yet the inefficiency of the private sector is relative, and it would be churlish to deny the incredible advances in living standards brought about by the modern business corporation. In the last 100 years, output per worker has gone up 50 times and, were it not for the appropriations of the state, living standards would have followed suit. The large business corporation deserves most of the credit for this staggering cornucopia.

State provision of services virtually guarantees the direst predictions of the 80/20 Principle. This is because it is impossible to pin down accountability for the value of services and very difficult to measure the relationship between inputs and outputs even at very aggregated levels; at disaggregated levels it becomes totally impossible. This is not because of the wickedness or cynicism of the state providers—it is intrinsic to a system where there is little customer choice, no need to measure performance and no rewards for providing superior value.

All organizations, especially complex ones, are inherently, and almost willfully, inefficient. What makes private-sector organizations less inefficient than their public-sector counterparts is the discipline of the market. This has been absent from the public sector, so that poor service providers do not perish and, even more importantly, good ones do not gain access to new resources. The 80/20 process of arbitrage is not allowed to operate. In the public sector, there is no point in 80/20 Analysis; it is virtually impossible to obtain meaningful, disaggregated data on performance, and, even were it possible, no one would have any imperative or incentive to do anything to encourage the few best-value providers and to take resources away from the many poor-value providers. Therefore, no great leaps forward in value are ever possible. And so, if we want to obtain more for less, one good way to begin is to deprive the state of all its service-provision functions.

The intelligent left has begun to realize this. The abolition of the state as provider does not necessarily mean a smaller role for the state as funder; the level of taxation and redistribution of wealth need bear no relationship at all to the extent of state service provision. Yet in practice, there will be a correlation. If the state does not give up most of its service-provision functions, the revolt against taxation and poor state value is likely to lead to lower levels of state funding. Conversely, if the state contracts out (whether to voluntary organizations or private-sector ones, or ideally to competition between both organizational types), it will be able to expand the volume and value of service provision at a cost that is low enough to be acceptable.

What does the 80/20 Principle imply about state economic intervention?

The one major area of controversy between left and right we have not yet examined is that of state intervention in the economy. The

80/20 Principle does not believe in the perfection of markets, because this is tempered by complex organizations that may operate very inefficiently. Yet decentralized markets, where consumers are able freely to assess relative value, offer the best spur to arbitrage and efficiency. In practice, state intervention nearly always favors the side of the producers (who can lobby effectively and sometimes, with varying degrees of honesty, subvert the state, which is always also concerned about short-term employment levels) against the interests of consumers. Antitrust policy is the only area where government tends to favor consumers; and even here the achievements over two-thirds of a century are marginal at best.

The 80/20 Principle implies that arbitrage and efficiency will be best served by the state intervening as little as possible in economic affairs. This is in marked contrast to the value of intervention in social matters (provided that the state does not directly offer services), where the potential for improvement by using the 80/20 Principle is massive. Waste for society as a whole can only be minimized by society reordering its affairs in a radical way; and the only mechanisms whereby this can happen are political.

THE 80/20 PRINCIPLE ASSERTS THE POTENTIAL FOR TERRIFIC PROGRESS

Whether the program implied by the 80/20 Principle belongs to the thinking left, the radical center, or the radical right, others will have to judge. Perhaps the 80/20 Principle can help end some of the sterile debates between the left and the right: those based on intellectual positions rather than vested interests. The key point about the principle is that it highlights the huge gaps in performance inherent in all aspects of life: the lack of balance between inputs and outputs, the way we deceive ourselves by thinking in terms of averages and overall performance, the difference between those few approaches that do things very well and the vast mass of mediocrity. The 80/20 Principle is therefore inherently restless, inherently ambitious, impatient of the status quo, and immovably wedded to the idea of progress—it asserts that we could make huge improvements to the wealth and happiness of every individual and to the quality of society as a whole.

The 80/20 Principle therefore offers the potential for honest and disinterested citizens to replace conventional political allegiances and start again. The politics implied by the principle are radical, ambitious, and even mildly utopian; they favor ambitious programs of focused social intervention; they have no illusions about the perfection of capitalism, corporations, or markets; yet they have little or no role for the state as provider of services and are extremely skeptical about the value of state economic intervention. The main value of the 80/20 Principle for the public good, as for personal and corporate good, lies in the insight it gives us into causes and results. The insight allows us to make great strides forward. Positive change is always possible and always disruptive. The prescriptions of the 80/20 Principle, in public policy as elsewhere, are radical, change seeking, and performance based.

Thus, my answer is that the 80/20 Principle does have moral force. It challenges us to arrange corporations (whether for profit or not for profit) and our societies so that the maximum possible resources are given to those few parts of activity that are tremendously useful to other people; and to ensure that the majority of resources that are currently not very productive see a multiplication of their effectiveness.

Progress: a past, present, and future fact

Why do we refuse to believe in humanity's potential to multiply effectiveness? In 1798 Thomas Malthus, an eccentric English cleric, worried in his *Essay on Population* "that the power of the population is indefinitely greater than the power in earth to produce subsistence for man."[9] Malthus was right about the multiplication of the earth's people, but he could not have imagined the increases in agricultural efficiency that were already underway. In the West we are now able to feed ourselves, yet agriculture has gone from employing 98 percent of the population to employing around 3 percent! And industry has produced quite incredible increases in wealth and output per head, increasing productivity by 3–4 percent compound per annum, or an increase of 50 times output per worker.

In our own lifetimes, we have seen the quality of consumer goods raised to levels of perfection and versatility which our grandparents could not have imagined; witnessed whole new categories of miraculous electronic products which have transformed both the home and the office and the boundary between them; watched as whole nations that were devastated, hungry, and demoralized have taken themselves from the edge of destruction to become thriving and outward-looking industrial leaders; seen most of the nations of Europe lose their national and ideological antagonisms and a whole new area of the world (in Asia) bootstrap its way to prosperity. All of these achievements have used the spirit of the 80/20 Principle, and many of the most spectacular gains, in quality, electronics, and computing, have knowingly used the 80/20 Principle to transform their effectiveness.

We see all this and yet we still cannot believe in the possibility of further dramatic progress. We imagine that we stand at the end of industry's ability to transform the world, that all the gains that can be made have been made and that the most we and our children can expect is a consolidation of current achievements. We do not believe politicians, we do not trust industry, and we have given up the habit of hope. We fear for our jobs and believe we may be experiencing the disintegration of civilized society.

If we accept the 80/20 Principle, we will temper these fears with a massive dose of optimism. Believe me, speaking as an experienced strategy consultant familiar with leading-edge "global" companies, there is still amazing scope to raise the effectiveness of industry. Yes, corporations have done very well, absolutely and in comparison to that great twentieth-century leech, the state organization. But no, they are currently not at all efficient or effective and an awesome amount of improvement is possible. So corporations are not suddenly about to stop their advances in productivity. They are only just beginning to use information technology properly, they have only recently rediscovered that customers and investors are more important than their own internal management processes, they are only now learning to compete effectively, and, most important of all, they are in the earliest stages of realizing how much waste and cost are being caused by their complexity.

I am absolutely confident in predicting that a combination of technology and a new determination of top executives to serve customers and investors, at whatever cost to their management structures, will lead a few corporations—remember that it only takes a few to prove that previous levels of achievement can be left well behind—to such astonishing success that, provided that markets remain tolerably free, we will marvel in 50 years' time at the transformation in living standards wrought by our corporations, to an even greater extent than we ought to marvel today at the progress in the past half-century.

And whatever our corporations achieve in their current role, there is a multiplier effect available to us, as the 80/20 Principle promises that there always is. In this case, we can easily identify it. It towers above us, in all its gleaming inefficiency, and it is called the state sector. Despite privatizations, the state sector, in the broadest sense, still consumes 30–50 percent of economic resources in most countries; in Great Britain, the home of privatization, it still consumes over 40 percent. Yet the intellectual case for state provision of services has been fatally undermined and few even on the left believe in it. If we privatized *everything*, including education and police services, but on a basis that ensured effective competition between current and potential service suppliers, and allowed nonprofits to compete on equal terms with for-profit corporations, we would see massive and continuous increases in value: more important than cost reduction, we would see terrific service improvements.[10] In education, for example, some schools and teaching methods are 50 times more effective than others, and information technology is still only being used intelligently by a tiny percentage of educators. If we remove the institutional barriers to arbitrage, to the spread of best practice, the consequences for people's lives, and for our economies, are almost unimaginable. If we used the 80/20 Principle in education as effectively as it has been used in computing, the multiplier effect would be amazing.

TAKE RESPONSIBILITY FOR PROGRESS

Put away your skepticism and your pessimism. These vices, like their opposites, are self-fulfilling. Recover your faith in progress. Realize that the future is already here: in those few shining examples, in agribusiness, in industry, in services, in education, in artificial intelligence, in medical science, in physics and indeed all the sciences, and even in social and political experiments, where previously unimaginable targets have been surpassed and new targets continue to fall like skittles. Remember the 80/20 Principle. Progress always comes from a small minority of people and organized resources who demonstrate that previously accepted ceilings of performance can become floors for everyone. Progress requires élites, but élites who live for glory and service to society, who are willing to place their gifts at the disposal of us all. Progress depends on information about exceptional achievement and the diffusion of successful experiments, on breaking down the structures erected by the mass of vested interests, on demanding that the standards enjoyed by a privileged minority should be available to all. Above all progress, as George Bernard Shaw told us, requires us to be unreasonable in our demands. We must search out the 20 percent of everything that produces the 80 percent and use the facts we uncover to demand a multiplication of whatever it is that we value. If our reach must always exceed our grasp, progress requires that we grasp whatever a minority has reached and ensure that it becomes the minimum standard for all.

The greatest thing about the 80/20 Principle is that you do not need to wait for everyone else. You can start to practice it in your professional and personal life. You can take your own small fragments of greatest achievement, happiness, and service to others and make them a much larger part of your life. You can multiply your highs and cut out most of your lows. You can identify the mass of irrelevant and low-value activity and begin to shed this worthless skin. You can isolate the parts of your character, workstyle, lifestyle, and relationships that, measured against the time or energy involved, give you value many times greater than the daily grind; and, having isolated them, you can, with no little courage and determination, multiply them. You can become a better, more useful, and happier human being. And you can help others to do the same.

NOTES
AND
REFERENCES

CHAPTER 1

1 Josef Steindl (1965) *Random Processes and the Growth of Firms: A Study of the Pareto Law* (London: Charles Griffin), p. 18.

2 Extensive research has revealed a very large number of short articles referring to the 80/20 Principle (usually called the 80/20 Rule) but failed to identify any books on the subject. If a book on the 80/20 Principle does exist, even if as an unpublished academic treatise, would a reader please let me know. One recent book, although not really about the 80/20 Principle, does draw attention to its significance. John J. Cotter's *The 20% Solution* (Chichester: John Wiley, 1995) provides in its introduction the right answer: "Figure out the 20% of what you do that will contribute the most to your success in the future, then concentrate your time and energy on that 20%" (p. xix). Cotter refers in passing to Pareto (p. xxi), but neither Pareto nor the 80/20 Principle (under any name) is mentioned outside the introduction, and Pareto does not even appear in the index. Like many writers, Cotter is anachronistic in attributing the 80/20 formulation itself to Pareto: "Vilfredo Pareto was a French-born economist who observed 100 years ago that 20% of the factors in most situations account for 80% of what happens (that is, 20% of a company's customers generate 80% of its profits). He called it Pareto's Law" (p. xxi). In fact, Pareto never used the expression "80/20" or anything like it.

What he called his "law" was in fact a mathematical formula (given in note 4), which is some way removed from (although the ultimate source of) the 80/20 Principle as we know it today.

3 Living with the car, (1996) *The Economist* (22 June): 8.

4 Vilfredo Pareto (1896/7) *Cours d'Economique Politique,* Lausanne University. Despite the conventional mythology, Pareto did not use the "80/20" phrase in his discussion of income inequality or anywhere else. He did not even make the simple observation that 80 percent of income was earned by 20 percent of the working population, although this conclusion could have been distilled from his far more complex calculations. What Pareto did discover, and what greatly excited him and his followers, was a constant relationship between the top earners and the percentage of total incomes they enjoyed, a relationship that followed a regular logarithmic pattern and could be charted in a similar shape whatever time period of country was taken.

   The formula is as follows. Call N the number of income earners who receive incomes higher than x, with A and m being the constants. Pareto found that:

$$\log N = \log A + m \log x$$

5 It should be stressed that this simplification was not made by Pareto himself nor, sadly, by any of his followers for more than a generation. It is, however, a legitimate deduction from his method, and one that is much more accessible than any explanation Pareto himself gave.

6 Harvard University, in particular, appears to have been a hotbed of Pareto appreciation. Aside from Zipf's influence in philology, the economic faculty demonstrated a hearty appreciation of the "Pareto law." For what is still the best explanation of this, see the article by Vilfredo Pareto in *Quarterly Journal of Economics*, 68, no. 2, May 1949 (President and Fellows of Harvard College).

7 For an excellent explanation of Zipf's law, see Paul Krugman (1996) *The Self-Organizing Economy* (Cambridge, MA: Blackwell), p. 39.

8 Joseph Moses Juran (1951) *Quality Control Handbook,* New York: McGraw-Hill, pp 38–9. This is the first edition, with a mere 750 pages compared to more than 2,000 in the current edition. Note that although Juran clearly refers to the "Pareto principle" and accurately distills its significance, the first edition does not use the term 80/20 at all.

9 Paul Krugman, op. cit., note 7.

10 Malcolm Gladwell (1996) The tipping point, *New Yorker*, 3 June.

11 Malcolm Gladwell, ibid.

12 James Gleik (1987) *Chaos: Making a New Science*, New York: Little, Brown.

13 See W. Brian Arthus (1989) Competing technologies, increasing returns, and lock-in by historical events, *Economic Journal*, vol 99, March, pp. 116–31.

14 Chaos theory explodes Hollywood hype (1997), *Independent on Sunday*, 30 March.

15 George Bernard Shaw, quoted in John Adair (1996) *Effective Innovation* (London: Pan Books), p. 169.

16 Quoted in James Gleik, op. cit., note 12.

CHAPTER 2

1 Author's calculation based on Donella H. Meadows, Dennis L. Meadows, and Jorgen Randers (1992) *Beyond the Limits* (London: Earthscan), pp. 66f.

2 Author's calculation based on Lester R. Brown, Christopher Flavin, and Hal Kane (1992), (London: Earthscan), p. 111, itself based on Ronald V. A. Sprout, and James H. Weaver (1991) *International Distribution of Income: 1960–1987*, Working Paper no. 159, Department of Economics, American University, Washington, DC, May.

3 Health Care Strategic Management (1995) Strategic planning futurists need to be capitation-specific and epidemiological, *Health Care Strategic Management*, 1 September.

4 Malcolm Gladwell (1996) The science of shopping, *New Yorker*, 4 November.

5 Mary Corrigan and Gary Kauppila (1996) *Consumer Book Industry Overview and Analysis of the Two Leading Superstore Operators* (Chicago, IL: William Blair & Co.).

CHAPTER 3

1 Joseph Moses Juran, op. cit. (see Chapter 1, note 8), 38–9.

2 Ronald J. Recardo (1994) Strategic quality management: turning the spotlight on strategies as well as tactical issues, *National Productivity Review*, 22 March.

3 Niklas Von Daehne (1994) The new turnaround, *Success*, 1 April.

4 David Lowry (1993) Focusing on time and teams to eliminate waste at Singo prize-winning Ford Electronics, *National Productivity Review*, 22 March.

5 Terry Pinnell (1994) Corporate change made easier, *PC User*, 10 August.

6 James R. Nagel (1994) TQM and the Pentagon, *Industrial Engineering*, 1 December.

7 Chris Vandersluis (1994) Poor planning can sabotage implementation, *Computing Canada*, 25 May.

8 Steve Wilson (1994) Newton: bringing AI out of the ivory tower, *AI Expert*, 1 February.

9 Jeff Holtzman (1994) And then there were none, *Electronics Now*, 1 July.

10 Software developers create modular applications that include low prices and core functions (1994), *MacWeek*, 17 January.

11 Barbara Quint (1995) What's your problem?, *Information Today*, 1 January.

12 See Richard Koch and Ian Godden (1996) *Managing Without Management* (London: Nicholas Brealey), especially Chapter 6, pp. 96–109.

13 Peter Drucker (1995) *Managing in a Time of Great Change* (London: Butterworth-Heinemann), pp. 96f.

14 Richard Koch and Ian Godden, op. cit. (see note 12); see Chapter 6 and p. 159.

CHAPTER 5

1 Henry Ford (1991) *Ford on Management,* intr. Ronnie Lessem (Oxford: Blackwell), pp. 10, 141, 148. Reissue of Henry Ford (1922) *My Life and Work* and (1929) *My Philosophy of Industry.*

2 Gunter Rommel (1996) *Simplicity Wins* (Cambridge, MA: Harvard Business School Press).

3 George Elliott, Ronald G. Evans, and Bruce Gardiner (1996) Managing cost: transatlantic lessons, *Management Review,* June.

4 Richard Koch and Ian Godden, op. cit. (see Chapter 3, note 12).

5 Carol Casper (1994) Wholesale changes, *U.S. Distribution Journal,* 15 March.

6 Ted R. Compton (1994) Using activity-based costing in your organization, *Journal of Systems Management,* 1 March.

CHAPTER 6

1 Vin Manaktala (1994) Marketing: the seven deadly sins, *Journal of Accountancy,* 1 September.

2 It is easy to forget the deliberate and successful transformation of society that arose from the idealism and skill of a few pivotal early-twentieth-century industrialists, who advocated the "horn of plenty" argument: that poverty, although prevalent, could be abolished. Here, for example, is Henry Ford again: "The duty to abolish the more disastrous forms of poverty and want is easily fulfilled. The earth is so abundantly fruitful that there can be ample food, clothing, work and leisure." See Henry Ford (1991) *Ford on Management,* intr. Ronnie Lessem (Oxford: Blackwell), pp. 10, 141, and 148. I am grateful to Ivan Alexander for showing me the draft of his new book, *The Civilized Market* (1997, Oxford: Capstone) whose first chapter makes this and many other points that I have borrowed (see note 3).

3 See Ivan Alexander (1997) *The Civilized Market* (Oxford: Capstone).

4 Quoted by Michael Slezak (1994) Drawing fine lines in lipsticks, *Supermarket News,* 11 March.

5 Mark Stevens (1994) Take a good look at company blind spots, *Star-Tribune* (Twin Cities), 7 November.

6 John S. Harrison (1994) Can mid-sized LECs succeed in tomorrow's competitive marketplace?, *Telephony*, 17 January.

7 Ginger Trumfio (1995) Relationship builders: contract management, *Sales & Marketing Management*, 1 February.

8 Jeffrey D. Zbar (1994) Credit card campaign highlights restaurants, *Sun-Sentinel* (Fort Lauderdale), 10 October.

9 Donna Petrozzello (1995) A tale of two stations, *Broadcasting & Cable*, 4 September.

10 Insurance agency consultant Dan Sullivan, quoted in Sidney A. Friedman (1995) Building a super agency of the future, *National Underwriter Life and Health*, 27 March.

11 A large number of articles about specific businesses and industries attest to this. For example, see Brian T. Majeski (1994) The scarcity of quality sales employees, *The Music Trades*, 1 November.

12 Harvey Mackay (1995) We sometimes lose sight of how success is gained, *The Sacramento Bee*, 6 November.

13 How much do salespeople make? (1994), *The Music Trades*, 1 November.

14 Robert E. Sanders (1987) The Pareto Principle, its use and abuse, *Journal of Consumer Marketing* 4, no. 1 (Winter): 47–50.

CHAPTER 7

1 Peter B. Suskind (1995) Warehouse operations: don't leave well alone, *IIE Solutions*, 1 August.

2 Gary Forger (1994) How more data + less handling = smart warehousing, *Modern Materials Handling*, 1 April.

3 Robin Field, Branded consumer products, in James Morton (ed.) (1995) *The Global Guide to Investing* (London: FT/Pitman), pp. 471f.

4 Ray Kulwiec (1995) Shelving for parts and packages, *Modern Materials Handling*, 1 July.

5 Michael J. Earl and David F. Feeny (1994) Is your CIO adding value?, *Sloan Management Review*, 22 March.

6 Derek L. Dean, Robert E. Dvorak, and Endre Holen (1994) Breaking through the barriers to new systems development, *McKinsey Quarterly*, 22 June.

7 Roger Dawson (1995) Secrets of power negotiating, *Success*, 1 September.

8 Orten C. Skinner (1991) Get what you want through the fine art of negotiation, *Medical Laboratory Observer*, 1 November.

CHAPTER 9

1 This phrase comes from Ivan Alexander (ibid., Chapter 2), whose thinking on progress I have shamelessly plundered.

2 Ivan Alexander (op. cit., see Chapter 6, note 2) remarks nicely that "though we are now aware that the riches of the earth are finite, we have discovered other dimensions of opportunity, a new compacted yet fertile space in which business can flourish and expand. Trade, commerce, automation, robotisation and informatics, though almost landless and spaceless, are unbounded domains of opportunity. Computers are the least dimensional machines mankind has yet devised."

CHAPTER 10

1 Quoted in *Oxford Book of Verse* (1961), p. 216.

2 The best and most progressive guide to time management precepts is Hiram B. Smith (1995) *The Ten Natural Laws of Time and Life Management* (London: Nicholas Brealey). Smith refers extensively to the Franklin Corporation and rather less extensively to its Mormon roots.

3 Charles Handy (1969) *The Age of Unreason* (London: Random House), Chapter 9. See also Charles Handy (1994) *The Empty Raincoat* (London: Hutchinson).

4 See William Bridges (1995) *JobShift: How to Prosper in a Workplace without Jobs* (Reading, MA: Addison-Wesley/London: Nicholas Brealey). Bridges argues, almost persuasively, that full-time employment by large organizations will become more the exception than the rule and that the word "job" will revert to its original meaning of "task."

5 Roy Jenkins (1995) *Gladstone* (London: Macmillan).

CHAPTER 12

1 Donald O. Clifton and Paula Nelson (1992) *Play to Your Strengths* (London: Piatkus).

2 Interview with J. G. Ballard (1989), in *Re/Search* magazine (San Francisco), October, pp. 21–2.

3 St. Paul was probably of even greater importance to the success of Christianity than was the historical Jesus. Paul made Christianity Rome-friendly. Without this move, fiercely resisted by St. Peter and most of the other original disciples, Christianity would have remained an obscure sect.

4 See Vilfredo Pareto (1968) *The Rise and Fall of Elites,* intr. Hans L Zetterberg (New York: Arno Press). Originally published in 1901 in Italian, this is a shorter and better description of Pareto's sociology than is his later work. The description of Pareto as the "bourgeois Karl Marx" came as a backhanded compliment in his 1923 obituary in the socialist newspaper *Avanti.* It is an apt description, because Pareto, like Marx, stressed the importance of classes and of ideology in determining behavior.

5 Except possibly music and the visual arts. Even here, however, collaborators may be more important than is generally acknowledged.

CHAPTER 13

1 See Robert Frank and Philip Cook (1995) *The Winner-Take-All Society* (New York: Free Press). Although they do not use the phrase 80/20, the authors are clearly talking about the operation of 80/20-like laws. They deplore the waste implied by such unbalanced rewards. See also the comment on the book in a perceptive essay in *The Economist* (25 November 1995, p. 134), on which I have drawn extensively in this

section. *The Economist* article notes that in the early 1980s Sherwin Rose, an economist at the University of Chicago, wrote a couple of papers on the economics of superstars.

2 See Richard Koch (1995) *The Financial Times Guide to Strategy* (London: Pitman), pp. 17–30.

3 G. W. F. Hegel (1953) *Hegel's Philosophy of Right,* trans. T. M. Knox (Oxford: Oxford University Press).

4 See Louis S. Richman (1994) The new worker elite, *Fortune,* 22 August, pp. 44–50.

5 This trend is part of the "death of management," whereby managers are rendered redundant and only the "doers" have a place in effective corporations. See Richard Koch and Ian Godden, op cit. (see Chapter 3, note 12).

CHAPTER 14

1 What follows is a highly simplified account. Those who want to take private investment seriously are referred to Richard Koch (1994, 1997) *Selecting Shares that Perform* (London: Pitman).

2 Based on the *BZW Equity and Gilt Study* (1993, London: BZW). See Koch, ibid., p. 3.

3 Vilfredo Pareto, op. cit.

4 See Janet Lowe (1995) *Benjamin Graham, The Dean of Wall Street* (London: Pitman).

5 Besides the historic P/E, which is based on the last year's published earnings, there is also the prospective P/E, which is based on future earnings as estimated by stock market analysts. If earnings are expected to rise, the prospective P/E will be lower than the historic P/E, thus making the shares appear cheaper. The prospective P/E should be taken into account by experienced investors, but is also potentially dangerous because the forecast earnings may not (and, as a matter of fact, often do not) materialize. See Richard Koch, op. cit. (see note 1), pp. 108–12, for a detailed discussion of P/Es.

CHAPTER 15

1 A telling chapter heading from Daniel Goleman (1995) *Emotional Intelligence* (London: Bloomsbury), p. 179.

2 See Dr. Dorothy Rowe (1996) The escape from depression, *Independent on Sunday* (London), 31 March, p. 14, quoting a forthcoming book *In the Blood: God, Genes and Destiny* by Professor Steve Jones (1996, London: HarperCollins).

3 Dr. Peter Fenwick (1996) The dynamics of change, *Independent on Sunday* (London), 17 March, p. 9.

4 Ivan Alexander, op. cit. (see Chapter 6, note 2), Chapter 4.

5 Daniel Goleman, op. cit. (see note 1), p. 34.

6 Ibid., p. 36.

7 Ibid., p. 246.

8 Ibid., pp. 6–7.

9 Dr. Peter Fenwick, op. cit. (see note 1), p. 10.

10 Quoted by Daniel Goleman, op. cit. (see note 1), p. 87.

11 Ibid., p. 179.

12 I am indebted to my friend Patrice Trequisser for pointing out this very important manifestation of the 80/20 Principle: you can fall in love in seconds and it can exert a dominant influence on the rest of your life. Patrice would not accept my caveat, since he fell in love at first sight more than a quarter of a century ago and is still very happily married. But of course, he is French.

CHAPTER 16

1 Charles Darwin (1839) *Voyage of the Beagle*, chapter on slavery.

2 *Guardian,* 3 February 1997.

3 Hans-Peter Martin and Harald Schumann (1996) *The Global Trap: The*

Assault on Democracy and Prosperity (Reinbek bei Hamburg: Rowohlt Verlag).

4 Richard Koch and Ian Godden, op. cit. (see Chapter 3, note 12), p. 210.

5 Quoted in David Osborne and Ted Gaebler (1992) *Reinventing Government* (New York: Plume), pp. 93–107.

6 Gordon Dryden and Jeannette Vos (1994) *The Learning Revolution* (Aylesbury: Accelerated Learning Systems), pp. 330–33 and 378–81.

7 See David Sadtler, Andrew Campbell, and Richard Koch (1997) *Breakup! Why Large Companies Are Worth More Dead Than Alive* (Oxford: Capstone).

8 Cop out (1996), *The Economist*, 30 March, p. 56.

9 Thomas Robert Malthus (1798) *An Essay on the Principles of Population as It Affects the Future Improvements of Society.* Malthus was an eccentric English parson who comes second only to Karl Marx in combining brilliant analysis with spectacularly wrong predictions.

10 The idea of privatizing *everything* may seem naïve or extreme. What, for example, about the army or the judiciary? This is too big a subject to cover here. Some shrivelled organs of the state might have to remain, but the public good, both in terms of value for money and the rights of citizens, will be best served by having the greatest possible number of functions run either by accountable commercial concerns or by accountable nonprofit organizations. No one has seriously tried to test out how far this principle could be pushed in practice. There is still a great deal of practical thinking to be done, but there can be no doubt which direction best serves liberty and prosperity.

INDEX

RICHARD KOCH is a successful entrepreneur, investor, and strategy consultant, who has based his own success on the 80/20 Principle. He has built multimillion-dollar businesses from scratch in hotels and has written and cowritten eight highly acclaimed books, the most recent being *Managing Without Management*.

He has advised the CEOs and chairmen of many blue-chip American and European corporations as a founder of the LEK Partnership, a partner of Bain & Co., a consultant with the Boston Consulting Group, and now through his own consultancy, Odyssey. He is nonexecutive director of many quoted and unquoted corporations, including Filofax, which has prospered greatly since he originated its rescue.